T0385276

STUDIES IN CHRISTIAN HISTORY AND THOUGHT

A Pledge of Love
The Anabaptist Sacramental Theology of Balthasar Hubmaier

STUDIES IN CHRISTIAN HISTORY AND THOUGHT

Series Editors

STUDIES IN CHRISTIAN HISTORY AND THOUGHT

A Pledge of Love

The Anabaptist Sacramental Theology of Balthasar Hubmaier

Brian C. Brewer

Foreword by H.W. Walker Pipkin

First published 2012 by Paternoster

Paternoster is an imprint of Authentic Media
52 Presley Way, Crownhill, Milton Keynes, Bucks, MK8 0ES

www.authenticmedia.co.uk
Authentic Media is a division of Koorong UK, a company limited by guarantee

09 08 07 06 05 04 03   8 7 6 5 4 3 2 1

British Library Cataloguing in Publication Data A catalogue record for this
book is available from the British Library

ISBN 978–1–84227–729–4

Typeset by Brian C. Brewer
Printed and bound in Great Britain for Paternoster

STUDIES IN CHRISTIAN HISTORY AND THOUGHT

Series Preface

This series complements the specialist series of Studies in Evangelical History and Thought and Studies in Baptist History and Thought for which Paternoster is becoming increasingly well known by offering works that cover the wider field of Christian history and thought. It encompasses accounts of Christian witness at various periods, studies of individual Christians and movements, and works which concern the relations of church and society through history, and the history of Christian thought.

The series includes monographs, revised dissertations and theses, and collections of papers by individuals and groups. As well as 'free standing' volumes, works on particular running themes are being commissioned; authors will be engaged for these from around the world and from a variety of Christian traditions.

A high academic standard combined with lively writing will commend the volumes in this series both to scholars and to a wider readership

To Amy
my encourager, my proof-reader, my companion in life

Contents

FOREWORD

I have been privileged to spend a number of years inside the life, writings and theology of Balthasar Hubmaier who lived ca. 1480-1528. In the decades of time with Hubmaier, I've come to understand that there have been misinterpretations of his life and work. Often, there has been a failure to accept Hubmaier as an authentic Anabaptist thinker and writer. Other interpreters have endeavored to make Hubmaier over in the theological viewpoints they themselves champion. There are some interpreters, particularly among Baptists, who have written with the intention of adopting Hubmaier as an inerrantist in his biblical understanding. In fact, Hubmaier was not likely to have been an inerrantist. He knew that interpretations and meanings in the biblical texts were too important to ignore if one were to respect and benefit honestly from the study and application of Scripture.

The sixteenth century was a time in which many unusually gifted theologians lived. New communities of faith appeared and separated from Rome. The names of Zwingli, Luther, Calvin, Menno Simons and Cranmer are among the most easily recognizable. Indeed, these were giants of faith whose leadership, writings and life stories joined with their followers to create the legacies that yet endure in the faith communities we identify as Protestantism. Less well known today in the recitation of the founders of the Protestant churches is the name of Balthasar Hubmaier. Yet, he was one of the most effective reformers of church and community. His educational grounding, high levels of personal energy, and personal abilities placed him among the premier reformers of his time. He has largely been forgotten in this role, likely enough because of his failure to found a community that would continue beyond his time.

The time in which Hubmaier functioned as a pastor and pastoral theologian was one of enormous change and uncertainty. The long-standing unity of Christendom reflected in the Roman Catholic Church had been shattered. Emerging Protestant churches of northern Europe called forth both measured and radical solutions. The alliances between church and empire had been advantageous in maintaining a unity of organization and power. There were few who saw any advantages to be gained by allowing the Holy Roman Empire or the Roman Catholic Church to come apart at the seams. Both pope and emperor and their respective followers were resistant to changes in empire and church. "Change" was not part and parcel of the mindset of existing rulers. Agitators who upset the comfortable patterns by which the institutions of the time functioned were not welcome. The existing status quo had produced a *homeostasis* that mostly kept the existing culture from threats of challenge and modification. The result was an enervating malaise dominating the soul of Western Europe.

Yet, change was coming. The leaders of the new expressions of church organization and worship were hunted by those in power. It was hoped that removing the select few who were the source of the troubles confronting church and empire would alleviate the predicaments in which the existing powers now found themselves. Luther, Zwingli, Hubmaier and Calvin, all significant Protestant leaders, were condemned by church and empire. Of this group, Hubmaier was captured and executed by the empire and Zwingli was killed in battle in Kappel in Switzerland at the beginning of the Counter Reformation there. It was a high price to pay for advocating change in the sixteenth century.

It is regrettable that the significance of Hubmaier as a pastoral theologian has been either ignored or not recognized. He left behind a significant number of writings, many of which are devoted to pastoral concerns. A prominent part of his pastoral theology pointed to the centrality of the sacraments in his thinking and ministering. It is well known that he cared about believer's baptism. But more than that, he had trained in the tradition of late medieval Catholicism. It is not surprising that he was inclined to take a much larger view of sacrament than has been readily recognized by rationalist-inclined theological writers of the 20th and 21st centuries. Yet this significant dimension of his reforming work has been virtually ignored.

It is a positive development among Reformation and Hubmaier interpreters to find a refreshing antidote for the lack of recognition of the vitality of sacramental thinking in the life and writings of an Anabaptist theologian, Balthasar Hubmaier. Brian C. Brewer presents us with an exceptional study of Hubmaier's sacramental thinking in the volume at hand. Brian, who was the first graduate of George W. Truett Theological Seminary at Baylor University, has acquitted himself well and indeed left the seminary and all interpreters of Hubmaier and the Reformation in his debt. In addition, Brian now teaches historical theology at his alma mater, Truett Seminary.

The volume at hand is the result of many years of ardent work on Hubmaier. It was first submitted as his doctoral dissertation at Drew University at Madison, New Jersey. I first met him there when I was given the privilege of serving on his dissertation committee. The most fortunate circumstances for Brian came as a result of the participation of two particular members of the committee. His advisor and the chair of his committee was Donald W. Dayton, a well-known American church historian who has distinguished himself not only in his publications but by advising doctoral students in theology for a number of years. I was pleased to see how both supportive and demanding Professor Dayton was of the work of his student, Brian Brewer. Brian was fortunate to have such a guide in the research and writing of his thesis.

In addition to Professor Dayton, Brian benefitted by the participation of James F. White on his committee. Professor White, who was one of America's leading interpreters of Christian worship, had retired after serving many years at the University of Notre Dame and was, at the time, serving as the Bard

Thompson Professor of Liturgical Studies at Drew University. Professor White gave Brian the gift of his expertise in the interpretation of liturgy, especially as the sacraments played a central role in the work of Hubmaier. It was no small gift.

I am pleased to say that Professor Brian C. Brewer, now Assistant Professor of Christian Theology at Truett Theological Seminary, has produced, as his initial scholarly book, this volume on Hubmaier, *A Pledge of Love: The Anabaptist Sacramental Theology of Balthasar Hubmaier*. I had the opportunity to send an initial typescript copy of the dissertation to the library at the International Baptist Theological Seminary in Prague, Czech Republic. I received in response a thoughtful and grateful expression of thanks from Ian Randall, the Anabaptist historian and theologian at Prague. Reformation studies and Hubmaier research are beholden to him. I read the original thesis several times and am happy to say that the study of the Reformation and of Anabaptism's leading early theologian, Balthasar Hubmaier, are in good hands.

H.W. Walker Pipkin
Formerly Professor of Church History and
Founder of the Institute of Baptist and Anabaptist Studies
International Baptist Theological Seminary
of the European Baptist Federation

Abbreviations

ANF	*Ante-Nicene Fathers*, (ed.) A. Roberts and J. Donaldson, 10 vols. (CLPC, 1885-96. Reprinted. Peabody: Hendrickson Publishers, 1994).
Hubmaier	*Balthasar Hubmaier: Theologian of Anabaptism* (trans and eds) H. Wayne Pipkin & John H. Yoder Scottdale: Herald Press, 1989.
LW	*Luther's Works* (St. Louis and Philadelphia: Concordia and Fortress, 1958-1986).
MQR	*The Mennonite Quarterly Review*
Schriften	*Balthasar Hubmaier Schriften* (eds) Gunnar Westin & Torsten Bergsten (Güthersloh: Gerd Mohn, 1962).
SW	***Selected Works of Huldreich Zwingli*** (ed.) Samuel Macauley Jackson (Philadelphia: University of Pennsylvania, 1901).
WA	*D. Martin Luthers Werke* (Weimar: Hermann Böhlaus Nochfolger, 1883-1993).
ZW	*Huldruch Zwingli Writings* (trans) E.J. Furcha (ed.) H. Wayne Pipkin (Allison Park: Pickwick Publications, 1984).

Introduction

Anabaptism, that "left-wing"[1] movement of the sixteenth century Protestant Reformation, has often been ignored or relegated to the footnotes of many historical accounts of Protestantism. Many Catholic and mainline Protestant scholars alike still hold erroneous stereotypes and continue to misunderstand the movement. Consequently, a more trustworthy history of Anabaptism has largely been left to the theological descendants of the Anabaptists, primarily Mennonite, Baptist and other believers' church[2] scholars. The fortunate result of such research has uncovered the pregnant thought of numerous sixteenth century leaders and established a better understanding of the events that surrounded the Anabaptist movement.

Subsequently, the works of such Anabaptist leaders as Conrad Grebel, Felix Mantz, Hans Hut, Leonhard Schiemer, Hans Denck, Dirk Philips and others have been recovered and increasingly appreciated. Yet, a number of scholars point out that only the works of Menno Simons rival the contribution of Balthasar Hubmaier to the formative theologies of Anabaptism, and none approaches Hubmaier among first generation Anabaptists in the development of the movement's early thought and Christian practice.

Balthasar Hubmaier is, undoubtedly, one of the most prominent names within Anabaptism. Such a place has been rightfully won, for Hubmaier was perhaps the most articulate defender of Anabaptist theology and its ordinal practices during the movement's fledgling years. Nevertheless, many students of the Reformation period too quickly associate Hubmaier's thought as being representative of Anabaptism, or even more inappropriately, as being common-

---

[1] "Left Wing of the Reformation" was Roland H. Bainton's nomenclature for various sixteenth-century groups which became disenchanted with the Lutheran and Zwinglian movements' relative conservatism of magisterially supported church reform. See his article, "The Left Wing of the Reformation," *Journal of Religion* 21 (1941), 124-34. George H. Williams popularized the analogous term "radical reformation" in his landmark study of Anabaptism, *The Radical Reformation* (Philadelphia: The Westminster Press, 1962), particularly xxvi-xxxi.

[2] Donald Durnbaugh introduced this term as a more precise label for "free" churches which claim some historical or typological tie to Anabaptism. See Donald F. Durnbaugh, *The Believers' Church: The History and Character of Radical Protestantism* (Scottdale: Herald Press, 1968), particularly 4-8.

place among the early Brethren.[3] Instead, this book will attempt to portray a Hubmaier who came to Anabaptist thought, and more specifically to an Anabaptist "sacramental" theology, through a different path from that taken by the other early leaders of the movement.

Hubmaier's Distinctive Sacramentalism

All leading sixteenth century Anabaptists arguably came to their radical reformed beliefs based upon somewhat similar basic theological tenets as a visible ecclesiology, evangelical soteriology or a pre-Pietist or semi-Pelagian notion of ethics as a response to the reigning medieval Augustinianism. However, no other first generation Anabaptist appropriated these beliefs demonstratively through a structured sacramental system as did Hubmaier. For Hubmaier, the rites of the church are forefront in the development of his theology, both as a Catholic professor and teacher and as an Anabaptist pastor and leader. His consciousness of worship, its proper practice, and its impact on congregational life and Christian ethics was pervasive throughout his works. To this end, this book will focus on Hubmaier's sacramental theology to bring a clearer understanding of the Waldshut reformer's Christian thought and distinct early influence on Anabaptism.

A study into the "sacramental" theology of any sixteenth century Anabaptist may, on first appearance, seem preposterous. Indeed, a cursory reading of the primary and secondary works of this radical movement implicates Anabaptism as a "non-sacramental" movement.[4] Anabaptism's descendants in the believers'

---

[3] John Howard Yoder, for instance, once observed that "in the sixteenth century there was christological originality among the Anabaptists (*though not in Hubmaier*)." See John Howard Yoder, "The Believers' Church Conferences in Historical Perspective," *The Mennonite Quarterly Review* [hereafter *MQR*] 65 (January 1991), 17 [italics mine].

[4] Most Anabaptist scholars tend to avoid the usage of the term "sacrament". Indeed, Walter Klaassen notes that "Anabaptism testifies uniformly that sacredness or holiness does not attach to special words, objects, places, persons or days. . . . There are no sacred *things*. 'The bread is nothing but bread.' . . . Therefore ordinary bread ought to be used and it should be treated like ordinary bread." Klaassen, *Anabaptism: Neither Catholic nor Protestant* (Waterloo: Conrad Press, 1973), 11-12, [italics his]. Here, while Klaassen does not name "sacrament" as a rejected term outright, the flavor of his writing certainly implies at least the spirit of Free Church antitransubstantiationism. John D. Rempel has noted that Anabaptism was both "anticlerical and antisacramental". See his "Mennonite Worship: A Multitude of Practices Looking for a Theology", *Mennonite Life* 55, no. 3 (September 2000), 1. Additionally, Thomas Finger notes that "Mennonites are thought to be a- or even anti-sacramental." See Thomas Finger, "Sacramentality for the Catholic-Mennonite Theological Colloquium" (April 2005), 28.

church today generally, though not unanimously, reflect this spirit.[5] Additionally, as James F. White points out, the term "sacramentality" is relatively novel.[6] As such, the application of such a modern definition into a classic period may appear anachronistic. Nevertheless, this book will argue that such an approach is not only appropriate but also enlightening of the development and implication of Hubmaier's thought.

Although the use of such terminology has been deemed an anathema by recent free church scholarship, such an approach is not completely reflective of the spirit of its forebears in the sixteenth century, particularly in Hubmaier in the first generation of Anabaptism, as well as Bernhard Rothmann, Pilgram Marpeck, Dirk Philips and Menno Simons among subsequent generations of early Anabaptists. The free church today, then, demonstrates a reluctance to utilize "sacrament" to describe some of its church practices, but this hesitation may be based more on events and influences after the Reformation period which limited or made suspicious use of this terminology and not squarely on the early Radical Reformation.[7]

Anabaptist scholarship has generally continued this anti-sacramental senti-

---

[5] The Christian Church (Disciples of Christ) historically has utilized this term and some Baptist traditions do not outright reject it. See Mark G. Toulouse, *Joined in Discipleship: The Shaping of Contemporary Disciples Identity* (St. Louis: Chalice Press, 1997), 159-160 and D. Duane Cummins, *A Handbook for Today's Disciples in the Christian Church (Disciples of Christ)* (St. Louis: Chalice Press, 1991), 25-30, for examples of the Disciples' usage of this terminology. Additionally, see Norman H. Maring and Winthrop S. Hudson, *A Baptist Manual of Polity and Practice*, revised ed. (Valley Forge: Judson Press, 1991), 145, for reference to historic Baptist use of this term. In this latter work, Maring and Hudson note that while "Baptists in general seem to prefer to speak of ordinances rather than sacraments,. . . there was a time when they were less hesitant to call the Lord's Supper a sacrament, and that term is still more common among British Baptists."

[6] James F. White, *The Sacraments in Protestant Practice and Faith* (Nashville: Abingdon, 1999), 13.

[7] This is especially true of those who understand "sacrament" to mean the dispensation instead of merely the conveyance of grace. As such, they would consider "sacrament" as nearly synonymous with "magical" and would thereby reject usage of such a term. Baptist linguist and Greek scholar A.T. Robertson opened his address to the 1911 convocation of the Baptist World Alliance in Philadelphia stating: "This is the one thing that Baptists stand for against the great mass of modern Christians. The Greek Church, the Roman Catholic Church, the Lutheran Church, the High Church Episcopalians, and the Sacramental wing of the Disciples attach a redemptive value to one or both of the ordinances. It is just here that the term 'Evangelical Christianity' comes in to emphasize the spiritual side of religion independent of rite and ceremony", here cited in R. Wayne Stacy, "Baptism" in R. Wayne Stacey (ed.), *A Baptist's Theology* (Macon, GA: Smyth and Helwys, 1999), 153. To Robertson's historic quote, Stacy himself adds: "believer's baptism by immersion in a nonsacramental sense is perhaps the *sine qua non* of Baptist theology . . .", here cited in Stacy (ed.), *A Baptist's Theology* 154.

ment, often by projecting their Mennonite and Baptist perspectives on their theological foreparents. To an extent, such an anti-sacramental position is appropriate. Grebel favored terminology which would avoid the implication of relapsing that which is spiritual to a sacramental form. He argued then for ceasing all priestly customs such as vestments, special bread and cup, and special water. Jakob Kautz wrote in his *Seven Articles* that "No word, no sign, no promise and no sacrament can make a man completely certain."[8] Melchior Hofmann spoke of priests as "sacrament sorcerers and conjurers" and accused Luther of making an idol of the sacraments. During his trial in 1570, one Anabaptist argued that the word "sacrament" did not exist in the Bible and should not be used in the church.[9]

These sentiments seem rather straightforward, then, as representative of Anabaptism. Consequently, when scholars encountered the works of Balthasar Hubmaier, they often made similar conclusions. For instance, Eddy Mabry notes:

> . . . Hubmaier also rejected the medieval term 'sacrament' itself. Historically the term 'sacrament' had meant the visible sign of an invisible grace, which communicated that of which it was the sign. Hubmaier rejected the notion that the sacraments conveyed grace. As they did not convey grace, but were only done in obedience to the commands of Christ, Hubmaier called them, not sacraments, but 'ordinances.'[10]

Mabry's research on this point exposes more his own modern Baptist convictions and less Hubmaier's true sacramental development in his theology.

More precisely, as a developing Protestant and Anabaptist, Hubmaier sought to transform the medieval notion of sacrament while still maintaining the use of its terminology. He wrote in his *Form zu taufen*:

> That we have called the water of baptism, like the bread and the wine of the altar, a 'sacrament'; and held it to be such, although not the water, bread, or wine, but in the fact that the baptismal commitment or the pledge of love is really and truly 'sacrament' in the Latin; i.e. a commitment by oath and a pledge given by the hand which the one baptized makes to Christ, our invincible Prince and Head, that he is willing to fight bravely unto the death in Christian faith

---

[8] Here cited in Gerhard J. Neumann, "The Anabaptist Position on Baptism and the Lord's Supper", *MQR* 35 (April 1961), 147.

[9] Neumann, "The Anabaptist Position on Baptism and the Lord's Supper", 147.

[10] Eddie Mabry, *Balthasar Hubmaier's Doctrine of the Church* (Lanham: University Press of America, 1994), 166.

under his flag and banner.[11]

Hubmaier's notion of the sacraments in his mature theological development did not disassociate itself from "sacramentality", but merely transposed it from the signs of water, bread and wine to their companion acts of oath and promise. For Hubmaier, the sacraments were firmly rooted in a well-formulated ecclesiology accompanied by strong doses of anthropology and ethics.

Like his Anabaptist colleagues, Hubmaier strongly affirmed the notion of a gathered fellowship of genuine believers who submitted themselves to baptism, the Lord's Supper, confession, and church discipline, in order to preserve a true church. The signs of baptism and the Lord's Supper, as such, were important features emblematic of this ecclesial transformation. It is unfortunate that Hubmaier did not have more time before his premature death to develop further his notion of the gathered community of believers to leave for his fellow Anabaptists and for posterity. Nevertheless, Hubmaier's extant writings indicate for him the importance of those signs and actions which were the fruits of the genuine church.

To those who criticized Hubmaier for his focus in ink and voice on these rites, Hubmaier responded in his *Von der brüderlichen Strafe*,

> So all of those who cry: 'Well, what about water baptism? Why, all the fuss about the Lord's Supper? They are after all just outward signs! They're nothing but water, bread and wine! Why fight about that?' They have not in their whole life learned enough why the signs were instituted by Christ, what they seek to achieve or toward what they should finally be directed, namely to gather a church, to commit oneself publicly to live according to the Word of Christ in faith and brotherly love, and because of sin to subject oneself to fraternal admonition and the Christian ban, and to do all of this with a *sacramental* oath before the Christian church and all her members, assembled partly in body and completely in spirit, testifying publicly, in the power of God.[12]

The signs testify to the genuineness of the gathered fellowship and must be accompanied by discipline. This was particularly important in light of Hubmaier's notion of the church as Christ's body on earth. Since he took seriously

---

[11] G. Westin and T. Bergsten (eds), *Balthasar Hubmaier Schriften* (Gütersloh: Gerd Mohn, 1962) [hereafter *Schriften*], 352; H. Wayne Pipkin and John H. Yoder (eds), *Balthasar Hubmaier: Theologian of Anabaptism,* Classics of the Radical Reformation, vol. 5 (Scottdale: Herald Press, 1989), [hereafter *Hubmaier*], 391. This latter work will be the translation cited, compared with the original, and will be hereafter amended when noted.

[12] *Hubmaier*, 384 [italics mine]; *Schriften*, 346.

the biblical tradition of Christ's ascension into heaven, His sitting on the right hand of God and His promise not to return until the great day of judgment,[13] Hubmaier reasoned that it was impossible for Christ to be present or contained in any object such as water or bread. The words of institution found in Luke and I Corinthians were interpreted by Hubmaier to be acts of memorial of Christ's presence, not invocations of Him. Instead, Christ's presence on earth was to be found in the body of disciplined believers. On this point, John D. Rempel rightly concludes:

> It follows from this that the dominical ceremonies of baptism and the Lord's Supper are not means of grace but responses to grace. Their agent is not God but the church and, within the church, the believers in it. These signs are part of what constitutes the church because they embody the condition of its existence, that is, the response of faith and obedience. For Hubmaier, *sacraments* are human pledges and witnesses that the gospel has been believed and acted on. In that indirect sense only are they signs that God is present and at work.[14]

God's indwelling presence, though, is prerequisite to such gathering, obedience, discipline and ritual signs. God's previous action in transforming the person inwardly through the preached Word by the work of the Holy Spirit provides comfort and strength to enter into the church's disciplined community. As such, Rempel testifies, "the word, without any relationship to the elements, functions sacramentally as the outward sign and means of an inward reality."[15]

Consequently, Hubmaier maintained the traditional view of the outward and visible as conveying the inward and spiritual realities. Nevertheless, the notion of "sacrament" was transferred from the signs themselves to their corresponding oaths and pledges taken with them. This approach and unabashed continued usage of medieval Christian and magisterial reformed language, albeit shifted into new contexts, places Hubmaier not as commonplace but as unique among his Anabaptist contemporaries in the first generation of Anabaptism. Yet his idea of Christian ethics in response to God's inner workings causes this Anabaptist to elevate the rites and proper practice of the ordinances of the church to a place of great significance in his writings and theology. This study into Hubmaier's sacramental theology should then serve to clarify the whole of his theology and bring greater light to the diversity of thought within early Anabaptism.

---

[13] *Hubmaier*, 336; *Schriften*, 303.

[14] John D. Rempel, *The Lord's Supper in Anabaptism: A Study in the Christology of Balthasar Hubmaier, Pilgram Markpeck, and Dirk Philips* (Scottdale, PA: Herald Press, 1993), 48 [italics his].

[15] Rempel, *The Lord's Supper in Anabaptism*, 49.

History of Research

Anabaptism has been a much ignored and maligned movement of the sixteenth century. Only in recent decades has mainstream scholarship begun to recognize the important role Anabaptism played during the Protestant reformation and in the development of several significant Christian ideals and traditions.

Excellent biographies have been published through the course of the twentieth century on Balthasar Hubmaier. The 1905 biography *Balthasar Hübmaier: The Leader of the Anabaptists*[16] was the groundbreaking study of Hubmaier in the English language. Written by Baptist church historian Henry C. Vedder, the book was a volume contribution to the *Heroes of the Reformation* series edited by Samuel Macauley Jackson. That Hubmaier was considered a "hero" of the sixteenth century Protestant movement was indicative of the changing attitudes in the last century towards Anabaptism. Vedder's book praised Hubmaier for his defense of biblical Christianity and provided an excellent biographical background for understanding the development of Hubmaier's sacramental theology. At the same time, Vedder downplayed Hubmaier's recantations and weaknesses.

In 1914 Carl Sachsse, theology professor in Bonn, published his work, *D. Balthasar Hubmaier als Theologe*, which evaluated Hubmaier's theological works and contribution to Reformation studies.[17] Sachsse argued that Hubmaier's views developed over time and, consequently, were exposed to numerous theological traditions and life experiences. Consequently, Hubmaier's theology was eclectic and revealed some doctrinal inconsistencies. Such inconsistencies could be extrapolated to affect his unique sacramental theology.

Most prominent among secondary works on Hubmaier was Torsten Bergsten's *Balthasar Hubmaier: Seine Stellung zu Reformation und Täufertum, 1521-1528*, published in 1961.[18] Bergsten's text, a fresh reconsideration of the life and thought of Hubmaier, was in such demand in Britain and America that it was translated and edited into an English version by Irwin Barnes and William R. Estep and published in 1978 under the title, *Balthasar Hubmaier: Anabaptist Theologian and Martyr*.[19] This text develops the theological similarities between Hubmaier and Zwingli, even on their ecclesiologies. Bergsten noted that while the Lord's Supper was a general common ground between these two, baptism was the main doctrine that divided the two reformers.

---

[16] Henry C. Vedder, *Balthasar Hübmaier: The Leader of the Anabaptists* (New York: G.P. Putnam's Sons, 1905).

[17] Carl Sachsse, *D. Balthasar Hubmaier als Theologe* (Berlin: Trowizsch & Sohn, 1914).

[18] Balthasar Hubmaier, *Balthasar Hubmaier Schriften* (Gunnar Westin and Torsten Bergsten, eds.; Gütersloh: Verlagshaus Gerd Mohn, 1962).

[19] Torsten Bergsten, *Balthasar Hubmaier: Anabaptist Theologian and Martyr* (trans. Irwin J. Barnes and William R. Estep; Valley Forge: Judson Press, 1978).

Christof Windhorst also added to the new interest in Hubmaier studies with his work *Täuferishes Taufverstandnis: Balthasar Hubmaiers Lehre Zwischen Traditioneller und Reformatorischer Theologie.*[20] Here, Windhorst presented a more contemporary view of Hubmaier. In particular, the author brought much insight into Hubmaier's baptismal theology as both borrowing from his medieval Catholic training and as utilizing a fresh, biblical approach to the sacraments.

In addition to these works, other scholars have explored one or another ordinance in Hubmaier's theology. Perhaps there has been no better study into the doctrine of baptism and its development in Anabaptism than Rollin S. Armour's doctoral dissertation at Harvard, *The Theology and Institution of Baptism in Sixteenth-Century Anabaptism*, later published as *Anabaptist Baptism: A Representative Study.*[21] Armour, a professor at Stetson and later Auburn University, analyzed the baptismal theologies of Hubmaier, Hut, Melchior Hofman, and Pilgram Marpeck. While such a work was significant for Anabaptist studies, Armour's text downplayed baptism's importance as a core issue in Anabaptism. A similar dissertation-turned-book written by John D. Rempel on the Lord's Supper was published in 1993. Titled *The Lord's Supper in Anabaptism: A Study in the Christology of Balthasar Hubmaier, Pilgram Marpeck and Dirk Philips*, the text offered new insights not only into Eucharistic theology but Anabaptism's broader critique of Catholic and magisterial reformed sacramentalism.[22]

Additionally, Eddie Mabry's 1982 dissertation, *The Baptismal Theology of Balthasar Hubmaier*, provided an excellent study of Hubmaier's medieval influences in developing his baptismal theology.[23] Mabry later revised and expanded his work into the book, *Balthasar Hubmaier's Doctrine of the Church*, published in 1994.[24]

Nevertheless, through the course of the twentieth century no scholar had taken the whole of Hubmaier's sacramental thought as the basis of research into his overarching theology. Studies on baptism and the Lord's Supper had certainly isolated slim segments of Hubmaier's theology for close investigation, yet no single study had adequately stepped back to comprehend his sacramental

[20] Christof Windhorst, *Täuferisches Taufverständnis: Balthasar Hubmaiers Lehre Zwischen Traditioneller und Reformatorischer Theologie* (Leiden: E.J. Brill, 1976).

[21] See both Rollin S. Armour, "The Theology and Institution of Baptism in Sixteenth-Century Anabaptism", *MQR* 38 (July 1964), 305; and Armour's *Anabaptist Baptism: A Representative Study* (Scottdale: Herald Press, 1966).

[22] John D. Rempel, *The Lord's Supper in Anabaptism: A Study in the Christology of Balthasar Hubmaier, Pilgrim Marpeck, and Dirk Philips* (Scottdale: Herald Press, 1993).

[23] Eddie L. Mabry, "The Baptismal Theology of Balthasar Hubmaier" (Unpublished dissertation, Princeton Theological Seminary, 1982).

[24] Mabry, *Balthasar Hubmaier's Doctrine of the Church* (Lanham: University Press of America, 1994).

thought as a whole, satisfactorily relating the ceremonial rites of the church to their corresponding sacramental promises in oath and covenant in Hubmaier's theology.

However, after the initial publication of this present work in the form of a dissertation at Drew University in 2003, Kirk R. MacGregor published in 2006 his revised dissertation from the University of Iowa under the title, *A Central European Synthesis of Radical and Magisterial Reform: The Sacramental Theology of Balthasar Hubmaier*. MacGregor argues that Hubmaier's sacramental theology depended heavily on Bernard of Clairvaux, a figure of importance to Hubmaier's mentor, Johannas Eck. With the caveat of arguing a "literary dependence" which does not speculate on whether Hubmaier had actually read Bernard or not, MacGregor argues that Hubmaier's sacramental thought was an amalgamation of Bernard of Clairvaux and Hubmaier's contemporaries in Martin Luther, Ulrich Zwingli and the Grebel circle.[25]

Another recent work of importance to Hubmaier studies is H. Wayne Walker Pipkin's 2008 publication, *Scholar, Pastor, Martyr: The Life and Ministry of Balthasar Hubmaier (ca. 1480-1528)*. This book, which is the published edition of Pipkin's 2006 Hughey Lectures at the International Baptist Theological Seminary in Prague, Czech Republic, outlines the changing perspectives within Hubmaier studies, Hubmaier's formative education and relationships in his early ministry, freshly reviews Hubmaier's conflict with Ulrich Zwingli, details the events of Hubmaier's Nikolsburg church and subsequent execution, and posits Hubmaier's "Baptist" theology.[26]

Similarly to MacGregor, the work presently in your hands posits Hubmaier as one who arrived at his mature, Anabaptist sacramental thought by conjoining his Catholic theological training to his magisterial and Reformation theology. However, Hubmaier's Catholicity may only safely be described as deriving from Johannes Eck and Hubmaier's own scholastic training, without conjecturing on the various strains of scholastic thought for his day. Instead, this book maintains that the retention of some of Hubmaier's Catholic thought influenced his understanding of baptism, the Lord's Supper and other church practices. The development of this thought provides greater insight into this Anabaptist thinker's consciousness of worship and ethical practice in the Anabaptist community of faith and helped to shape early Anabaptism and subsequent theologi-

---

[25] MacGregor further postulates that Hubmaier is not to be associated with the Anabaptists of Zurch but instead should be seen as a magisterial reformer who had accepted credobaptism. Kirk R. MacGregor, *A Central European Synthesis of Radical and Magisterial Reform: The Sacramental Theology of Balthasar Hubmaier* (Lanham: University Press of America, 2006), esp. 91-129.

[26] H. Wayne Walker Pipkin, *Scholar, Pastor, Martyr: The Life and Ministry of Balthasar Hubmiaer (ca. 1480-1528)* (Prague: International Baptist Theological Seminary of the European Baptist Federation, 2008).

ans and leaders of the movement.

Significance

Hubmaier's writings clearly reveal the importance he placed on the rites of the church within the development of his theology. While most studies on Hubmaier have provided general overviews of his life, ecclesiology or a single ordinance in his thought, little study has deeply probed Hubmaier's sacramentalism as a whole and the implicit connections between baptism, the Lord's Supper and other ethical responses to God's grace. To this end, this book will concentrate on Hubmaier's sacramental theology in order to elucidate further his theology and its distinct influence on Anabaptism.

To accomplish this goal, the first chapter of this book will set the theological context of Hubmaier's sacramental thought within a historic background of his life. This is to portray, as with all theologians, that doctrinal thought is not developed in a vacuum but is shaped by life experience and circumstance. Hubmaier, of course, is no exception to this. A trained Catholic priest who had attained a doctorate in theology, Hubmaier grappled with the tradition of his upbringing as he encountered the reformation writings of Luther, Zwingli and early Anabaptists. Consequently, the argument will be made that all of this life experience helped to shape Hubmaier's thought as unique among the first Anabaptists and his sacramental thought as nonpareil among his generation of Anabaptist peers.

Subsequently, the book will analyze the development of Hubmaier's doctrines of Eucharist, baptism, and other possible signs of sacrament individually in order to comprehend further Hubmaier's uncommon view of sacrament. The volume will then conclude by reviewing Hubmaier's liturgical contributions to Anabaptist worship and measure the possibility of any influence of Hubmaier's sacramental thought on later Anabaptism, the believers' church tradition and the church universal.

CHAPTER 1

The Sacraments in Hubmaier's Life and Theological Development

The study into the life of any thinker may provide avenues to understanding his or her thoughts and written contributions for posterity. Balthasar Hubmaier was shaped by his home life, his vast education, his wide reading of contemporary theology, his dialogue with other reformers, and, arguably, his staunch independence among magisterial and Anabaptist reformers.[1]

One of Hubmaier's greatest contributions to the believers' church tradition and to ecumenical dialogue as a whole was the development of his view of "sacramentality", a position which was unique among the very early Anabaptists. The Anabaptist Hubmaier saw the sacraments as neither "magical" rites with cleansing water and wine nor as mere symbols of redemption and memorial respectively. Nevertheless, he was steeped in the former tradition and lingered in the latter in order to complete his own unique theological sojourn. This exploration concluded with a notion of sacrament as an inward commitment accompanied by an outward pledge, the former as a believer's true covenant, the latter as his or her conveyance of such. Consequently, tracing Hubmaier's life-journey is worthy of the effort in order to bring light into his unusual assembly of Catholic, Protestant and Radical influences upon his thought.

Early Life and Education

"Hubmaier" means "farmer on the hill", and most researchers of his biographical material conjecture his upbringing to be not far removed from his surname.[2] Born into a lower class family between 1480 and 1485 in the town of

---

[1] Such independence, this book will argue, comes both theologically and, for a time, geographically.

[2] Indeed, in a document attributed to be an oration of Hubmaier written by his doctor father, Johannes Eck, upon the former's graduation from one of his schools, Eck states, "the narrow means of his [Hubmaier's] father's house was so embarrassing to him that he had to leave the high school for a time, and, to protect himself from want, became a school-teacher. . . ." Here cited in Henry C. Vedder, *Balthasar Hubmaier: The Leader of the Anabaptists* (New York: G.P. Putnam's Sons, 1905), 28-29. It seems evident then that Hubmaier's family was not well-off financially.

Friedberg,[3] five miles east of Augsburg, Hubmaier was approximately the same age as both Luther and Zwingli (b. 1483 and 1484 respectively). Little is known of Hubmaier's childhood years, save for an early development of Catholic piety and a strong veneration of the Virgin Mary as attributed to a staunchly Roman Catholic upbringing.[4] The child Hubmaier was baptized in the Catholic Church and later probably attended Latin school in Augsburg.[5] In 1503 Hubmaier began studies at the University of Freiburg, only to withdraw shortly thereafter because of dwindling finances. After teaching for a short period of time at a school in Schaffhausen, Hubmaier returned to Freiburg in 1507, probably after receiving his consecration as a priest at Constance. Upon his return to Freiburg, he quickly earned both a bachelor's and master's degree.[6]

Hubmaier's theological training was markedly different from that of many of his soon-to-be reformer contemporaries. Hubmaier was schooled in the more conservative tradition of German scholasticism representative of the late middle ages. This movement rejected the modern brand of Christian humanism which sought to decipher meaning in Scripture through philological exegesis. Erasmus and Jacques Lefevre d'Etaples were leading figures in this new approach to textual study in which original language, grammar and rhetoric were taken seriously. For Hubmaier and his conservative education, such innovation was superfluous.[7] The resulting interpretive cleavage between Hubmaier and his reformer counterparts in Zwingli, Luther, and Oecolampadius would be reflected in their early approaches to interpreting scripture.[8]

---

[3] Walker Pipkin notes the etymology of the name of Hubmaier's home town. Friedberg, Pipkin observes, is a word which means "peaceful mountain". Pipkin outlines the many playful ways Hubmaier would later appropriate his nickname as "Friedberger" in his later writings. See H. Wayne Walker Pipkin, *Scholar, Pastor, Martyr*, 37.

[4] Sydnor L. Stealey, "Balthasar Hubmaier and Some Perennial Religious Problems", *The Review and Expositor* XL, no. 4 (October 1943), 412. In his historic biography of Hubmaier, Henry C. Vedder surmised that "From the first he seems to have been inclined to piety and the service of God, and we shall not go astray if we attribute this inclination of heart to the influence of a Christian mother", Vedder, 25-26.

[5] Much of these details of Hubmaier's early life and education are surmised from the little records which remain about him during this period. For instance, when he registered at Freiburg, he was recorded as a cleric from Augustana diocese from Augsburg. Scholars have conjectured that such a notation suggests that Hubmaier received financial support from a benefice and would have attended the Cathedral school in Augsburg. For instance, see Pipkin, *Scholar, Pastor, Martyr*, 38.

[6] William R. Estep, *The Anabaptist Story: An Introduction to Sixteenth-Century Anabaptism* (Grand Rapids: Eerdmans Publishing Company, 1996), 78.

[7] Hughes Oliphant Old, *The Shaping of the Reformed Baptismal Rite in the Sixteenth Century* (Grand Rapids: William B. Eerdmans Publishing Company, 1992), 94.

[8] Walter Klaasen observed that Hubmaier's "approach was the unabashedly direct approach of the layman, whereas he viewed his educated opponents as using the tools of their scholarship to hide the truth and to confuse the simple." For an excellent explanation of Hubmaier's method of scriptural interpretation, see Klaasen, "Speaking in Simplicity: Balthasar Hubmaier", *MQR* 40 (Apr. 1966), 139-47.

While a student at Freiburg, Hubmaier studied under Johannes Eck, a leading nominalist, who himself was strongly influenced by the theology of Gabriel Biel.[9] This influence is most clear in terms of Hubmaier's continued appropriation of the classic late medieval nominalist distinction between God's absolute power, in which God is seen as capable of working in an unlimited capacity, and God's ordained power, in which God is viewed as choosing to set boundaries in the way God interacts with humanity, even in Hubmaier's later Anabaptist thought. Eck doubtlessly would have taught his pupils that God's decision to act in certain ways within the world (ordained power) did not curtail the divine faculty of sovereign freedom and omnipotence (absolute power).

The shape of late medieval nominalistic thought, made popular by Biel and didactically disseminated by Eck, emphasized the notion that the laws of nature and human interaction with the divine were based upon God's free choice to enter faithfully into covenant with the world.[10] God elects to remain faithful to the divine covenants of creation and redemption.

Humanity, likewise, is granted the freedom to respond to God's covenantal relationship. It is not completely broken in its fall into sin, but it is granted the gracious, though innate, capability of exercising righteous living in response to God's offer of a salvific relationship. Consequently, God's predestination is abridged into God's foreknowledge: God retroactively elects those whom God foreknew would have responded to the divine offer of covenant. As such, both God and humanity remain free, though God chooses to work within previously designated parameters.[11]

This brand of late medieval theology, as will be outlined subsequently in relationship to the sacraments, will impact Hubmaier's journey from Catholicism to Lutheranism to Anabaptism, as Hubmaier ultimately applied nominalist motifs to his sacramental theology. Namely, baptism and the Lord's Supper serve as the means for the human free will to enter into lasting covenant with both

---

[9] For further study into the question of Eck's appropriation of nominalism in his own theology, see Erwin Iserloh, "Die Eucharistie in der Darstellung des Johannes Eck", in *Reformationsgeschichtliche Studien und Texte*, 73/74 (Münster: Westfalen, 1950), 344.

[10] David Steinmetz notes that, for the nominalist, God's "fidelity is not grudging or coerced. It is a commitment freely and gladly assumed. In the last analysis the structures of creation and redemption rest on no other basis than a free and uncoerced decision of the sovereign will of God." See David C. Steinmetz, "Scholasticism and Radical Reform: Nominalist Motifs in the Theology of Balthasar Hubmaier", *MQR* 45 (1971), 126-27.

[11] Steinmetz, "Scholasticism and Radical Reform", 128. For further development of this concept, see also Kirk R. MacGregor, "Hubmaier's Concord of Predestination with Free Will", *Direction* 35, no. 2 (Fall 2006), 279-99.

God and the church. Johannes Eck then provided Hubmaier the pedagogical framework during these formative years around which Hubmaier' later theological developments and sacramental applications would be built.

Indisputably, Eck played a profound role in shaping Hubmaier's formative Catholic thought. This was evidenced overtly by Hubmaier's choice, upon Eck's recommendation, to follow his mentor to the University of Ingolstadt, where Hubmaier received his doctorate of theology in 1512 and was quickly made a member of the theological faculty. Remaining at his academic post, Hubmaier was appointed university preacher and chaplain of the university Church of the Virgin at Ingolstadt. Now steeped in Catholic education and tradition, Hubmaier was named vice-rector of the university by 1515. But his gifts in preaching brought him widespread acclaim in the region. Hubmaier himself recognized that his strengths were greater in homiletics than administration, and he subsequently accepted the prestigious call to be chief preacher of the new cathedral in the prominent city of Regensburg by early 1516.[12] Although Hubmaier had left the academy, evidence demonstrates an ongoing personal relationship between Eck and Hubmaier after this time.[13] Arguably, Eck's influence on Hubmaier's sacramental theology continued even after the latter's break from medieval Catholic theology to Anabaptism.[14]

---

[12] Estep, *The Anabaptist Story*, 79. Interestingly, Christof Windhorst notes that Hubmaier's move from Ingolstadt to Regensburg is a curious one and suggests a whole range of reasons for the move "from irregularities in the prorector's office up to a better endowed position in Regensburg." See his "Balthasar Hubmaier: Professor, Preacher, Politician", in *Profiles of Radical Reformers* (ed. Hans-Jürgen Goertz; Scottdale: Herald Press, 1982), 145

[13] Werner O. Packull reports the fascinating discovery in 1961 from the shelves of the University Library at Munich by Hans Wiedemann of a book given to Eck by Hubmaier. The cover page of the book, Platina's *Histories of the Popes*, contains the inscription in Eck's own hand: "Having been given by Balthasar Hubmaier, doctor of arts and theology, and public preacher at Regensberg, while Eck for reasons of recreation travelled by boat down the Danube to Vienna, so as to have comfort while sailing. July 18, 1516." A presumably later notation added: "This Balthasar first became a Lutheran, then a Zwinglian, thereafter he founded the sect of Anabaptists; he was burned at Vienna by King Ferdinand in March, 1529 [sic]." While some of the information written by Eck was misleading, interpretive or inaccurate, the discovery of the gift book does give credence to a continued relationship between the two as late as 1516. See Werner O. Packull, "Balthasar Hubmaier's Gift to John Eck, July 18, 1516", *MQR* 53 (Oct. 1989), 428-32.

[14] The lingering nominalism in Hubmaier's theology will be discussed more fully in chapter 3. Nevertheless, it is important to note here David Steinmetz's integral role in Anabaptist scholarship to bring this notion of medieval theology's continued influence on Hubmaier to the fore. See David C. Steinmetz, "Scholasticism and Radical Reform", 123-44, and his essay, "Balthasar Hubmaier (1485?-1528): Free Will and Covenant", in *Reformers in the Wings* (Philadelphia: Fortress Press, 1971), 200-208. Additionally, Walter Moore notes the parallels between Eck and Hubmaier, yet he is quick to point out that Eck did not conclude with the tripartite views of the human (body, soul, spirit) that Hubmaier manifested. See Walter Moore, "Catholic Teacher and Anabaptist Pupil: The Relationship Between John Eck and Balthasar Hubmaier", in *Archiv für*

The Possible Influence of Bernard of Clairvaux's Theology

Kirk R. MacGregor has argued that, during his theological training, Balthasar Hubmaier became highly influenced by the theology of the twelfth century French abbot and Cistercian reformer, Bernard of Clairvaux (1090-1153). MacGregor credits Bernard's writings as shaping Hubmaier's own sacramental thought, both as an early Catholic and even later as a Protestant reformer.[15] This theory is somewhat substantiated by Hubmaier's own use of Bernard's name in Hubmaier's cover letter to his 1526 treatise, *A Simple Instruction*, wherein the now Anabaptist reformer dedicated his work to Lord Leonhard von Lichtenstein at Nikolsburg. Within this letter, Hubmaier, now also schooled in humanism, playfully outlined the etymology of Leonhard's name as a person of "strength, manhood, and toughness", comparing such qualities to the biblical characters, Samson and David.[16] Almost in passing, Hubmaier compared his ruling authority also to the "bear" (*Bern*) of Bernard. In discussing David, Hubmaier mentioned Bernard's name with Leonhard's, cryptically stating "he strangled a lion and a bear". The apparently strange reference to Bernard (ostensibly Bernard of Clairvaux) at this juncture is now explained by MacGregor to be a reference to Bernard's sermon, *On the Second Baptism*, wherein the medieval abbot stated:

> Our first parents, most dearly beloved, were not overcome by the lion or the bear; no, they were seduced by the serpent. . . . Accordingly, dearest brethren, it behooves us to be baptized anew. Just as in baptism we are rescued from the powers of darkness and transferred to the kingdom of light, so in this second regeneration of the monastic vows we are refashioned in the light.[17]

This reference, MacGregor maintains, demonstrates Hubmaier's familiarity with not only Bernard's writings but particularly his understanding of ordination to the priesthood as a "second baptism", one which had an intrinsic effica-

---

Reformationsgeschichte 72 (1981), 79-93.

[15] As noted in the introduction of this book, MacGregor does not see Hubmaier as an Anabaptist akin to the Grebel circle but rather as a magisterial reformer who ultimately insisted on the exclusive practice of believer's baptism. See MacGregor, *A Central European Synthesis*, esp. 37-89.

[16] *Hubmaier*, 316.

[17] Originally cited in Bernard of Clairvaux, "On the Second Baptism", in *Sermons for the Seasons and Principal Festivals of the Year*, trans. by a priest of Mount Mellary (Westminster, MD: Carroll Press, 1950), 422-24; here cited in MacGregor, *A Central European Synthesis*, 21-22.

cy in sealing each priest's salvation in Christ. Thus, MacGregor ultimately argues, Bernard's influence was profound in shaping Hubmaier's sacramental theology and his own early sense of eternal security as a priest. This would come to the fore later when Hubmaier ultimately began rebaptizing some of his own congregants but initially demonstrated a reluctance to receive a second baptism himself due to his ordination. MacGregor suggests that Hubmaier was undoubtedly introduced to Bernard's writings, along with other patristic and medieval theologians, under the careful tutorship of Johannes Eck. Eck then inspired Hubmaier to be a high church sacramentalist in his early Catholic career.[18]

Regensburg Catholicity

Hubmaier's position in Regensburg was no tranquil retreat into what modern readers would characterize as typical priestly duties. As the leading priest of the city, he was apparently responsible for keeping the Jewish population under control. Controversy over the size and even existence of the Jewish community had stirred throughout the city for numerous years preceding Hubmaier's arrival. Indeed in such an intolerant time, Regensburgers viewed Jews as an economic blight and a scandal.[19] Regensburg was the only remaining, largely-populated German city not yet to expel its Jewish inhabitants, primarily due to the political backing of the Jews by Archduke Ferdinand. While various clergy-led skirmishes had ensued before his superintendency, Hubmaier's leadership brought about sweeping changes. Hubmaier viewed the Jewish population as an unnecessary burden on the Regensburg economy. In his sermons, he echoed

---

[18] MacGregor, *A Central European Synthesis*, 91.

[19] It seems that the reasoning given for such anti-semitic spirit in the city, though doubtless a rationalization, was the high interest Jews were said to have held on financial loans to the other Regensburg citizens. This, in the mind of Hubmaier and many others, was a form of sinful usury. Indeed, on one occasion, Hubmaier is credited with preaching, "Wir haben von Rom Bullen ausgebacht, kraft welcher jeder im Bann ist; der einem Juden zu seinen wucherischen Zinsen verhilft." ("We have brought papal bulls from Rome, by which anyone is excommunicated who assists a Jew in making a profit through usury"), and he later admitted in 1526 at a public hearing in Zurich to have preached against the "großen, überschwenglichen Wucher" ("the great, overwhelming profits") made by the Jews from those Christian citizens of the city. See Torsten Bergsten, *Balthasar Hubmaier: Seine Stellung zu Reformation und Täufertum, 1521-1528* (Kassel: J.C. Oncken, 1961), 77, and translations cited from Bergsten, *Balthasar Hubmaier: Anabaptist Theologian and Martyr*, 53. For further development of this theme within Hubmaier and his contemporaries, see also Michael Driedger, "The Intensification of Religious Commitment: Jews, Anabaptists, Radical Reform, and Confessionalization", in *Jews, Judaism, and the Reformation of Sixteenth Century Germany* (eds. Dean P. Bell and Stephen G. Burnett; Boston: Brill, 2006), 269-99.

what had been traditional anti-Semitic Christian themes that the Jews were blasphemers and mockers of Mary. Consequently, he stirred up the Christian population and instigated anti-Jewish violence in order to rid the city of its Jewish population.

Subsequently, he had the vacant synagogue destroyed and in its place built a chapel for pilgrimages in honor of the Virgin Mary (*zur schönen Maria*).[20] Pilgrims flocked to the new shrine where miracles were said to take place daily. Hubmaier, the ensconced Catholic, took upon himself, as the first chaplain of the new facility, to record each reported miracle in and around the building. Additionally, such a new religious attraction also allured an increased financial support for and donation of rich gifts to the church. Consequently, Hubmaier became the object of resentment by the local Dominican monasteries where a loss of popularity, and probably more importantly of money, was perceived because of the attraction of the new chapel. Such events demonstrate not only an unfortunate anti-Semitism in Hubmaier, a trait not unlike other Christians leaders – both Catholic and Protestant – in his day, but also the strength of late medieval Catholic thinking regarding Mariology, pilgrimages, and relics within his thinking at this juncture. Such outward expressions of Catholic theology suggest a Hubmaier who, one might at least conjecture, had not yet begun to challenge his scholastic training or entertain Reformation ideas.

Initial Reforms in Waldshut

Various suggestions have been made as to whether the controversy over the Jews or unexpected theological shifts in his theology caused Hubmaier to transfer his ministry from Regensburg to the quieter and more remote town of Waldshut in Hapsburg territory in early 1521. Regardless, its geographic location is of interest. Located on the upper Rhine between Schaffhausen and Basel, Waldshut offered both a quiet location for introspection and a crossroads between Luther's Wittenberg, Erasmus' and Oecolampadius' Basel, and Zwingli and Grebel's Zurich. Here Hubmaier was positioned geographically to observe and study the full gamut of the contemporary reformation movements of his time. Nevertheless, initially Hubmaier seemed to continue performing the duties of a medieval priest. For instance, Estep notes of Hubmaier that

---

[20] While John Howard Yoder noted the synagogue as "destroyed" during the anti-Semitic campaign with the chapel built on the site of the former structure, William Estep referred to the synagogue only as "deserted" and then "transformed" into the chapel. Thus, details as to whether the former structure was utilized remain unclear and disputed. See John Howard Yoder, "Balthasar Hubmaier and the Beginnings of Swiss Anabaptism", *MQR* 33 (Jan. 1959), 5 and Estep, *The Anabaptist Story*, 79.

During thunderstorms he stationed himself at the church door with the Host and blessed the clouds. At Easter and on other occasions, as when the Host was carried to the sick, he saw that everything was done with much pomp and ceremony. In fact, Waldshut had never before witnessed such elaborate processions or such impressive ritual. The reverend doctor reverenced Mary and all the saints and was in turn revered by the citizens of Waldshut.[21]

At this juncture, Hubmaier, the former theology professor, cathedral preacher and current parish priest, seemed to exhibit all the qualities of a cleric trained in late medieval Catholicism. Nevertheless, over the course of his ministry in Waldshut, Hubmaier and his parish in this quiet river town would undergo dramatic transformation.[22] The alteration of his sacramental theology became the most apparent modification in Hubmaier's mature theology. Hubmaier began to view the sacraments as human responses to God's initiative through which Christians would pledge their love to God and the church. The Catholic doctrine of *ex opere operato* was now intentionally absent from his developing sacramentalism.

Waldshut numbered no more than one thousand inhabitants at the time of Hubmaier's arrival and had only two churches, located near the upper and lower gates of the city. The move to Waldshut for Hubmaier was a great change of pace from the bustling Regensburg for the popular priest. Although he found the then placid city boring, Hubmaier found in it an ideal location for personal study and reflection on his own theological journey.[23] He initially remained faithful in Waldshut to the late medieval tradition of his training, gaining the confidence of his parish, even as the Reformation movement had made itself known in all parts of the Holy Roman Empire. Indeed, Johann Fabri, a former academic colleague and fellow pupil of Johannes Eck, observed from nearby Constance that his Waldshut colleague acted as a typical, even an outstanding Catholic priest during his first two years of ministry along the Rhine. Specifically, Fabri noted the great care Hubmaier took to venerate the Holy Sacraments, evidenced by Hubmaier's own creation of additional pomp and ceremony to the liturgy. Such practice apparently involved calling upon city council members to assist at the altar for the Eucharist at Eastertide.[24] Such attention to

---

[21] Estep, *The Anabaptist Story*, 80. See also Estep, "Balthasar Hubmaier: Martyr Without Honor", 6-7.

[22] Such a picture of this faithful, young Catholic priest belies the fact that years later his name would be listed by the Council of Trent beside Luther, Zwingli, Calvin and Schwenckfeld as a "heresiarch" whose writings were strictly forbidden. See Windhorst, "Balthasar Hubmaier: Professor, Preacher, Politician", 144.

[23] Estep, "Balthasar Hubmaier: Martyr Without Honor", 6.

[24] See Carl Sachsse, *D. Balthasar Hubmaier als Theologe* (Berlin: Trowitzsch & Sohn, 1914), 131, and Torsten Bergsten, *Balthasar Hubmaier: Anabaptist Theologian and Martyr*, 70. In the latter work, Bergsten noted of Fabri's observations: "Doubtless Fabri's description of Hubmaier's earlier work as a true servant of the church had the object of magnifying the guilt of his later apostasy and heresy. At the same time, Fabri's well-

ritual led Torsten Bergsten to observe that "Hubmaier exerted himself in his early years in Waldshut as a zealous champion of the Catholic sacramental system. Outwardly, he was a faithful son of the church, but inwardly, at the same time, a decisive religious and theological transformation was taking place."[25] Hubmaier's thought began to undergo some alteration in the following year of his ministry.

By the summer of 1522, Balthasar began an intensive study of the Scriptures, especially in the Pauline epistles.[26] He had become increasingly attracted to the writings of Erasmus and Martin Luther, leading him ultimately to journey to Basel. There he met Erasmus and Glarean, the former teacher of Conrad Grebel. Subsequently, Hubmaier visited other reforming Swiss cities to observe their progress and returned resolute to study Scripture more closely.[27] In the meantime, however, Hubmaier continued to say mass, baptize infants, and give extreme unction to the dying. Nevertheless, he had become increasingly anxious to see the Reformation transform his own community.

In the midst of his theological reconsiderations, Hubmaier received an invitation to return to the *Schönen Maria* in Regensburg in December of 1522. However, Hubmaier was now not the courtly cleric that the Regensburg congregation had remembered. At this juncture, he gradually began to manifest the marks of a clergyman open to the Reformation, most overtly in his style of preaching. He had commenced his Regensburg homecoming with a series of sermons on the Gospel of Luke. While not officially vacating his pulpit in Waldshut, Hubmaier agreed to perform clerical duties in Regensburg throughout the year of 1523. Yet, he joined a clandestine house meeting of radicals, led by a tanner, Hans Blabbans, for Bible study and study of Luther's writings. From a letter written two years later, Hubmaier seems to indicate that the study in this circle was the place of his theological breakthrough that transformed his preaching to exclusively biblical exposition.[28] The Regensburg church was unprepared for such preaching, and they found Hubmaier's plans for a reformation of Regensburg too abrupt and too daunting. He returned to Waldshut only three months later to attempt to reform the quiet town, to preach from the Bible instead

documented presentation is thoroughly reliable and, according to the author, Hubmaier acknowledged its validity."

[25] Bergsten, *Balthasar Hubmaier: Anabaptist Theologian and Martyr*, 70.

[26] Johann Loserth, "Balthasar Hubmaier", *Mennonite Encyclopedia* 2 (1956): 826.

[27] Estep, *The Anabaptist Story*, 80.

[28] Hubmaier wrote: "Further, I hear with great sadness how in your city of Regensburg, more men preach vanity than the pure word of God. That makes my heart ache; for what does not flow forth from the living word is dead before God. Therefore says Christ, 'Search the Scriptures.' He does not say, 'Follow the old customs – though I did nothing else when I was the first time with you. However, I did it ignorantly. . . . Within two years has Christ for the first time come into my heart to thrive. I have never dared to preach him so boldly as now, by the grace of God." This correspondence is not included among the published collected works of Hubmaier and is here cited only in Henry C. Vedder, 77-78 and Johann Loserth, *Doktor Balthasar Hubmaier und die Anfänge der Widerfäufer in Mähren* (Brünn: R.M. Rohrer, 1893), 41.

of the established doctrines and tradition of the Western church, and to reform his theology and practice of the sacraments.[29]

Luther's Influence

There is little debate that the writings of several reformers had deeply affected Hubmaier in the latter's journey from Catholic priest to Anabaptist reformer. Initially, most notable among these was Martin Luther's theological works, particularly Luther's arguments for *sola scriptura* and *sola fide*. Such reformation thought, along with attractive ideas of humanists and other evangelicals caused what Eddie Mabry calls an "inner religious crisis" for Hubmaier.[30] His own disillusionment with Catholic doctrine and practices had found resonance in confirming voices of more public disestablishment figures.

Luther's *Ein Sermon von dem neuen Testament, das ist von der Heilegen Messe*, written in 1520, profoundly shaped Hubmaier's thought, particularly regarding the sacraments. Luther's outline of *sola fide* in that document was interpreted by the Waldshut reformer as implying believer's baptism and rejecting the Catholic notion of sacraments effective *ex opere operato*, if taken, for Hubmaier, to its logical conclusion.[31]

Luther's later treatise, *The Pagan Servitude of the Church* (popularly known as *The Babylonian Captivity of the Church*) substantiates Luther's developing sacramental theology for the German Reformation. Here Luther wrote:

> For where there is the word of a promising God, there must necessarily be the faith of the accepting man. It is plain therefore, that the beginning of our salvation is a faith which clings to the Word of the promising God. . . . With plain words, life and salvation are freely promised, and actually granted to

---

[29] Scholars have conjectured as to the meaning of Hubmaier's sudden and apparently erratic departures from the Schaffhausen school, from Ingolstadt as prorector, from Waldshut and twice from Regensberg. Nevertheless, Pipkin and Yoder surmise that Hubmaier's first stay in Waldshut opened opportunities for his keen mind to begin in-depth study of various currents of non-establishment thought. Pipkin and Yoder, 17.

[30] Eddie Mabry, *Balthasar Hubmaier's Doctrine of the Church* (Lanham: University Press of America, 1994), 23.

[31] Rollin S. Armour, *Anabaptist Baptism: A Representative Study* (Scottdale: Herald Press, 1966), 24.

those who believe in the promise.[32]

Hubmaier would then have read such statements by the Wittenberg professor and interpreted for himself that the manifestation of faith in the individual was prerequisite for partaking in the sacraments, regardless of whether Luther intended this construal. Luther's writings from the early 1520s emphasized that the sacramental signs did not convey power in and of themselves (thus he rejected the Catholic *ex opere operato* understanding of the sacraments). The sacraments for Luther were only effective if accompanied by a testament or promise. Here Luther explained: "We may learn from this that in every promise of God two things are presented to us, the word and the sign, so that we are to understand the word to be the testament, but the sign to be the sacrament. Thus, in the Mass, the word of Christ is the testament, and the bread and wine are the sacrament."[33] For Luther, faith must be involved in the sacraments. Thus, for baptism, the German reformer would write: "The first thing to be considered about baptism is the divine promise, which says: 'He who believes and is baptized will be saved.' [Mark 16:16]."[34] This, however, did not mean to Luther that the water was salvific in itself but instead he maintained a nuanced understanding in which "the power of baptism depends not so much on the faith or use of the one who confers it as on the faith or use of the one who receives it."[35] Luther then repeatedly emphasized that the sacrament by itself does not justify or forgive but instead one's faith through the Word that the sacrament will justify is what fulfills God's promises.[36]

By 1521, Hubmaier was an avid reader of Luther's works.[37] He wrote a good deal of correspondence with acquaintances during this time regarding Luther, Oecolampadius, and other reformers. For instance, Hubmaier exchanged letters with a physician in Schaffhausen named Johann Adelphi in which the two expressed a shared interest in Luther's works and reforms. In one letter, Hubmaier stated that he was currently studying I and II Corinthians and was preparing to begin studying Romans. He also inquired what Adelphi thought of Luther's book, *Two Kinds of Righteousness*, noting also that he owned Luther's *On the*

---

[32] Luther, "The Babylonian Captivity of the Church", *Luther's Works* [hereafter *LW*] 36. Word and Sacrament, II (ed. Abdel Ross Wentz; Philadelphia: Muhlenberg Press, 1959): 39, 40.

[33] *LW* 36:44.

[34] *LW* 36:58.

[35] *LW* 36:64.

[36] See *LW* 36:65-66 and also Brian C. Brewer, "Radicalizing Luther: How Balthasar Hubmaier (Mis)Read the 'Father of the Reformation'", *MQR* 84, no. 1 (January 2010): 108.

[37] Mabry suggests that among early Anabaptists "perhaps no one was more influenced by the writings of Luther than Hubmaier", *Balthasar Hubmaier's Doctrine of the Church*, 32.

Holy Mass.[38] These remarks, made in passing, demonstrate Hubmaier's familiarity with Luther's writings by 1521.

The Waldshut priest was particularly moved by Luther's argument that faith was prerequisite to the sacraments. God's justification comes not through the sacraments but by faith. The sacraments are efficacious only because of faith in them.[39] For Hubmaier, such a view required an individual to manifest such faith, thus requiring believer's baptism and communion for there to be a genuine church.

In addition to Luther's profound argument for salvation *sola fide*, Hubmaier was deeply affected by Luther's foundational doctrine of *sola scriptura*. This doctrine precipitated Hubmaier's movement away from his medieval Catholic notion of tradition and church authority as equally important as the biblical witness. Scripture should not only be viewed as a check on patristics and church tradition but also as an authority in and of itself for all matters of faith and practice.[40]

While Hubmaier wrote little about Luther beyond the early 1520s, it is evident that the Wittenberg reformer played a significant role in shaping Hubmaier's reforming sacramental thought against the traditional Catholic doctrine of *opere operato* via Luther's doctrine of *sola fide*. Additionally, Luther aided Hubmaier in the latter's distancing from the scholastic tradition of his tutelage by presenting Hubmaier with an authoritative alternative to the church fathers and ecclesial authority through Luther's principle of *sola scriptura*.

Martin Luther's criticism of Catholic teaching on the sacraments and Luther's argument that the sacramental words should be viewed as words of proclamation were significant to Hubmaier's Protestant formation.[41] It is important to note here that Hubmaier's change of heart was initiated by sacramental reforms. The Lord's Supper and baptism became integral to Hubmaier's later

---

[38] Bergsten, *Balthasar Hubmaier: Anabaptist Theologian and Martyr*, 73. See also Brewer, "Radicalizing Luther", 104-105.

[39] Martin Luther, *D. Martin Luthers Werke*, I (Weimar: Hermann Böhlaus Nochfolger, 1897), 286 [hereafter *WA*].

[40] For instance, Hubmaier would write in 1526, "I test the holy fathers, councils, and human teachings by the touchstone of Holy Scripture, I John 4:1. If they measure up with it, then I am believing the Scripture. If they do not conform to it, I command them to get behind me, as Christ did to Peter when he was not minded according to the will of God, Matt. 16:23. This is also what Augustine desires, as well as Jerome, and also it is included in the papal laws that one should not believe any person beyond what one can prove with the Word of God, however holy one may seem to be. Paul also teaches us the very same. Even if an angel were to come down from heaven and preach to us another gospel, it should be accursed, Gal. 1:8. For one honors God in vain with human teachings, Isa. 29:13; Matt. 15:9", in "A Brief Apology", *Hubmaier*, 300; *Schriften*, 274.

[41] Christof Windhorst, "Balthasar Hubmaier: Professor, Preacher, Politician", in *Profiles of Radical Reformers: Biographical Sketches from Thomas Müntzer to Paracelsus* (ed. Hans-Jürgen Goertz; Scottdale: Herald Press, 1982), 147.

reforms, and he found much affinity with Luther's reworking of the Roman tradition. Hubmaier would ultimately adopt Luther's nomenclature of "sign" and "promise" but alter to definition of the latter to mean the human pledge or proclamation of love in response to God. Baptism would come to be the means through which each individual would pledge his love to Christ and promise to the congregation to follow in God's (and the church's) discipline. The Lord's Supper would become a communal pledge which reaffirmed the baptismal promise to serve and love one another. Hubmaier then transferred the origin of the pledge from God to the individual who responded to the divine initiative. What is unclear is whether Hubmaier misunderstood Luther or intentionally transferred the promise of the sacrament from God to the participant(s). Regardless, Luther's writing became foundational to Hubmaier's alteration in his own sacramental theology from the Catholic *ex opere operato* understanding to his own Anabaptist sacramentalism. Like Luther, Hubmaier would come to affirm that faith, and not the sacrament itself, is that which justifies.[42]

Erasmus and the Influence of Humanism

In 1521-22, the time he was encountering Luther's writings, Hubmaier was exploring the recent humanist works of Desiderius Erasmus of Basel.[43] Hubmaier's introduction to Erasmus undoubtedly came as a product of his ongoing relationships with humanists Beatus Rhenanus, Johann Sapidus, Johann Adelphius and Wolfgang Rychard.[44] Letters of correspondence in the early 1520s evince such theological exploration into humanism on Hubmaier's part. Consequently, it came as no surprise that Hubmaier would eventually encounter Erasmus' writings. In a letter dated October 1521 to Sapidus, the head of the grammar school in Schlettstadt, Hubmaier noted that he had read Erasmus' *Paraphrases in epistolas Pauli ad Rhomanos, Corinthios et Galatas* and *Ratio*

---

[42] For a much more extensive study of Luther's influence on Hubmaier's sacramental thought, see Brewer, "Radicalizing Luther", 95-115.

[43] Eddie Mabry observes that while Hubmaier's introduction to Erasmus may have come at this time, his interest in humanism probably came much sooner. In fact, there is evidence that Hubmiaer's doctor father, Johannes Eck, allowed for some of this humanistic influence as part of his eclectic scholastic nominalism. This is further buttressed by the fact that Hubmaier listened to the lectures of humanists John Faber and Urbanus Rhegius while serving as Eck's assistant at Freiburg. Nevertheless, Erasmus' works came as confirmation to Hubmaier's already formulating notion of free will through his late medieval upbringing, nominalist education, and previous exposure to humanist writings. See Eddie Mabry, *Balthasar Hubmaier's Doctrine of the Church*, 22-30.

[44] For a more thorough development of Hubmaier's relationship with these humanists, see Bergsten, *Balthasar Hubmaier: Seine Stellung zu Reformation und Täufertum*, 97-106.

seu compendium verae theologiae.[45] The school in Schlettstadt had become a center for humanism during this time, and Hubmaier also had written Sapidus for the purpose of recommending his nephew for consideration as a student. Hubmaier here seemed strongly to desire his nephew to learn humanistic thought. He wrote: "Make sure most learned man, that he in no way neglects the *Paraphrases* of Erasmus, his *compendium*, and the reading of Terence, by which you will be doing me a great favour."[46] If one were to interpret his words at face-value, Hubmaier's letter reflects a significant openness to if not complete acceptance of the humanistic school of thought and a movement away from his scholastic training. H. Wayne Pipkin then observes that from this and other letters to fellow humanists "Hubmaier demonstrated an awareness of key Erasmian texts that were popular among the humanist pastors of the region. Clearly Hubmaier was in tune with a circle of humanist pastors who found in Erasmus a programme for reforming the church along biblical lines."[47] While some scholars have interpreted his correspondence clearly to demonstrate Hubmaier's assent to humanism, others are more reluctant to concede Hubmaier as a full-fledged Erasmian.[48] Theologically, it is difficult to determine precisely to what degree Erasmus and his humanist contemporaries directly influenced Hubmaier's thought. Nevertheless, certain parallels are certainly present which helped to shape Hubmaier's sacramental theology and, as such, should be underscored.

The free will of humanity affected Hubmaier's thought more than any other characteristic in Erasmus' work. On this point, Hubmaier clearly mirrored Erasmus more than Luther. While the human after the fall is found in complete bondage to sin and is incapable of doing good in Luther's theology, Erasmus

---

[45] Here cited in n. 6, Bergsten, *Balthasar Hubmaier: Seine Stellung zu Reformation und Täufertum*, 57. See also Jarold Knox Zeman, *The Anabaptists and the Czech Brethren in Moravia 1526-1628: A Study of Origins and Contacts* (Paris/The Hague: Mouton, 1969), 125.

[46] Here cited in Darren T. Williamson, "The 'Doctor of Anabaptism' and the Prince of Humanists: Balthasar Hubmaier's Contact with Erasmus", *Erasmus of Rotterdam Society Yearbook Twenty-Seven* (2007), 43.

[47] Pipkin, "Scholar, Pastor, Martyr", 45.

[48] For instance, Bergsten pronounced from this that "Humanism fundamentally influenced Hubmaier in his development into a Reformer and an Anabaptist, and the impact that he thereby realized was of an enduring nature", Bergsten, *Balthasar Hubmaier: Anabaptist Theologian and Martyr*, 103. Thor Hall argues for both a direct influence from Erasmus and an indirect influence of Erasmus through Denck as influencing Hubmaier's doctrine of free will. On the other hand, Eddie Mabry downplays Erasmus' writings as a passing influence on Hubmaier and only as a corrective pull from Luther's notion of unconditional predestination. See both Thor Hall, "Possibilities of Erasmian Influences on Denck and Hubmaier in their Views on the Freedom of the Will", *MQR* 35 (April 1961), 160-170; and Mabry, *Balthasar Hubmaier's Doctrine of the Church*, 30.

held that God freely gives humanity complete freedom. In his *Diatribe de libero arbitrio*, Erasmus stated: "By freedom of the will we understand in this connection the power of the human will whereby humankind can apply to or turn away from that which leads unto eternal salvation."[49] Likewise, Hubmaier defined the doctrine:

> . . . since free will in the human being is nothing other than power, force, energy, or adroitness of the soul to will or not will something, to choose or flee, to accept or to reject good or evil, according to the will God, or according to the will of the flesh. . . .[50]

Though the parallels are striking both in theology and word choice, the works of these two thinkers require a more thorough reading in order to reveal some differences. For Erasmus, the freedom of humanity comes as a divine gift of grace. Hubmaier, on the other hand, reverts to his nominalist foundation of humanity's own capacity of the soul to respond to God.[51] Regardless, the similarities between them are apparent.

Differences appear between Erasmus and Hubmaier concerning the state of humanity after the fall. For Erasmus, humans lose their innately sown free will and know nothing of God outside a limited form of natural law. Only by grace are they restored to the freedoms they enjoyed heretofore.[52] Such a complete break from God is dissimilar to Hubmaier's anthropological development.

Hubmaier's general approach to humanity represents the classical trichotomous view of the spirit, soul and flesh.[53] Previous to the fall, all three substances were deemed "good" and enjoyed complete freedom. After Adam's trespass, each substance took on a different state from the other two as a consequence. The body or flesh of humanity is now completely corrupt and, because it can no longer choose good, is incapable of acting freely. The spirit, on the other hand, has gone completely unscathed. The spirit's freedom has remained "upright, whole and good."[54] It did not participate in the first sin, save for its imprisonment in the flesh. It still chooses freely and desires to do good (as one's conscience). The fall of humanity, then, occurred as a violation of this conscience as humanity acted against its own desire to do good.

---

[49] Originally cited from Desiderius Erasmus, *De Libero Arbitrio Diatribe*, in *Quellen zur Geshichtge des Protestantimus* VIII (Leipzig: A Deichert'sche, 1910), 19, here cited in Mabry, *Balthasar Hubmaier's Doctrine of the Church*, 26.

[50] *Hubmaier*, "Freedom of the Will", I, 443; *Schriften*, 393.

[51] Mabry, *Balthasar Hubmaier's Doctrine of the Church*, 26.

[52] Mabry, *Balthasar Hubmaier's Doctrine of the Church*, 29.

[53] "The spirit is whole also after the restoration. The flesh can do nothing at all. The soul, however, can sin or not sin", Freedom of the Will" I, *Hubmaier*, 442; *Schriften*, 392. Hubmaier argued the biblical foundation for this tripartite anthropology based upon I Thess. 5:23. See *Hubmaier*, 434; *Schriften*, 386.

[54] *Hubmaier*, "Freedom of the Will" I, 434; *Schriften, 386.

For Hubmaier, the soul is powerless, is now wounded and "sick unto death",[55] can still sin or not sin, but is entrapped within the corrupted body. The soul is incapable of choosing freely because of its loss of the knowledge of good and evil. While it can do little else at this point but sin and die, the Word of God can repair the soul's injured state. The Word reminds the soul what has been forgotten, the knowledge of good and evil. Subsequently, Hubmaier wrote that the soul "can now freely and willingly be obedient to the spirit, can will and choose good, as well as it was able in Paradise."[56] The soul, then, may join the spirit in desiring good and enjoy the resurrection of the heretofore dead flesh. Thus, all hinges upon one's response to the hearing of God's Word.

The regained freedom of the soul after its restoration in Christ, though, does not necessarily indicate that the human will choose to respond righteously. It simply returns the human to his or her status before the fall with the ability to choose sin or reject it. While the flesh is still worthless and dead in this life, one may choose against one's shell and with one's spirit by the grace acquired by Christ's intervention.[57]

As such, Hubmaier's anthropological development differed from humanism in general and Erasmus specifically. Nevertheless, the Waldshut reformer gleaned from Erasmus further justification for his developing sacramental theology. Indeed, Hubmaier argued even as late as 1526 that Erasmus supported his cause. In Hubmaier's *Old and New Teachers on Believers Baptism*, Hubmaier noted:

> [Erasmus] recounts all the articles of faith as they are contained in the *Symbolo Apostolorum*, [The Apostles' Creed] and adds these words: 'After you have taught the people these things and they believe what you have taught them, have repented of their prior life, and are ready henceforth to walk according to evangelical doctrine, then immerse them in water in the name of the Father and the Son and the Holy Spirit.' Here Erasmus publicly points out that baptism was instituted by Christ for those instructed in faith and not for young children.[58]

This passage reveals Hubmaier's defense of believer's baptism via Erasmus' writings. For Hubmaier, the freedom of the will would ultimately require a person to be cognizant of and able to choose God. Thus, baptism and the Lord's Supper are appropriately participated in by those adults who have freely confessed Christ.

Erasmus' interpretation of Scripture aided Hubmaier in coming to such con

---

[55] *Hubmaier*, 435; *Schriften*, 386.

[56] *Hubmaier*, 439; *Schriften*, 390.

[57] *Hubmaier*, "Freedom of the Will" I, 439-440; *Schriften*, 390.

[58] *Hubmaier*, "Old and New Teachers on Believers Baptism", 255; *Schriften*, 233.

clusions. Specifically, Erasmus' understanding of the word order in the Great Commission in Matthew 28[59] and his understanding of several passages in Acts[60] supported Hubmaier's mature Anabaptist thought. Hubmaier further expounded on Erasmus:

> He writes further on the second chapter of Acts (2:38): 'The Lord commanded the evangelical shepherds: Go forth and teach all peoples, baptize them, teach them to hold all things which I have commanded you,' Matt. 28:19. Teach those who are to be baptized the basic elements of evangelical wisdom. Unless one believes the same, then he is immersed in water in vain.[61]

Erasmus, then, played at least some role in the development of Hubmaier's sacramental thought, especially regarding baptism.

Additionally, Hubmaier was moved enough to visit Erasmus in Basel in June, 1522. There, Hubmaier discussed with the humanist the doctrine of purgatory and John 1:13 ("neither by the will of the flesh nor by the will of man").[62] In a letter to his friend Adelphius in late June, Hubmaier noted that Erasmus was of little help in the former's searching, that Erasmus "spoke freely but wrote cautiously".[63] Consequently, Balthasar was prepared to move elsewhere for more resonating dialogue.[64]

Nevertheless, the appeal of humanism had aided Hubmaier in his sacramental and theological transformation from medieval Catholic theology to a developing Protestant and ultimately an Anabaptist theology. Hubmaier was finally liberated to depart from his scholastic past and embrace Pauline theology, confessing a more humanist approach to biblical interpretation (though he still had not yet adopted humanism's philological technique of exegesis).[65] At the same time, however, such humanist influences on Hubmaier can be overstressed

---

[59] See Abraham Friesen, *Erasmus, the Anabaptists, and the Great Commission* (Grand Rapids: Wm. B. Eerdmans Publishing Co., 1998), 53.

[60] Acts 2, 8, 10 and 19 are all interpreted as corresponding to Matthew 28.

[61] *Hubmaier*, "Old and New Teachers on Believers Baptism", 255-256; *Schriften*, 233. Friesen notes this paraphrase of the Great Commission as important to Hubmaier. Here, teaching takes a priority prior to baptism. See Friesen, 53.

[62] Vedder, 54, and Bergsten, *Balthasar Hubmaier: Anabaptist Theologian and Martyr*, 74.

[63] See "Letter to Adelphius, June 23, 1522" (Vessenmeyer, 1826, 233f), here cited in Zeman, 125, n. 10. For further discussion of this correspondence, see Bergsten, *Balthasar Hubmaier: Seine Stellung zu Reformation und Täufertum,* 100-101.

[64] Nevertheless, Estep notes that "after visiting other Swiss cities and noting the progress of the Reformation, [Hubmaier] returned to Waldshut . . . more intent than ever on a study of the New Testament, which became increasingly the sourcebook of his theology", *The Anabaptist Story*, 80.

[65] Bergsten, *Balthasar Hubmaier: Anabaptist Theologian and Martyr*, 72-73.

when pertaining to anthropology, given Hubmaier's rich training in nominalist ideals of God's ordained use of power and the need for human response in
covenant. Consequently, attempts to perceive the level of humanism's influence
on this future Anabaptist's sacramental theology should be wisely measured and
tempered.

Zwingli and the Influence of Swiss Reform

Balthasar Hubmaier was undoubtedly influenced by Ulrich Zwingli of Zurich
in his theological transformation from a late-medieval priest to Anabaptist pastor. Zwingli's post-Enlightenment lens through which he viewed the Lord's
Supper and baptism as symbols of Christ's saving work for humanity would
inform Hubmaier's sacramental theology. Zwingli would write in his *Sixty-seven
Theses*: "Christ, having sacrificed himself once and for all, is for all eternity a
perpetual and acceptable offering for the sins of all believers, from which it follows that the mass is not a sacrifice, but is a commemoration of the sacrifice and
assurance of salvation which Christ has given us."[66] Zwingli would argue for
perceiving the elements of water, bread and wine as merely earthly, physical elements which powerfully represent Christ's work for humanity. He found Jesus'
words in John 6:63, "it is the spirit that gives life; the flesh is useless", as strongly
repudiating the doctrine of transubstantiation.[67] It is important to note, however,
that Hubmaier did not wholeheartedly assimilate himself to Zwingli's reformation ideas, even regarding the sacraments. Instead, the Waldshut reformer held
on to various elements of his Catholic past by translating some traditional notions of "sacrament" into evangelical categories. Zwingli may well have given
Hubmaier greater confidence in rebelling from his scholastic heritage, even regarding the sacraments, yet Hubmaier would ultimately find in Zwingli a nem-
esis rather than a confidante.

Hubmaier's Waldshut parish was positioned in the Black Forest along the
Rhine River. He once referred to this place as his "little nest" from which he
could fly down to Basel, Schaffhausen and Zurich to visit with his humanist
and reformation counterparts in Erasmus, Adelphi and Zwingli, respectively.[68]
Resettled in Waldshut by 1523, Hubmaier began a wide reading of reformation
and other dissident writings, which only added to his growing inclination to argue for church reform in his own parish.

---

[66] Ulrich Zwingli, "Sixty-seven Theses", cited in G.R. Potter (ed.), *Huldrych Zwingli*
(New York: St. Martin's Press, 1977), 22.

[67] See Zwingli, "On True and False Religion", here cited in S.M. Jackson and C.N.
Heller (eds), *Zwingli: Commentary on True and False Religion* (Durham, NC: Labyrinth
Press, 1981), 212-13.

[68] W.W. Everts, Jr., "Balthazar Hubmeyer", *Baptist Review* (No. 10, 1881), 203.

By the late spring of that year, Hubmaier apparently had begun correspondence with Ulrich Zwingli, the great reformer in Zurich. That Hubmaier had returned to Waldshut from Ingolstadt may be indicative of his reformation intentions. Waldshut was much closer to Zurich than his previous pastorate, and the town council ultimately sought to join the Swiss Confederation, seeking Zurich's protection from Catholic forces.[69] From Zwingli, Hubmaier probably learned the tactic of introducing changes in the liturgy gradually. But more importantly, Hubmaier and Zwingli began to correspond over issues about which they tended to agree, most notably their shared repudiation of issues in Catholic tradition concerning ecclesiology, particularly concerning the Lord's Supper and baptism. Hubmaier later noted that he and Zwingli shared a poignant conversation beside the Zurich moat on May 1, 1523. According to Hubmaier's later account, the two men discussed a number of articles Hubmaier had inscribed on a slate. A part of this discussion pertained to infant baptism, and they agreed that children should only be baptized after being instructed in the faith.[70] This, Hubmaier recalled, was their mutual belief as being the practice of the early church. Zwingli also confirmed such a meeting took place, *auff dem Zürch-graben*, but recollected only a discussion on the missionary and baptismal commands of Jesus in Mark 16:15-18[71] and how repentance corresponds to forgiveness in Luke 24:27.[72] Nevertheless, Hubmaier's impressions from this conversation proved to be formative in supporting his newly found convictions.

As a result of his relationship with Zwingli, Hubmaier was invited to participate in the Second Disputation in Zurich in October of the same year. During the First Disputation, in January of 1523, Zwingli had condemned the veneration of images as idolatry. Consequently, iconoclastic mobs broke out and severely damaged the crucifix hanging over the Niederdorf gate.[73] Subsequently, the Zurich Council called a Second Disputation to be held October 26-28 in

---

[69] Pipkin, *Scholar, Pastor, Martyr*, 49.

[70] "And after that in the same year, about Philip's and James' day, I conferred with you personally on the Zurich Graben about the Scriptures concerning baptism. There you said to me, rightly, that one should not baptize children before they have been instructed in the faith. That is the reason why in prior times they were also called catechumens", *Hubmaier*, "Dialogue with Zwingli's Baptism Book", 194-95; *Schriften*, 186-87.

[71] Interestingly, Rollin Armour points out that this text is the same biblical passage which caused the Zwickau prophets to argue against pedobaptism. See Armour, 20.

[72] Bergsten, *Balthasar Hubmaier: Anabaptist Theologian and Martyr*, 80. Nevertheless, Armour argues that such a concession by Zwingli, when combined with a third party's record of this meeting (Kessler's *Sabbata*) brings credence to Hubmaier's account: "It would also seem that Hubmaier is accurate in recounting that he himself questioned infant baptism at the time. Baptism was certainly discussed in the conversation; . . . [and] there is no identifiable reason for doubting the substance of his claim." See Armour, *Anabaptist Baptism*, 20.

[73] Bergsten, *Balthasar Hubmaier: Anabaptist Theologian and Martyr*, 82.

1523, proposing that the scriptural basis for the Western church's traditions supporting images and the mass should be discussed and explored. Hubmaier's input was valuable to the discussion. His active participation made public Hubmaier's shift to reformation theology.

Having been given the high honor of being seated next to Zwingli during the disputation,[74] Hubmaier argued for the basis on which reform in the church should take place:

> Now it cannot be denied, but is rather public, and clearer than the sun, that for several hundred years much error and abuse has been infiltrated into Christian practices and added to them by the devil, who never rests. This has also happened on these two subjects: namely, the images of the saints and the abuses of the mass. . . . For in all divisive questions and controversies only Scripture, canonized and sanctified by God himself, should and must be the judge, no one else: or heaven and earth must fall [Matt. 24:35].[75]

From this point of departure, Hubmaier publicly displayed not only his evangelical zeal, but also his own newly-found disdain for images. Citing Deuteronomy 27:15 ("'cursed is the person who makes a carved or molded image, which is an atrocity before the Lord God, and secretly places this image somewhere'"), he apparently silenced those who argued for the continued use of images in the church, provided they were not worshiped.[76] At the same time, Hubmaier urged for a more moderate enforcement of the removal of images, insisting that the local congregations "gather and decide unanimously without any disorder that the images shall be moved out and laid to sleep", subsequent to the right preaching of God and the working of God's fruits in each local fellowship.[77]

Hubmaier's disdain for images during this period may have implications for his developing sacramental theology. Symbols in and of themselves cannot ontologically appropriate "holiness" and, as such, are incapable of conferring grace. He maintained that only God and no images should be venerated by Christians. Neither should such images be kept in order to assist the believer in the contemplation of God's action, nor in order to elicit good works (as Jacob

---

[74] Bergsten notes of this that Hubmaier was "doubtlessly highly esteemed by Zwingli not only for his personal friendship but also for the prestige his presence lent the occasion", *Balthasar Hubmaier: Anabaptist Theologian and Martyr*, 82.

[75] *Hubmaier*, 23; *Schriften*, 716-17.

[76] *Hubmaier*, 24; *Schriften*, 718-19.

[77] While such an argument certainly may have been an attempt to head off the mob scene which took place previously that year, it may also display a new center for authority for Hubmaier: the local church over against a magisterial council. As such, Hubmaier may be intimating the beginnings of radical belief at this juncture. See *Hubmaier*, 26.

Edlibach had argued during the disputation). For Hubmaier, the Word of God serves this purpose,[78] and biblically ordained objects serve only as "outward visible signs" of God's previous action through covenant.[79] They assist only in the proclamation of such divine action. Consequently, Hubmaier deemed all images not authorized by Scripture as inappropriate and superfluous.

On the last day of the Zurich Disputation, Hubmaier argued boldly for more dramatic changes to the mass. He articulated his belief that the Eucharist was a memorial, not a sacrifice. It is "a proclamation of the covenant of Christ, in which there is a remembrance of his bitter suffering and his self-sacrifice."[80] Additionally, he put forth his view that this action was an "outward visible sign and seal through which we are made completely certain of the forgiveness of our sins",[81] and that Christ's sacrifice was accomplished on the cross. Consequently, the mass should first be completely consistent with and a form of proclamation of the Word of God. Second, it should be rendered in the language of the common people, so that it might be understood. Last, the congregation should be allowed to partake of both elements, for Christ said "Drink ye all of it!" (Matt. 26:27).[82]

However, careful analysis of Hubmaier's words during this disputation demonstrates a theologian who is not merely mirroring Zwingli's Eucharistic theology. During the discussion on the mass, Hubmaier may have reflected more of Luther's understanding of the real presence of Christ within the elements than Zwingli's mere symbolism. Sounding somewhat like Luther during Luther's own subsequent debate with Zwingli at the Marburg Colloquy in 1529, Hubmaier charged Zwingli of making double-talk in the latter's interpretation of Christ's words of institution: *Hoc est corpus meum*. Hubmaier was recorded as scolding the Zurich reformer:

> Hence I implore and warn you, dear Zwingli, for the sake of God, that you from now on withhold such glosses and worthless discourses as you employed, for instance, in the words of Christ concerning the Supper where you gratuitously turned an *est* into a *significant*. . . . If you had preserved the straightforward understanding of the words spoken by Christ, then much harm would have been prevented.[83]

---

[78] ". . . for it is impossible that the Word of God should be preached and not bring works and fruits in that whereto it was sent from God [Isa. 55:10]", *Hubmaier*, 26.

[79] *Hubmaier*, 27.

[80] *Hubmaier*, 27.

[81] *Hubmaier*, 27.

[82] *Hubmaier*, 28.

[83] The German transcript of this citation can be found in *Transcript of the Second Zurich Disputation* in Emil Egli and Georg Finsler, *Huldreich Zwingli Sämtliche Werke* 2 (Leipzig: M. Heinius Nachfolger, 1908), 786; here citing the English translation in Kirk MacGregor, *A Central European Synthesis*, 120.

It is unclear from this passage and cannot be assumed that Hubmaier was still advocating medieval sacramentalism or even Lutheran notions of a holy union of Christ's presence with the elements.[84] Instead, Hubmaier probably disagreed with Zwingli's approach to biblical hermeneutics in altering the plain meaning of the verb *est*. Instead, as Hubmaier would later argue, the elements of bread and wine were Christ's body and blood *in remembrance*. Thus, Hubmaier may not have completely disagreed with Zwingli's ultimate interpretation but was repudiating what he may have seen as a lax and irresponsible use of the biblical text in arriving at such a position. Regardless, one may safely agree with Kirk MacGregor's observation that "even when the two reformers were on the best of terms, they were not in agreement on every matter" and that Hubmaier demonstrated some independence from Zwingli's version of reformation theology.[85]

While the development of Hubmaier's Eucharistic thought will be taken up in the next chapter, the alteration of his sacramental theology at this point is indicative of his new theological convictions as a whole. That the mass should be understood by the people demonstrates Hubmaier's belief that sacraments are the Christian's responses to grace, not divine actions carried out *ex opere operato*. Borrowing from Luther's notion of *sola fides* and applying his understanding that faith requires intellectual assent,[86] Hubmaier insisted that the sacraments, in this case the mass, must be comprehensible by those witnessing and partaking. Congregants are no longer seen as ontologically transformed through the external rites of church. It is Christ and a Christian's covenant with God that does this. Instead, the mass becomes an outward sign of the memorial of Christ's action and each Christian's concurrence with Christ's covenant.

Beyond these interactions of 1523, it becomes difficult to argue a significant, on-going influence of Zwingli on Hubmaier and even more problematic to characterize him as a Zwinglian disciple. Although the two theologians certainly shared ideas with one another during this period, more often than not utilizing similar language,[87] their meanings often stressed differing ends within evangelical paradigms.[88] A leading difference within this paradigm was the

---

[84] Kirk MacGregor argues that this passage evinces that Hubmaier still believed in "some form of real presence" of Christ in the Supper. See MacGregor, *A Central European Synthesis*, 120.

[85] MacGregor, *A Central European Synthesis*, 120.

[86] Mabry, *Balthasar Hubmaier's Doctrine of the Church*, 37.

[87] For examples, see Mabry's development of Zwingli/Hubmaier parallels in their writings, *Balthasar Hubmaier's Doctrine of the Church*, 41-42.

[88] Mabry points out that even Zwingli's and Hubmaier's apparent agreement on the sole authority of scripture in matters of faith displays divergence of opinion when hermeneutically applied. While Hubmaier limits the church's actions to what Scripture specifically permits, Zwingli allows for certain functions when Scripture does not explicitly forbid them. Infant baptism, for instance, would become the most highly debated issue between these two, based primarily upon these differing allowances within their biblical exegeses. See Mabry, *Balthasar Hubmaier's Doctrine of the Church*, 43-44.

emphasis, for Zwingli, on God's initiating action for sacramental recollection contrasted with Hubmaier's insistence that the sacraments focus on the human pledge to covenant with God's grace and action. While such divergence in their thought seems semantic within the scope of their general agreements, it would be enough to pit one leader against the other in future written debates.

Further Reforms in Waldshut

Upon his return to Waldshut, Hubmaier seemed to be emboldened by his now public theological assertions. He prepared a similar disputation to be held in Waldshut in which he outlined his reformed beliefs in his *Eighteen Articles* (*Achtzehn Schlussreden*). Estep notes that "it is evident from their content that he had completely overhauled the scholastic theology characteristic of his Freiburg and Ingolstadt days."[89] Although his work contained Lutheran and Zwinglian characteristics, particularly Zwingli's *Sixty-Seven Articles*, Hubmaier's own *Articles* demonstrated some original thought. Here he publicly espoused the sole authority of scripture in matters of faith, the importance of faith alone to make a person holy, the importance of the mass as memorial and not a sacrifice, the Christian obligation to support the needy, and the inconsequentiality of chastity for the priesthood.[90] Not surprisingly, Hubmaier subsequently removed all images from the Waldshut sanctuary, abolished laws on fasting and began to conduct services in German. Additionally, he married Elisabeth Hügeline, the daughter of a wealthy Waldshut citizen. While the Waldshut citizenry quickly joined in Hubmaier's reforms, the other clergy were slower to conform.[91]

The Catholic hierarchy received notice of Hubmaier's reforms in Waldshut and requested the Waldshut City Council to dismiss the priest and replace him with another "who does not hold to Luther's condemned doctrines".[92] Though the city council continued to support its priest, Hubmaier ultimately wanted to avoid further conflict or endanger Waldshut. He left his beloved congregation in September of 1524, taking refuge in a Benedictine monastery in Schaffhausen. While displaced from his parish, Hubmaier wrote his famous treatises, *Concerning Heretics and Those Who Burn Them* (*Von Kertzern und ihren Verbrennern*) and *Axiomata or Theses Against Eck* (*Axiomata – Schlussreden gegen Eck*). Hubmaier probably penned both writings to defend himself against the church's charge of heresy.[93]

---

[89] Estep, *The Anabaptist Story*, 82.

[90] *Schriften*, 71-74; *Hubmaier*, 32-34.

[91] Johann Loserth, "Balthasar Hubmaier", in *Mennonite Encyclopedia* 2 (1956), 827.

[92] Cited in Estep, *The Anabaptist Story*, 84.

[93] In the latter work, Hubmaier generally designated himself as in the same camp as that of Ulrich Zwingli. See *Hubmaier*, particularly 51-53. See also John Howard Yoder, "Balthasar Hubmaier and the Beginnings of Swiss Anabaptism", 6.

Hubmaier's opponents worked incessantly to have the reformer extradited to Austria. Not feeling secure in his political future in Schaffhausen, Hubmaier was coerced to return to his post and was reestablished as Waldshut's chief preacher by November.[94] One Waldshut opponent to Hubmaier wrote that Hubmaier returned "as if he were the emperor himself".[95] In gratitude, peasants gathered around the city to form a type of military force against invasion by Catholic authorities. Hubmaier himself took his turn standing guard at the city wall.

While Hubmaier had been shaped both by Luther's and Zwingli's brands of reformation theology, by the time of his return to Waldshut, he was quickly moving in the direction of Anabaptist theology, especially in the development of his ecclesiology and sacramental practices. Hubmaier had particularly become displeased with Zwingli's ambivalence on the issue of baptism. Hubmaier perceived Zwingli as periodically ready to defend believer's baptism, while at other times reluctant to push the Zurich city council and its churches too far. By the time Zwingli had reached a decision to continue holding to a form of pedobaptism,[96] Hubmaier's convictions had led the Waldshut priest to conclude that the rite should be reserved exclusively for confessing adults.

Rollin Armour notes that of the three major reformers of the southern region of German-speaking Europe (Zwingli, Martin Bucer, and Oecolampadius), by 1525 only Oecolampadius was still open to a reconsideration of infant baptism.[97] In a letter to Oecolmpadius in January of that year, Hubmaier argued for

---

[94] Loserth, 827.

[95] Here cited in Estep, "Balthasar Hubmaier: Martyr without Honor", 8.

[96] Geoffrey W. Bromiley notes of Zwingli's change of heart and mind on baptism that "it is difficult to say what brought about the decisive change in Zwingli's view of the matter. Perhaps he was influenced by the sectarianism of the Anabaptists, or their revolutionary tendencies [in their correspondence with Thomas Müntzer], or more likely their tendency to depreciate the Old Testament. It may even be that he gained something from Luther's resolute opposition to the Zwickau prophets. Above all, he must have seen that the appeal to Scripture meant something far bigger and deeper than simply the citation of one or two proof-texts." Bromiley, *Zwingli and Bullinger*. Library of Christian Classics, XXIV (Philadelphia: Westminster Press, 1963), 119. Pipkin and Yoder, on the other hand, note that "Zwingli's early doubts about the propriety of infant baptism were soon quieted by his concern for the maintenance of the visible Christian community as a civil and social order." See *Hubmaier* [hereafter all editorial notations in this collection of writings will be cited as "Pipkin and Yoder"], 79.

[97] Armour, 22. Hughes Oliphant Old observes regarding the correspondence between Hubmaier and his reformed counterparts in Oecolampadius and Zwingli that the latter two reformers "did not give Hubmaier's questions anything like the attention they deserved, or anything like the attention he demanded" and that they "doubtlessly had other things on their minds which they considered more important [than discussing baptism]." See Hugh Oliphant Old, *The Shaping of the Reformed Baptismal Rite in the Sixteenth Century* (Grand Rapids: William B. Eerdmans Publishing Co., 1992), 95.

the importance of credobaptism, calling infant baptism a "vessel without wine". Though this letter will be developed further in subsequent chapters, it is significant to note at this point that Hubmaier stressed that baptism and the Lord's Supper both comprise a "bond with God" and must be returned to their "nature and genuine purity" in order to restore a purer form of Christianity.[98]

This 1524 letter also reveals the liturgical reform Hubmaier had already put into place pertaining to the practice of baptism. Citing Matthew 19:14 ("Let the little children come to me", etc.) as his justification for modifications, he wrote:

> I like to assemble the congregation in the place of baptism,[99] bringing in the child. I exposit in the native tongue the gospel text: 'Children were brought . . .' (Matt. 19:13). As soon as his name has been given to him, the whole congregation on bended knee prays for the child, entrusting him to the hands of Christ, that he may be ever closer to the child and pray on his behalf. If there are parents of a sick child at a given time, who most earnestly wish the child to be baptized, I baptize it. In this matter, I take on sickness myself along with the sickly little ones, but only for a time, until better instructed. But as for interpreting the Word, I do not give ground in the least respect.[100]

Thus, while he still continued to practice pedobaptism for insistent parents of sickly children, Hubmaier had already begun conforming his conventional praxis to his theological beliefs, substituting infant baptism with a service of consecration. Such a liturgical innovation, of course, came out of his new sacramental conviction that baptism comes as a symbolic reenactment of the spiritual bond between God and the believer. Since the very young are incapable of making such a pledge in response to God's grace, an alternate ceremony of dedication is substituted to recognize spiritually this rite of passage.

---

[98] *Hubmaier*, 70.

[99] Pipkin and Yoder note here that "Hubmaier probably means that he gathers the assembly at the baptistery, so as to make the new ceremony something like the old one. But the phrase may also mean 'in lieu of baptism'", n. 17, p. 72.

[100] *Hubmaier*, 72.

Relationship with and Conversion to Anabaptism

How Hubmaier came to his Anabaptist convictions is, to a degree, uncertain. Although there is evidence that Hubmaier had been in contact with various magisterial reformers and that he certainly would have met and perhaps had spoken on behalf of Conrad Grebel during the Zurich Disputation,[101] Hubmaier's contacts with the Swiss Anabaptist leaders beyond this are ambiguous. Pipkin and Yoder note that while Hubmaier had begun to share the basic convictions of the developing "left wing" of the Zurich Reformation, he did so "without participating in their meetings or in the psychological dynamics of the coming to birth of Zurich Anabaptism."[102]

Only by early 1525 did Hubmaier return to Zurich, now finding a theological kinship in the Swiss Brethren. He had spoken without complete devotion to either Zwingli or the Brethren at the disputation, though Hubmaier seemed to have found firmer theological footing in the Anabaptist camp now a little over a year later.[103] Hubmaier's entrance into radical Protestant thought, then, probably came generally independently of his counterparts in Zurich.[104]

Hubmaier's Eucharistic thought carried a stronger emphasis of human response to the memorial of Christ's death than did Zwingli's by calling on the congregation to pledge their love for and forgiveness of one another. Additionally, Hubmaier's baptismal theology became even more markedly distinct from Zwingli's. After a thorough exploration of the Bible, Hubmaier found no basis

---

[101] Pipkin and Yoder note that Conrad Grebel opened that portion of the debate on the mass but "immediately deferred to 'those who can speak better.'" Subsequently, "Baltassar Fridberger" stood to give articulate opening remarks on the subject. See *Hubmaier*, 26-29.

[102] Pipkin and Yoder, 79. Eddie Mabry affirms this point, noting that "there is no real evidence that [Hubmaier's] next actual contact with [the Swiss Brethren] came before 1525. By this time, of course, they had made a complete break with Zwingli, had set up their own reformation in Zurich and the surrounding areas, and were already practicing believer's baptism", Mabry, *Balthasar Hubmaier's Doctrine of the Church*, 50.

[103] Mabry, *Balthasar Hubmaier's Doctrine of the Church*, 50.

[104] Kirk MacGregor observes that "it is critical to remember that before 1524, the point at which infant baptism first became an issue in the Zurich Reformation, Hubmaier was already refusing to administer the rite, of which he served as a leading opponent since at least 1523, and was baptizing mostly believers from that point forward". Thus, while one might argue that Hubmaier was an Anabaptist or at least moving in that direction before the Grebel circle officially broke from Zwingli on the issue of baptism and before he himself was rebaptized, MacGregor actually argues that Hubmaier never technically was an Anabaptist but was instead a magisterial reformer who had rejected infant baptism. See MacGregor, *A Central European* Synthesis, 121, 124. While an original argument and one that highlights Hubmaier's independence and unique features as a reformer, such a position tends to mitigate the numerous theological parallels between Hubmaier's reforms and those of Swiss Anabaptism.

for pedobaptism because he could find no such teaching explicitly mentioned in Scripture.[105] Consequently, Hubmaier's reworking of his sacramental theology remained significantly distinct in its orientation from the Grebel circle throughout the remainder of his life, as Yoder argues, "precisely because he came to the problem of baptism as a trained thinker dealing with a theological problem".[106] While it is true that Hubmaier began reading pamphlets by Karlstadt and Müntzer which also criticized the pedobaptist practices of the Roman Church,[107] his convictions were not projected upon him by others but came only after his own exhaustive study. One might perceive, for this reason alone, how Hubmaier's independence from the Grebel circle allowed him to develop a sacramental theology that differed somewhat from the former Zwingli followers. Even though other Anabaptists held for the continuation of baptism and the Lord's Supper as "ordinances" only, Hubmaier disclosed a sacramental theology that outlined these signs of water, bread and wine as accompanying and following sacramental pledges or covenants made with God.[108] While he had arrived at these conclusions intellectually, Hubmaier was slow in executing them liturgically, particularly with regard to baptism. A great catalyst in this process was a visit by Wilhelm Reublin of Wytiken.

After the Anabaptists were expelled from Zurich, the radical reformers spread across the region to areas which might be more receptive to their beliefs. Reublin, one of the original Swiss Brethren and a former disciple of Zwingli, came to Waldshut. From Reublin Hubmaier learned that the practice of adult baptism had taken place in Zurich. Up to this point, Hubmaier believed that all modifications to baptism in the church, save for his own moderate reforms, were only made in theological theory, not actually in ecclesiastical practice. Reublin probably spent a few days at the end of January 1525 in Waldshut. Before he left, he is said to have baptized a few citizens.[109]

Yet, Hubmaier was still insistent upon the traditional magisterial Protestant position of attaining the support of the town council before making any dramatic moves with church practice, especially regarding the sacraments.[110] Probably in an attempt to do just this, he issued a challenge, not a debate which would name time and place, indicating to the Waldshut government his intentions of liturgical reform. Pipkin and Yoder note that this came in the shape of a "*pro forma* challenge . . . which, by virtue of its having been issued, will certify

---

[105] Mabry, *Balthasar Hubmaier's Doctrine of the Church*, 50-51.

[106] Yoder, 7.

[107] Windhorst, "Balthasar Hubmaier: Professor, Preacher, Politician", 149.

[108] These "pledges" regarding the Eucharist and baptism will be outlined in the next two chapters, respectively.

[109] Pipkin and Yoder, 78.

[110] For this reason, MacGregor refers to Hubmaier as "the Magisterial Radical Reformer", *A Central European Synthesis*, 108.

his right to move on in the direction indicated."[111] Regardless, in his *Public Challenge to All Believers in Christ*, Hubmaier made an even stronger statement regarding the practice of baptism:

> Whoever wishes to do so, let him prove that infants should be baptized, and do it with German, plain, clear and unambiguous Scriptures that deal only with baptism, without any addition. Balthazar Freidberger offers in his turn to prove that the baptism of infants is a work without any basis in the divine Word, and this he will do with German, plain, clear, and unambiguous Scriptures that deal only with baptism, without any addition. Now let a Bible, fifty or one hundred years old,[112] as the right, proper, and true arbiter be placed between these two positions. Let it be opened and read aloud with imploring, humble spirit, and then let this dispute be decided and once for all brought to a conclusion. Thus I shall be well content for I want always to give God the glory and allow his Word to be the sole judge; to him I herewith desire to submit and subject myself and all my teachings. Truth is Unkillable.[113]

While apparently certain of his convictions regarding baptism at this juncture, Hubmaier may well have not seen the applicableness of his words to himself. Kirk MacGregor notes that in the same month of this writing, Hubmaier and Waldshut were visited by Anabaptist converts from Zurich who offered to baptize Hubmaier as a follower of Anabaptism. MacGregor conjectures that Hubmaier may well have refused this offer because of his understanding of his own ordination as a priest:

> . . . Hubmaier retained his regenerative doctrine of ordination, probably derived from Bernard of Clairvaux, by ontologically grounding this ceremony in the power intrinsic to the sacrament of baptism and necessary for the reconciliation of penance, the restoration of grace flowing from which is a requirement for worthily partaking of the Eucharist. Relying upon his holy orders, therefore, it seems clear that Hubmaier fully believed that both the temporal and spiritual punishment for his past, present, and future actual sins had been remitted through his Bernardian spiritual 'second baptism,' relieving him of any need to engage in a physical second baptism.[114]

---

[111] Pipkin and Yoder, 79.

[112] Rollin Armour notes that Hubmaier's desire for an older biblical text, "fifty or one hundred years old", probably arose out of a questioning of the recent translations in Wittenberg and Zurich. See Armour, *Anabaptist Baptism*, 24.

[113] *Hubmaier*, 80; *Schriften*, 106-107.

[114] MacGregor, *A Central European Synthesis*, 122.

However, in April of 1525, Reublin returned to Waldshut and was received warmly. Reublin continued to articulate Anabaptist principles, particularly baptism, to Hubmaier and his congregation and found in the Waldshut priest "a ready hearer and speedy convert."[115] Though Hubmaier had already been completely congenial to adult baptism in theory and had made modest modifications to that end in his services, his complete conversion to this principle and practice came on this occasion. Pipkin observed that "the peasants' unrest nearby and the initial successes of the revolt, which included participants from Waldshut, may well have accelerated the adoption of Anabaptism in the city."[116] Interestingly, MacGregor argues that Hubmaier may have been refusing to baptize infants for several months (thus baptizing believers only) before Reublin's arrival. Only now did Hubmaier begin to apply those rebaptizing convictions to himself since he heretofore was depending upon a medieval view of understanding his ordination as securing his own salvation. That Hubmaier immediately renounced his ordination as a priest following his baptism gives some credence to MacGregor's hypothesis.[117]

On Holy Saturday, April 15, Reublin baptized Hubmaier and approximately sixty members of his congregation. According to one account, effort was made to make the rebaptism of Hubmaier as public as possible by baptizing him in the pulpit of the church before the entire congregation.[118] The following day, Easter Sunday, Hubmaier then baptized over three hundred church-goers,[119] including most of the city council, from a milk pail which had been filled with water from a well, brought into the sanctuary and placed on the font. At some point after the service, the font was then thrown into the Rhine as a papal relic.

In these insurgent acts, one might see the developing sacramental theology taking place in Hubmaier and his Waldshut congregation. Objects used to convey the grace found in the sacraments are now no longer viewed as ontologically "holy" in and of themselves. As a result, Hubmaier would introduce the use of plain bread in the Supper, and in this case, utilized plain well water with the most ordinary of farm instruments, a milk pail. The font, on the other hand,

---

[115] Vedder, 111.

[116] H. Wayne Pipkin, "The Baptismal Theology of Balthasar Hubmaier", in *Essays in Anabaptist Theology* (Elkhart: Institute of Mennonite Studies, 1994), 88.

[117] MacGregor, *A Central European Synthesis*, 121-23.

[118] See Johnson, 69.

[119] Claus-Peter Clasen implied that the entire congregation was baptized on this weekend, numbering the congregants of the Waldshut church in 1525 at 360. See Clasen, *Anabaptism: A Social History, 1525-1618* (Ithica, NY: Cornell University Press, 1972), 62. William Estep indicates that the three hundred baptisms actually took place the entire week following Easter and not merely on Easter Sunday. See his "Balthasar Hubmaier: Martyr Without Honor", 8.

suggested an inherent sacredness of the water in the minds of these villagers. Consequently, such ornate liturgical fixtures were viewed as vestiges of the Catholic notion of *ex opere operato* and were not coextensive with the intentionally commonplace symbolism which is to accompany a believer's response to grace. As a result, the Waldshuters concluded that such fixtures must be discarded.

The Waldshut liturgical reforms continued through Easter week with the baptisms of dozens of other parishioners.[120] On Easter Monday the Lord's Supper was celebrated, and on Tuesday the congregation was said to have been given "the bread of heaven" and all had their feet washed. This was recounted as having been done "in the attempt to reproduce the exact order of the New Testament churches, [though] there were certain to be some extravagances, resulting from a hasty and unwise literalism."[121]

Hubmaier, the Anabaptist

Immediately following his baptism and his resignation as parish priest, Hubmaier was elected pastor of the newly converted Anabaptist congregation in Waldshut. While the other reforms he had enacted previous to this point allowed him to remain conscientiously with the Roman church, the sacramental pledge symbolized here by waters of baptism seemed to replace Hubmaier's vows of the priesthood and caused him to abandon his holy orders. This point will be developed further in chapter three of this book.

The newly baptized congregation inaugurated a congregational polity structure. Additionally, the old system of benefices supported by enforced tithes was abolished as the congregation pledged to meet the pastor's financial needs. Consequently, even tithing could be viewed as part of one's sacramental vows. As with baptism and the Lord's Supper, the new Anabaptist church in Waldshut was based on voluntarism. Thus, while not all the citizens of Waldshut joined with Hubmaier's Anabaptism, Hubmaier's church was comprised of those who had responded publicly to their perception of God's working in their lives. The new Anabaptist church then was made up of those who were rebaptized through credobaptism, as the new baptism became the entrance into the visible church in Waldshut. That such a demarcation took place between old members and the newly baptized demonstrates that Hubmaier's Anabaptist sacramentalism was already inherently tied to his new ecclesiology of a believers' church.

Soon after these events, Conrad Grebel visited Waldshut, probably to recognize Hubmaier as an Anabaptist leader. This action exposed Hubmaier as a

---

[120] Vedder believed some seventy to eighty more individuals were rebaptized the week following Easter Sunday, 112.

[121] Vedder, 112.

prominent public leader of the radicals, which would be seen as both a "place of honor and dishonor" among those in the region.[122]

In the months to follow, Zwingli and Hubmaier would exchange a number of public pamphlets, particularly pertaining to the sacraments. Both men would argue that the sacraments were covenant signs, but Zwingli would find in the Old Testament custom of circumcision a paradigm in which the covenant sign belonged to the family and not the individual. Consequently, he contended that faith was not necessary before the sacraments were enacted.

Hubmaier would parry in several works by underscoring the important role of the individual in understanding the covenant of faith before entering into its symbolic ceremonies. The Waldshut reformer seemed reluctant to enter public debate at this point. He occasionally wrote of what seemed to be an introverted sentiment or a cautious demeanor by claiming that he wished he could stay in his "barrel and cave and not at all to creep out into the light, not that [he] feared the light, but in order that [he] might remain in peace."[123] He expressed that he "had hoped that someone else would have done such [a work]."[124] Hubmaier seemed at home in Waldshut and appeared to have preferred the quiet life of a river town cleric to that of an outspoken theologian and reformer. Nevertheless, his path was set. His doctrine must be defended. Hubmaier would be the leading defender of Anabaptist sacramentality, not only because he was Anabaptism's only trained theologian, but also because faith and the sacraments were still vitally important to this former Catholic priest and professor. Such a defense, Hubmaier believed, was divinely driven; "The human heart undertakes also to do something for itself," he mused, "but God directs and controls according to his pleasure."[125]

Writings and conflict between the magisterial and radical reformers throughout the region would be heightened over the course of the year. As the Peasants' War reached a climax with the defeat of the proletariat in the battle of Griessen (east of Waldshut) on November 4, 1525, Waldshut's last ally had surrendered.[126]

---

[122] Vedder, 113.

[123] *Hubmaier*, 97; *Schriften*, 119.

[124] *Hubmaier*, 97; *Schriften*, 119.

[125] *Hubmaier*, 97; "Des menschen hertz nymbt auch wol etwas für sich, aber Gott schickts und richts nach seinem gefallen", *Schriften*, 119.

[126] Zeman, 127. Hubmaier is often credited with not only theological leadership in Waldshut but also political leadership in opposing Ferdinand's regime. Loserth notes that "Hubmaier became the soul of [the peasants'] resistance. . . . There is no doubt that he encouraged the city of Waldshut in its resistance against the Austrian government which led to armed intervention, and himself took part in the preparations for battle. Contemporaries and later writers have actually considered him the instigator of the Peasants' War", 827. While this theory provides much fodder for debate, it seems to contradict Hubmaier's own statement that "no preacher in all the regions where I have been has taken more pains and done more work by writing and preaching than I have that the government be obeyed; for it is of God", Loserth, 827. Although this issue is not directly pertinent to the development of Hubmaier's sacramental theology, this writer would argue parenthetically that whatever the extent of Hubmaier's involvement in the Peasant revolt, such participation only underscores his care for the disenfranchised. This support paralleled Hubmaier's concern

Consequently, Hubmaier could not reach Zurich for further disputations on the sacraments. Zwingli had used this theo-political situation to isolate the Anabaptist community in Waldshut from its allies. While Hubmaier requested other public debates with Zwingli, even after his own eventual departure from the region, Zwingli never answered such requests. Pipkin and Yoder wrote, "Unfortunately, the dialogue was never to take place. The distance between the two Reformers, so near in so many ways theologically if not in spirit, was never to be overcome."[127]

The Austrian army under the command of Ferdinand, brother of Emperor Charles V, defeated the peasants and turned its attention to Waldshut. Once again, Hubmaier knew the only way to save the city was to flee; this would be his final farewell to his beloved river town and its congregation. On December 5, 1525, Hubmaier and his wife fled Waldshut, only one day before the Austrians took the city. Though he would have preferred escaping to Strasbourg or any of a handful of other destinations, the army blockades allowed him only to flee through the Swiss countryside to Zurich.[128]

---

for those disenfranchised from the cup of the Eucharist reflected in his maturing theology.

Evidently, Hubmaier helped compose letters for the Waldshut citizenry in their dialogue with Austria and in attempts to secure political (and theological) alliances. What was important to protect and fight for in Hubmaier's mind was not the removal of feudal burdens but merely the freedom of religious practice. As Loserth notes, "if the people of Waldshut would only be granted religious liberty, they would be ready to fulfill all their obligations as Austrian subjects", 828. For further discussion of this theo-political issue, see James M. Stayer, "Anabaptists and future Anabaptists in the Peasants' War", *MQR* 62 (Apr. 1988), 99-139, a variation of which makes up a chapter in Stayer's excellent study, *The German Peasants' War and the Anabaptist Community of Goods* (Montreal: McGill-Queen's University Press, 1991), 61-92; and lastly, see Tom Scott, "Reformation and Peasants' War in Waldshut and Environs: a structural analysis" [2 parts], *Archiv für Reformationsgeschichte*, 69 (1978), 82-102, and 70 (1979), 140-69.

[127] Pipkin and Yoder, 168.

[128] Estep, *The Anabaptist Story*, 91-92. George H. Williams notes that the day following Hubmaier's departure from Waldshut, the vicar-general, John Faber, said mass and the town returned to its Catholic allegiance. See Williams' classic study of Anabaptism, *The Radical Reformation* (Philadelphia: Westminster Press, 1962), 137. It is recorded that by Christmas of 1525, the Abbot of St. Blasien sang High Mass in Waldshut's principle church and that "Christians who had adhered to orthodox beliefs had been very glad to be able to return to them". See Bergsten, *Balthasar Hubmaier: Seine Stellung zu Reformation und Täufertum, 1521-1528*, 353 and Bergsten, *Balthasar Hubmaier: Anabaptist Theologian and Martyr*, 271.

Hubmaier, the Recantor

By mid-December of 1525, Hubmaier had reached the city and was provided shelter by Henry Aberli, an Anabaptist preacher, in an inn called the Green Shield. But the city of Zurich was no safe-haven for Anabaptists, and within three or four days Hubmaier's presence was discovered. He and his wife were imprisoned by the city council under the pretense of restraining them, as Zwingli put it, from "hatching out some monstrosity."[129] Either when he was in prison or in response to his earlier requests, the city council surprisingly granted a public disputation between Hubmaier and Zwingli. Also present were such renowned figures as Leo Jud, Oswald Myconius, Komtur Schmid, Sebastian Hofmeister, four members of the city council, and an obscure school teacher from Zurich named George Bender. Though accounts differ both in Zwingli's and Hubmaier's records and in historical research, one can conclude that the debate, much of which pertained to sacramental theology, was fervid and heated.[130]

During this closed disputation, Hubmaier defended his sacramental beliefs, particularly that baptism should follow and be a public pledge of one's faith and, hence, be reserved for adults and not for young children. Zwingli argued that baptism was for Christians and their children.[131] While the Anabaptist theologian undoubtedly defended his stance lucidly, Hubmaier surprisingly agreed at the disputation's conclusion to recant his baptismal teachings. But before he made his final statement, he asked to speak alone with Jud, Myconius, and Hofmeister, all of whom had allegedly at one time also questioned the validity of infant baptism.[132]

Hubmaier read his recantation before the Small Council at the end of the day and before the Council of Two Hundred on the day following. Records indicate that in his recantation Hubmaier agreed with Zwingli's understanding and practice of the sacrament of baptism as replacing circumcision and promised there-

---

[129] Cited from Zwingli's letter to Peter Gynoraeus (August 31, 1526), in *Huldreich Zwingli: The Reformer of German Switzerland, 1484-1531* (trans. Samuel Macauley Jackson; New York: G.P. Putnam's Sons, 1901), 253.

[130] Estep, *The Anabaptist Story*, 91-92. The details of this debate will be further outlined in the subsequent two chapters on the Lord's Supper and baptism.

[131] While no public records were made of this disputation, Vedder believes that Hubmaier's *Dialogue with Zwingli's Baptism Book* "gives internal evidence of having been rewritten after the author's actual dispute with Zwingli", n. 1, p. 119. For Hubmaier's possible recollection of this debate, see *Hubmaier*, 170-233. Although Hubmaier's account, naturally, made himself appear the victor, Zwingli later would write: "It was determined that I should discuss with him in a friendly manner the baptising of infants and Catabaptists, as he earnestly begged first from prison and afterwards from custody. I met the fellow and rendered him mute as a fish", as cited in Samuel Macauley Jackson, *Huldreich Zwingli: The Reformer of German Switzerland*, 249.

[132] Estep, *The Anabaptist Story*, 92.

after to abstain from emphasizing the sacraments as a response of faith to God by an adult and, additionally, to cease in his own practice of rebaptizing.[133]

But such a recantation was not enough to satisfy Zwingli. In addition, Hubmaier was ordered to read his recantation to the congregation at Fraumünster after Zwingli had delivered his sermon address. Yet in a surprise move, instead of recanting, Hubmaier recanted his recantation before the congregation. Zwingli later wrote a colleague stating:

> Then a form of recantation was drawn up, not in accordance with any formula of the Council or of anyone, but by his own hand. And when he had read this in the church to which the name Abbey is given, and the address which I delivered to the people had been finished, he straightway denied the recantation in the presence of the whole assembly.[134]

Hubmaier is said to have cried: "Oh what anguish and travail I have suffered this night over the statements which I myself have made. So I say here and now, I can and will not recant."[135] And the rebellious Anabaptist then proceeded to maintain his Anabaptist sacramental principles, specifically that only believer's baptism was appropriate and justifiable in the Scriptures. Hubmaier was cognizant of the fact that to retreat from his beliefs on baptism would occasion the surrender of the remainder of his overarching sacramental theology which emphasized a Christian's ethical response to God's initiating grace and a public promise to live for Christ. An abdication of his notion of believer's baptism and the Lord's Supper would ultimately violate Hubmaier's Anabaptist ecclesial principle of the visible church. Subsequently, Hubmaier was said to have been "violently interrupted, hurried away, and thrown into [the Wellenberg] prison, where he was treated with great rigor",[136] while Zwingli silenced the congregation from the other pulpit and described Hubmaier as being possessed by the devil for his outbreak.

Hubmaier's second imprisonment was an ordeal of emotional and physical torture. Throughout this tribulation, he continued to write and pray.[137] Yet, under the duress of the rack, Hubmaier again uttered a required recantation which he agreed to commit to writing in order to be released from prison and torture.

---

[133] "So I have meditated much about love, and have at last been moved to abandon my conviction that one should not baptize children, and [to conclude] that in rebaptizing I have been in error", *Hubmaier*, 151-52; *Schriften*, 148.

[134] Cited from Zwingli's letter to Gynoraeus (Aug. 31, 1526), in *Huldreich Zwingli: The Reformer of German Switzerland*, 254-55.

[135] Recorded here in Johannes Kessler, *Johannes Kesslers Sabbata mit kleineren Schriften und Briefen* (eds. Emil Egli and Rudolph Schoch; St. Gallen: Fehrsche Buchhandlung, 1902), 151.

[136] Vedder, 129.

[137] His *Twelve Articles of Christian Belief* was written in the Wellenberg prison during this time.

Though much less severe in its content, even to the point of being a sort of apology for and not against adult baptism, Hubmaier's statement satisfied Zwingli contingent upon Hubmaier's agreement never to preach or baptize in the Canton of Zurich again.

Interestingly, such a punishment was interpreted by magisterial reformers and their historians as an act of mercy on the Anabaptist leader. Oswald Myconius, who wrote the first biography of Ulrich Zwingli in 1532, recorded, almost parenthetically, the events as follows:

> Doctor Balthasar Hübmaier was the head of the Catabaptists, not long before a friend and companion in the gospel, but a little while after a most violent foe [to Zwingli]. He first broke out in writings and then after he had escaped from Waldshut, a town on the Rhine, and had secretly entered into Zurich, being apprehended, he resisted by word of mouth in the court-house in the presence of the deputies only. Then he requested the Senate that he be permitted to confer with Leo Jud, Sebastian Hofmeister, and me [Myconius or "Oeconomus"]. His wishes were complied with a second time. We laboured with this man so that he promised to recant the next day. Therefore in this mind coming the day after into the church from the court-house, he ascended the pulpit after Zwingli was come down and confirmed all he had taught before, moved thereto he pretended because he [Zwingli] had put so much stress upon constancy, the miserable man judging that his pertinacity was constancy! Returned to prison he was altogether hidden until by the kindness of Zwingli he was secretly sent away, not without a guide and travelling money, and came to Constance, where he so loaded the man [Zwingli] with abuse that he was forced to apologize to the brethren. But enough about the Catabaptists![138]

Regardless of whether the sentence of exile came as an expression of kind mercy or added discipline, Hubmaier left Zurich ashamed, humbled and disappointed with the weakness of his flesh. Estep passionately noted that "for the man who failed to defeat [Hubmaier] in debate resorted to the base tactics of the inquisitor".[139] Now discredited by the movement for which he had served as an articulate spokesman, Hubmaier left Zurich in secrecy to his last haven.

---

[138] Oswald Myconius, "The Original Life of Zwingli", here cited in Ulrich Zwingli, *Early Writings* (ed. Samuel Macauley Jackson; Durham, N.C.: The Labyrinth Press, 1912), 15-16.

[139] Estep, *The Anabaptist Story*, 94.

Hubmaier, Preacher of Nikolsburg

Records indicate that Hubmaier made his way through Constance, then Augsburg, and finally arrived in Nikolsburg, in Moravia, by July 1526. According to legend, Hubmaier encountered Hans Denck for the first time in Augsburg and won him over to Anabaptism during this brief stay.[140]

Nikolsburg was not an unwise choice for Hubmaier to set up residence. Moravia was the only province in Europe where Hubmaier could find a more than temporary habitation, and the townspeople seemed ready to welcome the tarnished leader. Vedder noted that

> here [Moravia] was a new experience indeed for the Anabaptists! Everywhere they had been despised, persecuted, counting them-selves fortunate if barely permitted to live: here they not only found themselves tolerated, but saw their rulers actually embracing their faith, publicly avowing it, and using their wealth and power to pro-mote the preaching of a pure gospel.[141]

While the town was primarily made up of followers of Luther and Zwingli, Moravia was ripe for Anabaptism, and Hubmaier seemed to arrive to harvest the returns.[142] In only a brief time, he won the leading preacher, Martin Goschl, who subsequently was married,[143] and the leading nobleman, Leonhard von Liechtenstein, for Anabaptism.[144] Pipkin observes that "the force of Hubmaier's personality must have been substantial, for soon after he arrived, Prince Leonhard allowed Balthasar to take over the development of the Christian community in Ni[k]olsburg."[145] Nikolsburg soon became a center for the Anabaptist move-ment. Somewhere between two thousand and ten thousand people were said to have been converted and baptized in the year Hubmaier ministered in this city. The Nikolsburg church became Anabaptist, imitating the Waldshut parish pat-tern. The news of the growing Anabaptist community within this climate of tol-erance resulted in a massive migration of persecuted dissenting Christians and Anabaptists from other German-speaking regions into Moravia.[146]

The time was also fruitful for Hubmaier personally. Not only did he find profound success in preaching, but he also wrote voluminously during this pe-

---

[140] Vedder, 142. For further discussion on the Denck-Hubmaier encounter and its pos-sibly exaggerated importance in Anabaptist historiography, see Werner Packull, "Denck's Alleged Baptism by Hubmaier: Its Significance for the Origin of South German-Austrian Anabaptism", *MQR* 47 (October 1973), 327-38.

[141] Vedder, 152.

[142] Estep even espoused that "the influence of Huss was still felt in the area", *The Anabaptist Story*, 94.

[143] Pipkin and Yoder, 339.

[144] Estep, "Balthasar Hubmaier: Martyr without Honor", 9.

[145] Pipkin, *Scholar, Pastor, Martyr*, 83.

[146] Estep states that "this marked the beginning of one of the most fruitful periods in Anabaptist history", *The Anabaptist Story*, 94.

riod. Leonhard von Liechtenstein secured the services of printer Simprecht Sorg of Zurich, who moved his entire print shop to Moravia in order to publish Hubmaier's complete Nikolsburg works.[147]

Probably encouraged by the von Liechtenstein family to write a defense of his faith and actions, Hubmaier produced his *Brief Apology* in order to clear his name from religious and political criticism. Though covering numerous subjects concisely, Hubmaier emphasized his tenaciously held sacramental thought that the Lord's Supper and baptism come as symbolic responses to the public covenant made by confessing Christians with God and their congregations.[148] Additionally, Hubmaier wrote prolifically on several other theological topics and published several more works while in Moravia. While writing some seventeen pamphlets in Nikolsburg, Hubmaier also used this peaceful retreat as a place to construct a literary defense of Anabaptist theology. Of these seventeen treatises written between 1526 and 1527, no less than eleven dealt specifically with the sacraments of the church.[149] Throughout, he consistently emphasized the sacraments as vows made in response to God's grace, followed by their corresponding ceremonial signs in water, bread and wine.[150]

Hubmaier, the Martyr

Hubmaier's extensive writing in the year he spent in Nikolsburg may have resulted from some prophetic urgency. He may have known that his time for such work was limited. As his books and reputation spread throughout the region of Moravia, Hubmaier and the growing Anabaptist movement once again caught the attention of Ferdinand I. When Moravia came under his jurisdiction after the death of King Louis of Hungary and Bohemia, Ferdinand used his expanding powers to drive the Anabaptists out of this heretofore peaceful region. The Austrian authorities insisted that Hubmaier be extradited, officially not because of any theological beliefs but because of his political involvement in the Peasants' War in Waldshut.[151] Steinmetz argues that "the Moravian nobility, who would have resisted extradition on charges of heresy, were not willing to risk their lives to protect someone who was charged with treason".[152] Hubmaier and his wife surrendered to the Austrians. They were subsequently taken to Vienna

---

[147] Loserth, 828. Steinmetz records the printer's name as "Froschauer", additionally noting that the man had already been forced to leave Zurich because of his Anabaptist views, 201-202.

[148] *Hubmaier*, 302-303; *Schriften*, 275-76.

[149] Vedder, 154.

[150] Hubmaier would publish, along with other works concerning sacramental theology, his *Christian Catechism*, the earliest-known Anabaptist catechism (which shall be elucidated upon later).

[151] Nevertheless, Bergsten notes that though Hubmaier was accused of and officially arrested for political crimes, "there can be no doubt that it was also for his work as an Anabaptist which had caused the king to take this step", *Balthasar Hubmaier: Anabaptist Theologian and Martyr*, 378.

[152] Steinmetz, *Reformers in the Wings*, 202.

and imprisoned at Kreuzenstein castle on the Danube in August of 1527. One historian has observed that during this occasion while undergoing intense questioning and torture in prison and

> under the pressures of ill health, the inevitable death sentence, and his characteristic openness to the truth, [Hubmaier] succeeded in seriously compromising his former position at several points. But he refused to back down on baptism, the Lord's Supper, and his previous denial of the existence of purgatory.[153]

The sacraments, in particular, were too important now for Hubmaier's reformation thought. Hubmaier's sacramentalism at this juncture played a paramount role in the development of his Anabaptist theology. Baptism and the Lord's Supper were more than ceremonial rites of the church to the Anabaptist leader. Instead, they represented the sacramental promises in oath and covenant in response to God's grace, and as such played a pivotal role in reforming the worship and ethical practice of the church.

Hubmaier's resistance to disavow this sacramentality contributed to his execution. While tortured on the rack on March 3, 1528, Hubmaier this time refused to recant, confess or receive last rites from a priest.[154] On March 4, 1528, Hubmaier "on account of [his] crime and condemned heresy [was] condemned to the fire".[155] Subsequently, he was led to his place of execution the following day. Sources indicate that upon appearing at his execution site, Hubmaier recited Bible verses to himself as words of comfort. Upon arrival at the scaffold and before a large group of people, Hubmaier cried out in his Swiss dialect, "O my gracious God, grant me grace in my suffering!" He then turned to the crowd and asked pardon if he had offended anyone, and Hubmaier expressed forgiveness toward his own enemies. As the wood was lighted, the Anabaptist leader cried out, "O my heavenly Father! O gracious God!" and when his hair burned, "O Jesus!" Hubmaier then died of smoke inhalation.[156] The dean of the philosophical faculty at the University of Vienna, Stephen Strügel, who witnessed the execution, remarked that Hubmaier was "fixed like an immovable rock in his heresy."[157] Three days later, Hubmaier's wife was thrown from a large bridge into the Danube with a stone tied around her neck and drowned.

While Balthasar Hubmaier officially was put to death for his involvement in

---

[153] Estep, *The Anabaptist Story*, 102.

[154] Estep opines that "the man, who for the sake of 'unity of the church' had recanted his position on baptism in Zurich and still later appeared at Graitzenstain, discovered hitherto unknown fortitude when faced with his own imminent death." Estep, "Balthasar Hubmaier: Martyr without Honor", 10.

[155] Vedder, 242.

[156] These last statements of Hubmaier, though not recorded in Hubmaier's collection of works, are all cited in Loserth, 833.

[157] Estep, *The Anabaptist Story*, 103.

the Peasants' War, his execution did not dispatch the theological principles for which he was persecuted his entire Anabaptist career. Central to those principles was Hubmaier's sacramentality which emphasized the human promise made in response to God and accompanied by the signs of water, bread and wine. For Hubmaier, these elements, used only in the context of one's confession of faith and affirmative answer to the divine offer of salvation, were crucial to restoring the visible church. In this radical reformer's thought, a free human decision is prerequisite to the reception of baptism and Eucharist. As such, these are covenantal actions exclusively on the part of mature believers. Hubmaier had understood the church not to encompass an entire geographic community but to be a voluntary society of baptized believers.[158] Transformed by God's reconciliation and their acquiescence to its covenant, Anabaptist Christians were to strive for righteous living confirmed in their sacramental pledge of love to God and their community of faith.

This theological development within Hubmaier's thought, accompanied by Hubmaier's gifts of leadership and polemics, proved to be an enormous threat to both Catholic and Zwinglian proponents. Other Anabaptists who held similar views to Hubmaier's likewise often met similar fates. Nevertheless, the Anabaptist movement continued, at times with vigor, for subsequent generations. Hubmaier's perceived "immortal truth"[159] found firm footing on a sacramental theology which emphasized the importance of faith preceding the sign.

---

[158] Steinmetz, *Reformers in the Wings*, 207.

[159] "Die Warheit ist untödtlich", Hubmaier's favorite motto, came at the conclusion of several of his works. Yoder rendered this phrase "Truth is unkillable" while Pipkin prefers "Truth is immortal". See Pipkin and Yoder, n. 12, p. 42 and n. 10, p. 76, respectively. For Pipkin's later explanation of their difference in translation, see his book, *Scholar, Pastor, Martyr*, 103-107.

CHAPTER 2

The Lord's Supper as Sacrament

Any study into Hubmaier's sacramental thought and development undoubtedly would bring significant focus to his baptismal theology. Such focus is not unwarranted, particularly given Hubmaier's own apparent unrelenting concentration on that rite throughout his Anabaptist writings. Nevertheless, the Anabaptist leader entered into theological debate on the subject of the Lord's Supper before he broached the matter of water baptism. This study will then follow Hubmaier's form and begin by analyzing his Eucharistic thought first.[1]

Those who maintain a general knowledge of Anabaptist theology may permit that the movement's distaste for the Catholic mass and understanding of the proper role of the practice of the Lord's Supper is not expressively discrepant from Zwingli's own appropriation of the Eucharist. Both Zwingli and the Anabaptist tradition affirmed that the Supper was observed "in memory of the Lord and as a sign of brotherhood in the body of Christ. These are the two principle points."[2] Indeed, Hubmaier's early dissenting thought differed little from that of the Zurich reformer's. On the other hand, one may not simply conclude that Hubmaier's mature theology when collated to Zwingli's was completely unoriginal. The later Hubmaier was no Zwinglian. This portion of the study, then, will seek to outline the development of Hubmaier's doctrine and practice of the Lord's Supper, the unique role it played in Anabaptist liturgy and, most importantly, its overarching contribution to Hubmaier's sacramental thought.

The Development of Hubmaier's Eucharistic Thought

Little public information exists as to Balthasar Hubmaier's understanding and practice of the Lord's Supper before his appearance at the Second Zurich Disputation in October 1523. Nevertheless, various second-hand reports indicate that the younger Catholic priest was unusual only in his fervor for

---

[1] This writer will use such terms as *Eucharist*, *Lord's Supper* and *communion* interchangeably to refer to the Protestant or Anabaptist understanding of the rite and will use *mass* to distinguish the Catholic terminology of the same.

[2] Gerhard J. Neumann, "The Anabaptist Position on Baptism and the Lord's Supper", *MQR* 35 (April 1961), 147.

Catholic sacramentality during his first stays in Regensburg and Waldshut.[3] Yet by late 1522, Hubmaier had changed course and manifested enthusiasm for reforms in Zurich, and Zwingli subsequently invited him to join the second disputation in the city several months later.

While in Zurich, Hubmaier spoke boldly about perceived liturgical and hermeneutical distortions by the Roman church from the biblical pattern, comparing current Catholic practice to a lost donkey or ox having fallen into a pit out of which it must be helped immediately.[4] From this striking introduction, Hubmaier stated:

> Now it cannot be denied, but is rather public, and clearer than the sun, that for several hundred years much error and abuse has been infiltrated into Christian practices and added to them by the devil, who never rests. This has also happened on these two subjects: namely, the images of saints and the abuses of the mass.[5]

One of Hubmaier's first public statements since the commencement of his Waldshut pastorate, then, pertained to this perception of the misapplication and misemployment of the mass in Catholic theology and practice. While not fully developed, Hubmaier's sacramental thought was already incongruent with Roman Catholic practices.

At the end of the second day of the disputation, as attention was called once again to the Roman mass, Hubmaier continued in his argument:

> Concerning numerous abuses in the mass – which I would rather call a testament of Christ or a memorial of his bitter death – without doubt this is the main point of the abuses, that we interpret the mass as a sacrifice. In order to be on record on that subject, which concerns me, and since I want to let myself be taught by all Christian believers according to God's will but only through Scripture [I conclude that] I have not been taught otherwise than that I must with my dear brothers in Christ Huldricho Zuinglen and Leone Jud confess that the mass is not a sacrifice but a proclamation of the covenant of Christ, in which there is a remembrance of his bitter suffering and his self-sacrifice, who offered himself once for all on the cross, and never more will again be offered; and that this is done by an outward visible sign and seal through which we are made completely certain of the forgiveness of our sins. And he who celebrates the mass otherwise is sealing a letter that has not yet been written. . . .

---

[3] Estep, *The Anabaptist Story*, 80.

[4] *Hubmaier*, 22-23; *Schriften*, 716.

[5] *Hubmaier*, 23; *Schriften*, 716.

Christ speaks: *Hoc facite* ['do this']. He does not say, *Hoc offerte* ['Sacrifice this'].[6]

Clearly, Hubmaier denounced the traditional Catholic understanding of mass as a sacrifice. In its stead, he proposed this act of worship be viewed as a recurrent remembrance on the part of the believing congregation of Christ's one-time sacrifice on Calvary. Additionally, he articulated his understanding that this visible act serves as a "proclamation of the covenant of Christ".[7] The proclamation is performed by this "outward visible sign and seal" so that the participating believers are assured of divine absolution.

Even as they come very early in Hubmaier's career as a dissenting Christian, these statements nevertheless disclose an unfolding sacramental theology which stresses the human response on the part of the believer to the covenant or promise of God and whose public testimony of such response is performed through outward visible signs instituted by God as revealed through Scripture. The Lord's Supper for Hubmaier, then, does not transfer grace but expresses through the act of memorial by symbol the grace already received by the participants through the historical event represented, namely Christ's passion.

Here Hubmaier revealed and even conceded his thought as being a part of the Zwingli camp. He completed his rhetorical contribution to the Zurich Disputation by outlining five basic summarizing principles regarding the Lord's Supper, principles with which Zwingli and the other reformers would have readily accepted. First, he maintained that the mass is not a sacrifice but a sign instituted by Christ to confirm the faith of the believer. Second, the priest must preach only the "pure, true, clear Word of God" during the mass, of which the elements are a sign.[8] Similarly, third, the Supper is a proclamation of Christ and therefore must utilize the Word of God. Fourth, the mass should be read in the tongue of the people gathered, "for doubtless Christ did not speak Calcuttish with his disciples at the Last Supper but rather aloud and understandably."[9] Since the Supper is a form of proclamation of the Lord, "to celebrate the mass quietly and not proclaim is to silence the Lord."[10] Last, both the bread and the wine should be shared with all desirous of participation. For Christ said, "Drink ye all of it! [Matt. 26:27]".[11]

Such convictions, while newly found for the Waldshut priest, were generally representative of at least the majority of those gathered at the Zurich disputa

---

[6] *Hubmaier,* 27; *Schriften,* 786. Hubmaier cites Matthew 26:26-28; Luke 22:19ff; Mark 14:22-24; I Corinthians 11:23-26; and Hebrews 7 and 9 as scriptural supports for his view.

[7] *Hubmaier,* 27; *Schriften,* 786.

[8] *Hubmaier,* 28.

[9] *Hubmaier,* 28.

[10] *Hubmaier,* 28.

[11] *Hubmaier,* 28.

tion. Nevertheless, as shall be discussed later in this chapter, Hubmaier's own appropriation of dissent from Catholicism would, over time, take on a somewhat different meaning than that of Zwingli or even those Swiss Anabaptists who departed from the Zurich leader under Conrad Grebel.

Upon his return to Waldshut, Hubmaier proposed to imitate Zwingli's disputation and, in turn, effect ecclesial reforms in his own city. Paralleling Zwingli's sixty-seven theses that outlined the proposed discussion for the first disputation in Zurich, Hubmaier compiled his own *Eighteen Theses Concerning the Christian Life*. Here again he emphasized his own perception of the proper form for the Supper, representing two of his theses:

> 5.   The mass is not a sacrifice, but a memorial of the death of Christ, for which reason it cannot be offered either for the dead or for the living. Hereby requiem masses and memorial masses of the seventh day, the thirtieth day, and of the anniversary collapse.
> 6.   As often as such commemoration is held, the death of the Lord shall be proclaimed in the tongue of every land. Here all dumb masses [*stummende messen*] fall on one heap.[12]

Written in the spring of 1524, Hubmaier's *Theses* represents a Zwinglian-type critique of the Roman mass. This public statement differs little from his more exhaustive proclamation in Zurich months earlier. Indeed, other points among his *Theses* buttress Hubmaier's insistence that every believer may appeal directly to God without priestly liaison and is capable of discerning whether his or her priest is biblically consistent in his preaching and liturgy by the parishioner's own use of the Scriptures.[13] Consequently, Hubmaier enervated the authority of both the priest and the sacrament in its intermediary functions between God and the layperson.[14] Instead, the Christian is liberated to approach God with reliance solely upon Christ as Mediator. At the same time, Hubmaier reemphasized that the mass be said in the vernacular since it serves as a form of proclamation of and memorial to Christ's historic sacrifice on Golgotha. Thus, while his Eucharistic thought was still evolving, by 1524 Hubmaier had already begun to emphasize the importance of communion as an act to be received and

---

[12] *Hubmaier*, 32-33; *Schriften*, 73. A "dumb mass" (*stumende messen*) is one in which the words of the ceremony are not heard or understood by the congregation.

[13] "8. Since every Christian believes and is baptized for himself every one should see and should judge by Scripture, whether he is being rightly fed and watered by his shepherd", *Hubmaier*, 33; *Schriften*, 73.

"9. Since Christ alone died for our sin, in whose name alone we are baptized, so shall only he be appealed to as our sole Intercessor and Mediator. Here all pilgrimages fall away", *Hubmaier*, 33; *Schriften*, 73.

[14] Rempel, 53.

comprehended by the laity. Nevertheless, he continued to reflect Zwingli's emphasis on the elements themselves as they serve as visible signs to offer assurances of one's remission from sin. Gradually through the ensuing years, though, Hubmaier insisted more strongly that the sacrament was not bound to a visible sign but was, more precisely, one's witness to God's effective and saving work.

At this juncture, Hubmaier's Eucharistic thought became more distinct from Zwingli's. Although much of Hubmaier's newly found presumptions about the Supper emerged from Zwingli's Christological understanding of personal faith (i.e., faith only in the sacrifice of Christ on the cross as atonement for believers), Zwingli's approach continued to emphasize a significant role from the priest or deacon in administering the sacraments. Hubmaier, undoubtedly also influenced by Karlstadt and the Grebel circle,[15] began to stress a more biblically strict view that did not require this priestly function.[16] From this point, one might observe an overarching ecclesiological divergence develop between the Grebel circle with Hubmaier on the one hand and Zwingli with the Zurich council on the other.

Perhaps the beginning of such theological cleavage in Hubmaier's works from Zwingli's thought might be identified in the Waldshut priest's *Several Theses Concerning the Mass*, published in 1525.[17] From the outset of this piece, Hubmaier continued to articulate the Zwinglian idea that the Supper was "commemoration of [Christ's] suffering and proclamation of his death until he comes to us again."[18] Likewise, he argued that the Lord's Supper was an "outward sign or symbol

---

[15] See both Ronald J. Sider, *Andreas Bodenstein von Karlstadt: The Development of His Thought, 1517-1525* (Leiden: E.J. Brill, 1974), 5, and Rempel, 50.

[16] Rempel notes that "it mattered greatly . . . whether the deacon gave the bread in communion or whether each communicant took it for oneself. The two practices expressed different understandings of the church", 50.

[17] Interestingly, earlier that year Hubmaier wrote to Oecolampadius stating, "We have written twenty theses on the Eucharist, also several rules on preparing the table of the Lord, which writings I would willingly have sent on to you but they are no longer in my hands". See *Hubmaier*, 69. Whether Hubmaier's *Etliche Schlußreden vom Unterricht der Messe* was a form of these earlier twenty theses is difficult to ascertain. Carl Sachsse attempted to recover the original twenty theses in his *D. Balthasar Hubmaier als Theologe* (Berlin: Trowitzsch & Sohn, 1914), 13-14. Westin and Bergsten note that "Es ist jedoch anzunehmen, daß die Schrift nach dem 16. Januar entstand, sonst hätte Hubmaier sie wahrscheinlich mit anderen Worten, als es geschah, in seinem Brief an Oekolampad erwähnt", 101. Pipkin and Yoder observe the probability that "the present [extant] text is not those [twenty] theses but is probably a reworked treatise based on the earlier outline". See Pipkin and Yoder, 73.

[18] *Hubmaier*, 74; *Schriften*, 102.

instituted by Christ." Hubmaier then applied this symbol to the congregation: "[it] signifies to us how he offered his body for us and shed his blood so that we also do the same for the sake of our neighbor."[19]

These three claims (memorial, proclamation, and outer symbol) comprise a distinctively Zwinglian triad and summarily introduce Hubmaier's Eucharistic thought to that date in 1525 in this treatise. Nevertheless, Hubmaier began to synthesize Zwingli's (and to some degree Karlstadt's) works in a unique way.[20] Hubmaier argued in this treatise that those participants in the Supper who do not manifest the willingness to sacrifice for the other congregants

> perjure their oath to Christ; for where the Lord Christ went, Prince and Head of his church, we do not want to follow, although we present ourselves to be members of the church in the reception of this symbol, also to do the same for all those who with us are members of the body of Christ, which is his church.[21]

Although Hubmaier did not precisely articulate it, one might observe the development of this thinker's notion of sacrament as not the visible sign itself but the covenant that accompanies or is recalled by the sign. In further support of this development, Hubmaier stated that "one should always pay more attention and that more seriously to the things signified by the word symbols than to the symbols themselves. For outside of their signifying, the same mean nothing and are in vain."[22]

Through such statements, the reader might observe in Hubmaier's thought intimations of a notion which shall be developed in the future more thoroughly, namely, that the Supper and baptism are visible signs of the covenants to which they correspond. By participating in them, the believer is proclaiming his or her response to God's initiative and promising both God and congregation that he or she will abide in Christ. Ultimately, the true sacraments (the means by which grace is conveyed) will be transferred to such promises. Hubmaier, in Zwinglian-like fashion, had already removed such ontological meaning from the signs themselves. They became merely "word symbols".[23] While Hubmaier still maintained that this sign is a "symbol instituted by Christ", there was no longer language present regarding its power to assure believers of their remission of sins.[24] Such an omission suggests Hubmaier's ultimate break with Zwingli, as

---

[19] *Hubmaier,* 74; *Schriften,* 102.

[20] See Westin and Bergsten, 101, and Rempel, 54. The former editors indicate Hubmaier's reliance upon these sources while the latter author argues for "the originality at work in Hubmaier's borrowing".

[21] *Hubmaier,* 74-75; *Schriften,* 102.

[22] *Hubmaier,* 75; *Schriften,* 103.

[23] *Hubmaier,* 75; *Schriften,* 103.

[24] Indeed, one should note carefully the language used in Hubmaier's writing: It is the Spirit which makes the congregation alive and assures them of eternal life while the bread and wine are word symbols of his love. The word symbols may serve as *anamnesis*

the Supper was no longer to be viewed as divinely instituted but instead will serve as a human witness to Christ's passion for the forgiveness of the sinner.[25] The Christian then responds to such witness through Christ-like sacrifice for others in the fellowship. The metaphysical force of this symbol is thereby reduced while the ethical implication is enhanced. Nevertheless, the power of "sacrament" is maintained by the initial divine action of covenant to which the ordinal signs serve as symbols, anthropologic response, and pledges to God and congregation.

Zwingli utilized the association of *res* and *signum* through the language of Augustine. This is not to say, of course, that Zwingli associated one metaphysically with the other. Quite to the contrary, what he argued in his *On the Lord's Supper*, in essence, is that the sign cannot be the thing signified. Instead, as the congregation participates in communion through the act of *anamnesis* (remembering), they represent the altruistic sacrifice of Christ.[26]

Hubmaier likewise applied the signs of the Supper to the congregation as a communion. What then made Hubmaier's theology distinct at this point had as much to do with his ecclesiology as his sacramentality. For Hubmaier, the *res* was the *visible* church, the Body of Christ which voluntarily responds in covenantal obedience to God, symbolized here by the signs of communion:

> As we now have communion with one another in this bread and drink
> of the Christ meal, so also should the body and blood of all of us be
> shared with each other, just as the body and blood of Christ is shared
> with us all. This is the meaning of the word *symbol* when we eat and
> drink together.[27]

The degree to which the individual must respond to God voluntarily became a primary point of departure for Hubmaier from Zwingli. Even as Hubmaier's work at this point still relied upon his Zurich mentor, the level of personal, ethical response in community differed. One may note Hubmaier's stress on ethics in correspondence to a believing community in his conclusion of *Etliche Schlussreden vom Unterricht der Messe*:

> We conclude that the bread and wine of the Christ meal are outward
> word symbols of an inward Christian nature here on earth, in which
> a Christian obligates himself to another in Christian love with regard

---

for Christ's saving love, but it is the Spirit through the Word which assures the Christian of eternal security. While this may seem semantic, it nevertheless reveals the level of Hubmaier's reductionism in restoring, at least his mind, a biblical understanding of communion.

[25] Rempel, 50.
[26] Rempel, 52.
[27] *Hubmaier*, 75; *Schriften*, 103.

> to body and blood. Thus as the body and blood of Christ became my
> body and blood on the cross, so likewise shall my body and blood
> become the body and blood of my neighbor, and in time of need theirs
> become my body and blood, or we cannot boast at all to be Christians.
> That is the will of Christ in the Supper.[28]

For Hubmaier, if the ceremony were made up of those who did not so commit their lives to share and sacrifice with one another, the worshipful act is rendered meaningless. Neither the officiating priest by his authority nor the elements *ex opere operato* can effect a righteous response in the participant. Instead, the participant must willingly manifest such an attitude through obedience, with the divine covenant acting as stimulus. The promise both to God and to the congregation becomes the essence of Hubmaier's sacramentalism.

Balthasar Hubmaier's contribution to Eucharistic thought, at this point, is this transposing of the Supper from the elements themselves to the individual worshipper acting in communion with his or her fellow celebrants. At the same time, however, Hubmaier did not elevate humanistic thought to the level of arguing for the sacraments as mere expressions of good works on the part of the believer. Hubmaier understood the Lord's Supper (and we shall see also with baptism[29]) as a response to God's initial saving work. Hence, though a rite shared with the members of the church, the Supper is a promise to love God and church in response to God's grace.[30]

Hubmaier's *Unterricht der Messe* reveals several contributing theological factors which helped shape his Eucharistic and overarching sacramental thought, particularly his usurpation of soteriological and pneumatological themes. These two contributing factors come to the fore in his discussion on "word symbols":

> But the Spirit makes us alive, and the Spirit comes with the Word
> which then assures the human being of eternal life, as the bread and
> wine are word symbols of his love, by which we remember how he,
> Christ, was our Christ, and how we also are always to be Christ to
> one another. [31]

---

[28] *Hubmaier,* 76; *Schriften,* 104.

[29] In his *On the Christian Baptism of Believers* written later in 1525, Hubmaier stressed God's sovereignty in such action: "God gives [the promise of salvation] to whomever he wants. He knows his own, John 3. Nobody will tear out of the hands of Christ those whom the Father has given to him", *Hubmaier,* 100. Instead, the sacraments come as a proscriptive means of response to God's own salvific promises.

[30] Rempel, 56-57.

[31] *Hubmaier,* 75; *Schriften,* 103.

One can deduce from this and other passages that Hubmaier understood the human experience of the presence of Christ (as the second person of the Trinity) as historic and eschatological only. During this present interim time, the Holy Spirit solely acts as God's interacting agent with humanity. It is the Spirit that moves humans to saving knowledge through the written Word. The Supper at this point in Hubmaier's thought then comes as a means for commemorating Christ's historic interaction with humanity and one-time sacrifice.[32] The Spirit, on the other hand, acts as the catalyst for belief within the person before participation in the meal and reassures the believing participant of the promise of salvation during the commemorating rite.

In turn, this theological approach also carries ecclesiological implications. In Christ's present absence from earth (and current presence only on the right hand of the Father), the church is called to act in his stead as the Body of Christ on earth:

> . . . we also are always to be Christ to one another. We all are one bread and one body – we all, who have fellowship in one bread and in one drink. As one little kernel does not keep its own flour, but shares it with the others, and a single grape does not keep its juice for itself, but shares it with the others, so should we Christians act – or we eat and drink unworthily from the table of Christ. For the bread which we break means and commemorates the communion of the body of Christ with us, that he is our own, for he gave his body for us through the drink of the communion of his blood which he poured out for the forgiveness of our sin.[33]

This later passage reveals the ethical and ecclesiological trajectory of Hubmaier's maturing thought. The early Hubmaier had implied that the Supper was a time of communion with Christ; such language now begins to be diminished for Christ being shared in community with one another.[34] The elements now serve as reminders to the congregation to act as Christ to each other through the bond of unity. Like grains of wheat, each believer is ground to the others. The

---

[32] Mabry observes that "For Hubmaier, as for the Anabaptists, the Supper was not a matter of Christ's presence with the believer at the celebration of the Supper, either by being bodily eaten or symbolically there; but rather, the believer went back in memory to be with Christ in His suffering on Calvary. Through remembering the suffering of Christ, the believers also remembered their own origin and past as a covenant people, and witnessed to their unique relationship with the suffering Christ by observing His suffering on the cross throught [sic.] the observance of the Lord's Supper", *Balthasar Hubmaier's Doctrine of the Church*, 172.

[33] *Hubmaier*, 75; *Schriften*, 103.

[34] Rempel rightly notes of this former reference to Christ being shared in the elements as "a remnant of the traditional view of the mass, temporarily existing side by side with the elements which are soon to squeeze it out", 56.

elements then become outward word symbols of "an inward Christian nature here on earth, in which a Christian obligates himself to another in Christian love with regard to body and blood."[35]

Thus, while baptism was understood as an initial pledge of love in response to God's saving grace, Hubmaier viewed the Supper as the continuous covenantal and ethical response in Christian community of each believer's willingness to love, serve and sacrifice for the others. The breaking of the one loaf and drinking of the one cup attend as reminders of this communal pledge. Consequently, the subjective appropriation of this understanding is incumbent upon the individual participant for such a remembrance to be spiritually effective. Hubmaier apparently admonished the members of his congregation of their sobering responsibilities:

> Before eating from the table of the Lord, the person should test himself and recollect whether he is so minded toward his neighbor
> . . . . In the Christ meal one should proclaim the death of Christ, and obligate and bind oneself together with body and blood in brotherly service through this visible word symbol and not come together merely for the sake of eating and drinking. Just this Paul calls communion or fellowship, I Cor. 10:16.[36]

While Hubmaier's thought still parallels much of Zwingli's theology of the Lord's Supper, certain elements from other sources emerge as well. That Christ is not present at the commemorative meal but was corporeally present at the Last Supper suggests a reliance upon Karlstadt. Also borrowed from Karlstadt was Hubmaier's view of the grain and grapes mixed and poured, respectively, to make one loaf and one cup.[37] Nevertheless, Hubmaier's own appropriation of such resources brought to bear a unique synthesis of reformed and radical thought.[38]

---

[35] *Hubmaier*, 76; *Schriften*, 104.

[36] *Hubmaier*, 76; *Schriften*, 103.

[37] Karlstadt, *Karlstadts Schriften aus den Jahren 1523-1525*, I (Halle: Max Niemeyer, 1957) 13, 20. Additionally, Windhorst and Rempel both point out Hubmaier's usage of Karlstadt. See Christoph Windhorst, "Das Gedächtnis des Leidens Christi und Pflichtzeichen brüderlicher Liebe: Zum Verständnis des Abendmahls bei Balthasar Hubmaier", in *Umstrittenes Täufertum, 1525-1975* (ed. Hans-Jürgen Goertz; Göttingen: Vandenhoeck & Ruprecht), 122, and Rempel, 54.

[38] Indeed, Eddie Mabry argues that "while Hubmaier agrees with Zwingli and the Anabaptists that the Supper conveys no grace to the recipient, and that it must be preceded by faith, he adds quite a bit more than they do to his own view of what the Supper does represent. All of this suggests that while these various line [sic] of theology may have had their impact upon Hubmaier's thinking, he was basically an independent thinker; and, as such, he produced a doctrine of the Lord's Supper which was . . . essentially his own", *Balthasar Hubmaier's Doctrine of the Church*, 177.

Though greatly influenced by Zwingli's theology, Hubmaier manifested increased and intentional cleavage from Catholic, Lutheran, and Zwinglian Eucharistic conceptions in his text, *A Simple Instruction* (*Einfältiger*), written in late 1526. Some scholars have noted that Hubmaier wrote this treatise "at the height of his influence as an Anabaptist",[39] and such observations are valid given his gravitas at this point as a popular and heroic Anabaptist reformer in Moravia. This tract, more polemical in spirit than his previous works on the Supper, was published in two editions, which probably testifies to its importance to the theological dialogue taking place in that region. *A Simple Instruction* served also as Hubmaier's most expansive explication of his mature Eucharistic thought as an Anabaptist.

After a lengthy dedicatory eulogy to Leonhard von Lichtenstein of Nickolsburg, which detailed the creative philological study of Leonhard's name outlined in the previous chapter, Hubmaier opened the main body of his thesis by delineating some fifteen various approaches made in church history to understand the Eucharist.[40] These include variations of trans- and consubstantiation. All of the theories, Hubmaier argued, reveal the disunity of "opinions and conjectures"[41] found in the papal rules and ancient and modern schools of thought. Nevertheless, he maintained that such theological division should in no way hinder, confuse or bring harm to the "pious Christian". Instead, the individual believer looks not to church traditions or human authorities but only to God and "judges for himself according to [God's] simple Word, and looks about himself so that he is not misled by anyone whereby the blind together with the blind leaders would fall into the ditch."[42]

Thus, beginning with such a derogatory opening, Hubmaier immediately distanced himself from Roman and Lutheran approaches to the rite of the Lord's Supper. He continued his diatribe by disassociating himself from the Karlstadtian and Zwinglian camps, respectively, as well, particularly on the issue of interpreting the words of institution for the Supper:

---

[39] Pipkin and Yoder, 314.

[40] Interestingly, the first sentence of the main body of this text contains Hubmaier's first depreciatory use of the word "sacrament". Here he stated: "In ancient times there has always been great disunity on the sacrament (as they called it) of the alter." [. . . "*in dem Sacrament* (*als man es genennt*) *des Alltars*."] *Hubmaier*, 319 and *Schriften*, 290. Despite this apparently pejorative spirit regarding the term, Hubmaier did not discontinue its usage but simply transferred the "sacramentality" from the representative rite to the human pledge in covenant with God and church to which he believed it pointed.

[41] "*Opiniones und won* [*Vermutungen*]". *Hubmaier*, 320; *Schriften*, 290.

[42] Hubmaier here set up his subsequent discussion on biblical hermeneutics appropriate for the believer in discerning sound biblical theology and, in so doing, argued vehemently for the autonomy of each believer before God. See *Hubmaier*, 321; *Schriften*, 291.

Second, since indeed also with the present-day teachers who write on the Supper of Christ are to be found disagreements and arguments about the word of Christ, 'This is my body,' many write that the trope or type of this Word lies hidden in the little word *hoc* or *this*. That is, that this little word *hoc* does not point to the bread but to the body of Christ. The others use the little word *est* for *significat*, that is, *is* for *signifies*, thus: 'The bread signifies my body.' Which opinion can never be forced with clear and orderly Scriptures nor conquered, . . . It does not satisfy the human conscience; it gives more cause for erring and confusing the entire Bible than to satisfying or overcoming the adversaries. For if this is the practice then no one would be certain as to where *est* |is| stands in the Scripture for *significat* |signifies| or for itself. And in the end there would be so many fights over words as there are *ests* and *ises* in the Bible. So I would maintain just with the same authority and with the same arguments that this bread must be the body of Christ and thus *is* is taken in the Old Testament for *is*, Genesis 1:3: 'God said let there be light and there was light.' Likewise in the New Testament: 'And the word became flesh', John, chapter 1, John 1:14. Therefore, in this saying, 'This is my body', the *is* must also be used in this way.[43]

This passage clearly demarcated Hubmaier from the popular tropistic interpretations of Scripture. Karldstadt held that the words *"Hoc est corpus meum"* referred not to the loaf but to Christ; Zwingli had rendered *est* as *signifies* in order to justify the Eucharist as memorial. Such tropistic techniques seemed to Hubmaier to be arbitrary interpretations of otherwise straightforward textual hermeneutics.

From this pivotal juncture, the Moravian leader then disclosed his own approach to biblical exegesis based upon three general rules of interpretation. First, wherever scripture is "dark" or unclear, it should be placed with accompanying biblical texts that are "brighter" or clearer. In cases where texts are obscure based upon their brevity, longer paralleling passages in Scripture may bring greater perspicuity. Hubmaier then displayed such a case with four passages dealing with the Supper: in Matthew, Mark, Luke and Corinthians. Since the first two gospels utilize the words in question more laconically (what Hubmaier touts as *micrologi*, using Christ's words in the most succinct way), the passages from Luke and Paul should be used as hermeneutically illuminating texts to buttress interpretation.[44] Because the latter passages include the sentence of Christ: "Do this in remembrance of me", one may easily infer that the bread serves as the *corpus Christi* in *anamnesis*.

---

[43] *Hubmaier*, 321-22; *Schriften*, 291.
[44] *Hubmaier*, 322-23; *Schriften*, 292.

Hubmaier further explicated his hermeneutical approach in his second point on biblical exegesis: *"Talia sunt subiecta qualia permittuntur ab eorum predicatis,* that is: The preceding words should be understood according to the following words."[45] In this case, a literal rendering of a short passage may be undermined by the figurative and logical elucidation that follows. Thus, to interpret Christ's *"Hoc est corpus meum"* literally is to curtail the fuller intent of biblical doctrine. While he praised those contemporaries (primarily Catholics) who rendered *est* in its simpliest form[46] as *is* and thus implied the broken body at the meal to be the actual Savior's body, Hubmaier argued that such an interpretation severs the full and simple meaning of the passages:

> In the power of this saying everyone must confess and say that this baked bread is the body of Christ who was crucified for us. Now, however, this bread in itself is not the body, for this bread was not crucified and did not die for us, so the bread must be the body of Christ in remembrance, so that all the words of Christ can remain in their plain and simple sense. . . . For these words, 'in my memory,' testify in the entire previous saying that the breaking, distribution and eating of bread is not a breaking, distribution, and eating of the body of Christ, who is sitting at the right hand of God the Father in the heavens, but all that is a remembrance of his being broken and distributed in suffering. It is also an eating in faith, that he was thus taken, broken, and divided for us, so that we remember this and be aware of his death.[47]

For Hubmaier, at least in this case, the logical explanation of broader collateral biblical passages outweighed a literal rendering of shorter passages. Consequently, he delineated a hermeneutical basis for his separation from Catholic literalism and Zwinglian tropism.[48]

---

[45] *Hubmaier*, 324; *Schriften*, 293.

[46] Walter Klaassen notes that "for Hubmaier the Scriptures were clear and transparent and pure and luminous and simple." See Klaassen's classic study of Hubmaier's biblical exegesis and arguments in "Speaking in Simplicity: Balthasar Hubmaier", *MQR* 40 (April 1966), 139-47 [citation from 143].

[47] *Hubmaier*, 324; *Schriften*, 293-94.

[48] On this point, Rempel views Hubmaier's second hermeneutical rule was based more on logic than in rendering the "natural" meaning of words in order to deduce their meaning. While this may have been the result of Hubmaier's exegetic movement in the Eucharistic passages, his stated intent seemed to attempt to restrict interpretation within the confines of corresponding biblical passages. To further substantiate this viewpoint, Hubmaier later argued: "Here you see clearly, where one wants to determine a right conclusion out of the Scriptures, that one does not make patchwork and present half Scriptures, but sets all the Scriptures of one kind of matter wholly and completely together, and after that, to introduce a perfect final judgment", *Hubmaier*, 327; *Schriften*, 295. See Rempel, 59, for his view.

Hubmaier's third rule for biblical exegesis pertained to his interpretation of Christ's phrase "in memory of me". The use of such terminology in Scripture serves as a type in Hubmaier's thought to draw all previous words within the corresponding passage into the category of *anamnetic* thought. For example, he compared such passages to daily speech regarding wooden images. The believer would say of an image: "'That is Our Lady, St. Peter, or St. John,' and it is not they, but only the memory of them by the institution of human beings, whereas the former is by the institution of Christ."[49] For Hubmaier, Christ's words "in memory of me" have the force to characterize all other Eucharistic passages within this memorializing form of speech.

Hubmaier then concluded this section of his *Einfältiger* by proposing five counter-arguments to his own hermeneutical rules with his own answers in response in hopes of thereby suppressing opposing criticism. Most striking among these was his final counter-argument and answer couplet that testified to the stringency to which Hubmaier held Christ's earthly absence[50] and future kingdom. To the probable question of how he would handle the statement by Jesus in Mark 14:25: "Truly I say to you that I will not henceforth drink from the fruit of the vine until the day that I drink it anew in the kingdom of God", Hubmaier surprisingly cited the Emmaus road narrative in Luke. Hubmaier pointed out that the disciples did not recognize the Christ even during the meal until he took the bread, blessed it and broke it. What is noticeable about Hubmaier's consideration of this passage was his interpretation that the disciples only recognized Christ through this action "as in the memorial sign".[51] For Hubmaier, then, such an event is powerful only in its reminiscence of the Last Supper and does not seem to carry any post-passion Eucharistic implications. Even the Emmaus meal, for this Anabaptist's theology, was a reinforcement of the ongoing institution of the Supper as a recollection of Christ's death (in accordance with I Corinthians 11:26: "For as often as you eat this bread and drink this cup . . .").[52]

This line of argumentation set the stage for the next section in Hubmaier's thesis: that Christ is no longer bodily present to humanity but will return bodily

---

[49] *Hubmaier*, 324-25; *Schriften*, 294. Later in his treatise, Hubmaier would provide this "parable": "I see an image of Emperor Nero and say that is Emperor Nero. The speech is false in itself. If, however, I say, that is Emperor Nero in memory, then it is now true. Thus also if one says of a statue of Maximilian, that is Emperor Maximilian, then the speech is false, for he is no longer here. But if one says that is Emperor Maximilian of praiseworthy remembrance, then now one sees apparently that these words, *praiseworthy memory*, have the character, type and nature of directing the entire speech and previous words to the late Maximilian", *Hubmaier*, 327 [editor's italics].

[50] Rempel also makes this observation, 59-60.

[51] *Hubmaier*, 328; *Schriften*, 297.

[52] See Rempel, 59-60 and *Hubmaier*, 328; *Schriften*, 297.

in the "hour of the last judgment".[53] Hubmaier outlined four separate biblical passages, Matthew 26, Mark 14, I Corinthians 11 and excerpts from Acts, to substantiate this claim. He then broke down each passage phrase by phrase, adding to each an explanation and a theological theory, as in the form of a biblical commentary. Each passage combined Hubmaier's first exegetical principle of understanding the simple meaning of the text with his subsequent principles of deducing meaning from longer parallel passages and with those phrases and sentences which follow. Thus, while he arguably remained true to his three principles for exegesis, he belied the hermeneutical consistency of such principles through their praxis.

In the Matthean passage of Christ's words of institution (26:26-30), for example, Hubmaier presented salient points in interpreting several of the biblical phrases. "As *they* were eating", for instance, provided evidence for Hubmaier that the Supper is a communal event, and thus not one to be celebrated privately, even for those with infirmities.[54] In another phrase, Christ "gave thanks", which Hubmaier interpreted to mean that the congregation is to bless and thank God (through prayer) and not make a consecration, as was the Catholic practice. Lastly, Christ concludes this passage with his prophetic statement that he would not again partake from the "fruit of the vine" until the last days. From this phrase, Hubmaier noted that even Christ articulated the element within the cup as from a fruit, not from his veins or any other supernatural source. "Therefore Christ clearly called it a fruit of the vine and not blood, to prevent future error."[55]

Such phrases show Hubmaier's simplistic approach to biblical exegesis and interpretation. Yet when he applied his additional principles, such simplistic and literal interpretations broke down. This is particularly true of his interpretations of Christ's statements "this is my body" and "this is my blood" from the same passage. Here, Hubmaier's modest literalism is substituted for a more complicated biblical collage. These statements of Christ are not to be taken literally in this case, but only figuratively by the interpolation of Christ's and Paul's words ("in remembrance") in Luke and Corinthians, respectively, within the Matthean passage. While such a move stays within Hubmaier's stated principles, it suggests to the reader that Hubmaier's exegetical principles were formed retrospectively to concluding his Eucharistic perspectives and created to justify his theological ends.

Hubmaier's interpretation of the Mark passage (14:22-26) contained similar argumentation. Of interest in this passage, though, was Hubmaier's discussion

---

[53] *Hubmaier*, 329; *Schriften*, 297.

[54] *Hubmaier*, 329 [italics mine]; *Schriften*, 297. Rempel rightly notes from this the probability that Hubmaier sought "to invalidate private masses, the reservation of the sacrament for the sick, and masses where a congregation does not commune and only the priest partakes", 60.

[55] *Hubmaier*, 331; *Schriften*, 298.

of the timing of Christ's words with the actions of the Last Supper. Hubmaier pointed out that Christ blessed the cup, the disciples drank from it, and then afterward Christ proclaimed, "This is my blood". Here Hubmaier questioned:

> Now then, on the basis of these words how could the wine be transformed into blood as our sacrificers and consecrators pretend, forcing us to believe such against the clear words of Christ by means of sword, fire and water, since faith is a work of God and not of the hangman?[56]

The timing of Christ's words, in Hubmaier's mind, proved transubstantiation as a problematic concept if the disciples had already imbibed the element before Christ's transforming proclamation.

In his discussion of the Eucharistic passage from I Corinthians (11:23-29), Hubmaier again broached the topic of Christ's present absence from the earth in arguing the Supper as a "remembrance, a memorial meal, and a reminder of the suffering of Christ, and not a sacrifice."[57] What seems peculiar is Hubmaier's insistence that Christ's words, said naturally while *present* among the disciples, portray the Supper as a reminder to the believer of Christ's historic bodily presence and sacrifice even while in earthly absence. By stating "Do this in my memory", Hubmaier maintained, Christ "lead [sic.] them away from his natural body, which profits nothing, John 6:63."[58] If Christ were present, Hubmaier argued, his admonition to celebrate the Supper "in memory" would be spurious.

Finally, Hubmaier's final set of passages, three excerpts from Acts, all point to the Christ's risen (and not earthly) reality. Utilizing Acts 1, Hubmaier outlined the biblical pericope of Christ's ascension and the angel's promise that Christ "will come as you have seen him ascend into heaven."[59] From Acts 7:48-50 and Acts 17:24, Hubmaier argued that Stephen's citation of and Paul's reference to Isaiah 66, respectively, buttress the claim of Christ's earthly absence. From the first of these passages, Stephen is recorded as arguing: "But the Most High does not live in temples made with hands. As he says through the prophet, 'Heaven is my throne and the earth my footstool. . . .'"[60] From this point Hubmaier inferred that the Catholic mass was an attempt to manipulate God, comparing it to a puppet play for children.[61]

Thus, while he attempted to distance himself somewhat from Zwingli's and Karlstadt's tropistic interpretations of the meal, Hubmaier saved his most caustic

---

[56] *Hubmaier*, 331; *Schriften*, 299.
[57] *Hubmaier*, 333; *Schriften*, 300.
[58] *Hubmaier*, 333; *Schriften*, 300.
[59] Acts 1:11, here cited in *Hubmaier*, 334.
[60] Here cited in *Hubmaier*, 335; *Schriften*, 302.
[61] *Hubmaier*, 336; *Schriften*, 302.

remarks for the Roman literalism. Indeed, Bergsten notes Hubmaier's use of the derogatory term "Mass-priests" (*Messpfaffen*) throughout the *Instruction*.[62] In the first edition of this work, this term appeared as *Moesspfaffe* and in the second as *mäosspfaffe*. *A Brief Apologia*, a work written by Hubmaier at approximately the same time as the *Instruction*, explained these as wordplays. In this latter text, Hubmaier noted that the word "mass" is found only once in the Bible. He stated:

> Daniel writes about it that Maoz is an idol set up by the antichrist, 'which must be honored with gold, silver, precious stones, and everything costly,' Daniel 11:38. Consequently I attach to the priest's mass just as much value as I do to the Frankfurt fair [*Frankfurter Messe*], for there is nothing there but daily buying and selling, only that in the priest's mass this takes place spiritually. Yea, O Christ, who drove the Gadarene swine into the lake, come with your whip and drive such simoniacal merchants out of thy temple![63]

Hubmaier's philological play showed how this idol god is *ma'ozzim* in Hebrew and *Maozim* in Latin. For Hubmaier, these comprised the origin of the modern *Messe* and imply its meaning as idol worship. Such was Hubmaier's sardonic temperament in these polemical writings.

Hubmaier's *Einfältiger*, the longest of his texts dealing with the Supper and the only text that delves deeply into his understanding of the words of institution, demands further reflection. Consequently, this book shall address such issues as theological reflection along with Hubmaier's other Eucharistic writings later in this chapter.

The Supper in Hubmaier's Liturgical Practice

Hubmaier's final work that focused on the Lord's Supper, *A Form for Christ's Supper* (*Eine Form des Nachtmahls Christi*), came not in the cast of a theological tract for the purpose of debate but as a liturgy for practice in worship. Such an extant writing, along with his liturgical records on baptism and the ban, is invaluable to Anabaptist research for understanding the movement's appropriation of its theology within congregational praxis in the sixteenth century.

Scholars point out that this work, written in Nikolsburg in 1527, probably emerged during a time of relative peace for Hubmaier and his flock, "when there was a context for properly structuring congregational life and practice."[64] It is accompanied by two other orders of worship written by Hubmaier during

---

[62] Bergsten, *Balthasar Hubmaier: Anabaptist Theologian and Martyr*, 344.

[63] *Hubmaier*, 302-303; *Schriften*, 276.

[64] Pipkin and Yoder, 393.

the same period, one on baptism and one on the ban. Yet scholars observe that the liturgy for the Supper, which falls between those for baptism and the ban respectively, is more conducive to and beneficial for reconstructing Moravian Anabaptist worship because of its liturgical comprehensiveness.[65] Additionally, the text's completeness has permitted its adaptation for worship in some contemporary churches.

From the outset of reading Hubmaier's *Nachtmahl*, one might easily be persuaded that Hubmaier's composition of instructions and liturgy is representative of sixteenth century free church evangelicalism. He argued initially, for instance, that the rite of the Supper should make use of commonplace elements: "Then they should prepare the table with ordinary bread and wine. Whether the cups are silver, wood, or pewter, makes no difference."[66] Additionally, he pressed basic Protestant demands such as the use of the vernacular and the avoidance of the canon of the mass. That vestments are not to be worn by priests but congregants are encouraged to be "respectably dressed and should sit together in an orderly way without light talk and contention,"[67] signifies Hubmaier's understanding of sacrament as a human action. No longer is this ceremony in a private language (i.e., Latin) with special elements taken by selected people (the wine reserved only for the clergy); all God's people are full participants of common elements made sacrosanct only by memorial of Christ's holy act on the cross and by the congregational promise that Calvary's remembrance elicits. However, Hubmaier radically redefined "God's people", restricting access to the table to those who had been "properly" baptized and had spiritually prepared themselves. Regardless, Hubmaier's introduction suggests a Zwinglian influence in its relative simplicity and an apparent absence of Catholic ritual, including the mingling of water with the wine.[68]

While characteristic of reformed and radical theology of his time, none of these arguments seems terribly surprising to the reader at this juncture after surveying Hubmaier's previous didactic expositions. Nevertheless, this liturgy, when read more thoroughly, reveals some of Hubmaier's most innovative thought and a unique synthesis of the variety of Christian traditions exemplifying this Anabaptist's unusual theological sojourn.

Before outlining the words, scriptures and prayers of communion, Hubmaier proceeded into this liturgy by placing emphasis on a time of preparation for the meal. Again, Hubmaier stressed the importance of individual and congregational understanding before participating in the sacrament. If this act is truly to be a communal response and binding pledge and not an *ex opere operato* work, then such instruction is requisite and significant. Thus while he spearheaded an Anabaptist movement in its first generation to undercut the canon mass, Hubmaier nevertheless did not leave the rite in a void. In its stead, the Moravian reformer set a fixed

---

[65] Rempel, 73.
[66] *Hubmaier*, 394; *Schriften*, 355.
[67] *Hubmaier*, 394; *Schriften*, 355.
[68] Rempel, 73.

liturgical formula into place that is unique to the radical movement.[69] *Nachtmahl*, then, manifests an interesting combination characteristic of classical form and allusions to Zwinglian theology, accompanied by radical rhetoric that is consistent with Hubmaier's nonpareil and synthetic theology.

The opening section is one in which the priest leads the congregation in preparation for the table. Every participant was called upon to "begin by accusing himself" before God and offering up penitential prayers.[70] Furthermore, Hubmaier provided a suggested prayer for the priest as he "first of all should fall on his knees with the church and with heart and mouth" offer up remorseful and confessional words.[71]

The priest continues such strong leadership in the service by guiding the people to sit and hear the "Scriptures concerning Christ", a compendium of Jesus' life, works, teaching, passion and resurrection "so that the eyes of those who are gathered together may be opened".[72] Naturally, such subjective cognition and responsibility on the part of the entire community would not be as necessary for a more medieval approach to the Supper in which the elements act sacramentally in conveying or distributing God's grace. But Hubmaier's stress on the ethical response of the believer becomes the core of the sacrament in his mature theology, transposed from the signs of bread and wine to their companion act of covenantal pledge on the part of the believer to God and one another. This time of preparation, personal reflection and confession is essential, in Hubmaier's mind, for an appropriate sacramental promise to take place, followed by its symbolic gesture in partaking of the Eucharistic elements in memorial of Christ's initial work of salvation.

For Hubmaier, this human promise should be made as a response to hearing the proclamation of the Gospel of Christ. While the hearer is free to respond as the Spirit leads, "there must be diligence so that the death of the Lord is earnestly proclaimed, so that the people have a picture of the boundless goodness of Christ, and the church may be instructed, edified, and led, in heartfelt fervent and fraternal love."[73] If communion is a pledge to God, in part, by Christian

---

[69] Rempel observes that "*Nachtmahl* is the final stage in that process of the renewal of eucharistic worship [for Anabaptism]", 74.

[70] *Hubmaier*, 394; *Schriften*, 355.

[71] *Hubmaier*, 394; *Schriften*, 355.

[72] *Hubmaier*, 394; *Schriften*, 355. Hubmaier suggested that this compendium might include John 8:12; I Corinthians 10 or 11; John 13, 14, 15, 16 or 17; or even Sirach 2. The fact that Hubmaier still referenced apocryphal literature signifies the vestiges of his lingering Catholicism even in his mature Anabaptist theology.

[73] *Hubmaier*, 395; *Schriften*, 356. Interestingly, following his proposed sermon outline for this occasion from the Emmaus episode in Luke 24, the manuscript calls on the congregation prayerfully to respond in hymnody: "Stay with us, O Christ! It is toward evening and the day is now far spent. Abide with us, O Jesus, abide with us. For where thou art not, there everything is darkness, night, and shadow, but thou art the true Son, light, and shining brightness, John 8:12. He to whom thou dost light the way, cannot go astray."

unity in love for one another, such subjective meditation and recollection must take place in order to engender this sacramental response in community effectively.

The final prelude to communion included a time of appropriate questions by those with less understanding and response by those more learned regarding the Christian faith. Then the priest would read I Corinthians 11 and lead the congregation in a period of self-examination, "for whoever eats and drinks unworthily, eats and drinks a judgment upon himself, as he does not discern the body of the Lord."[74] Self-evaluation and judgment serve as prevention to divine condemnation, lest one participate without such spiritual reflection.[75] Consequently, as will be discussed further in the fourth chapter, one may perceive that spiritual discipline was of greatest importance within the community of faith, especially in relation to the sacraments.

For Hubmaier, any Christian's self-examination is comprised of four basic parts: First, one should spiritually hunger for the bread and thirst for the drink of heaven. Here Hubmaier noted that "if the spiritual eating and drinking does not first take place, then the outward breaking of bread, eating and drinking is a killing letter", and is a "hypocrisy".[76] Here again Hubmaier made clear that the spiritual act precedes and is separate from the symbolic enactment in the sacrament.[77] Indeed, it is the spiritual response in prayer and promise before God

---

[74] I Cor. 11:14 here cited in *Hubmaier*, 396; See also *Schriften*, 357.

[75] One natural question which would arise from such an expression is how sinful humans might be made worthy for communion. Later in the *Nachtmahl* Hubmaier answered this question: ". . . who can sit at the supper table with a good conscience? Answer: One who has thus taken to heart and has thus shaped himself in mind and heart and senses inwardly that he truly and sincerely can say, 'The love of God which he has shown me through the sacrifice of his only begotten and most beloved Son for the payment of my sins . . . has so moved, softened, and penetrated my spirit and soul that I am so minded and ready to offer my flesh and blood, further more so to rule over and so to master it, that it must obey me against its own will'", *Hubmaier*, 399-400; *Schriften*, 359. Thus, what is humanly impossible because of sinful flesh is made possible by the inward anointing of God's Spirit. The power of God becomes stronger in the Christian than the temptation to give into iniquity. When one surrenders to sin, he or she confesses such sin to God and thus "reigns and rules mightily over the restless devil of his flesh.
. . . So everyone who is a Christian acts and behaves so that he may worthily eat and drink at the table of the Lord", *Hubmaier*, 401; *Schriften*, 360.

[76] *Hubmaier*, 397; *Schriften*, 357.

[77] Rempel summarizes well Hubmaier's sacramental ethic here, stating that "the inward reality, the coming of the Spirit, happens prior to the Lord's Supper; the outward reality happens after it. The sacrament is not the cause but the consequence of faith and obedience. This familiar refrain rounds out the argument of these pages. Our communion with Christ is not given through the breaking of bread; it precedes the ritual of the Supper and has been sealed in our inner nature because Christ came in the flesh. His incarnation is a promise of self-offering, fulfilled in the church. It could be called a sacrament just as the believers' willingness to offer their bodies is a sacrament", 76.

that maintains a higher priority than does the outward breaking of bread and drinking of the cup.

Hubmaier's second point for self-examination highlights his Anabaptist ethic towards God and others. Here he argued that those who prepare themselves for the table must be thankful in words and through deeds toward God, that such an attitude be one of sacrifice just as Christ had offered himself for the believer. Hubmaier's transition to communal ethics played the key role at this juncture. He noted:

> But since Christ does not need our good deeds, is not hungry, is not thirsty, is not naked or in prison, but heaven and earth are his and all that is in them, there he points us toward our neighbor, first of all to the members of the household of faith, . . . that we might fulfill the works of this our gratitude toward them physically and spiritually, feeding the hungry, giving drink to the thirsty, clothing the naked, consoling the prisoner, sheltering the needy. Then he will be ready to accept these works of mercy from us in such a way as if we had done them unto him. . . . From this it is certain and sure that all the good that we do to the very least of his, that we do to Christ himself.[78]

Thus, the ethic to love one another in the Anabaptist community, for Hubmaier, is the believer's best expression of his or her love for and praise to God.

Only after such ethical expression takes place can the Moravian Anabaptist participate in communion. For in Hubmaier's mature theology, the Eucharist comes as a way of "saying, testifying, and publicly assuring" the community of this communal pledge.[79] The act of partaking of bread and wine comes as public symbolism of what has preceded. It is not insignificant that at this point Hubmaier uses the words "sacrament" and "sworn pledge" interchangeably, for one's promise before God and then the community becomes the basis of Hubmaier's sacramentalism. The outward act is only meaningful when preceded by the inward action of the heart:

> This is the true fellowship of saints, I Cor. 10:16. It is not a fellowship for the reason that bread is broken, but rather the bread is broken because the fellowship has already taken place and has been concluded inward in the spirit, since Christ has come in flesh, John 4:27. For not all who break bread are participants in the body and blood of Christ, which I can prove by the traitor Judas, Matt. 26:25.

---

[78] *Hubmaier*, 397; *Schriften*, 357.
[79] *Hubmaier*, 398; *Schriften*, 358.

> But those who are partakers inwardly and of the spirit, the same may
> also worthily partake outwardly of this bread and wine.[80]

Hubmaier further elucidated this argument by comparing the public act of
Eucharist to that of baptism. One is baptized in water, he reasoned, not in order
to believe but because one has believed. In the same way, one takes communion
not to be in fellowship but because one already has committed to this fellowship
inwardly, "that each one should also sacrifice and pour out his flesh and blood
for the other."[81]

Thus, "sacrament" in Hubmaier's theology is not the objective working of
God but the subjective response to God on the part of the believer. While baptism served as an individual response on the part of the baptizand, the action in
water only as symbolic seal of the prior pledge of the candidate before God (as
shall be discussed thoroughly in the next chapter), the Supper represented the
community's love for one another following its pledge to love in response to
God's grace.[82] The rites of water, bread and cup are public testimonies to inward
pledges of Christian faith in and love for God and neighbor.

These symbolic rites, then, if comprehended correctly by the Anabaptist congregation, play a central role in the life of the church for Hubmaier. On this point,
one may observe how emphatically Hubmaier placed their role. He argued:

> If now one had no other word or Scripture, but only the correct under-
> standing of water baptism and the Supper of Christ, one would have
> God and all his creatures, faith and love, the law and all the prophets.
> So whoever makes a mockery of the Supper of Christ, the Son of Man
> will mock before God and his angels.[83]

Thus, while Christians should confess their sins in preparation for the Supper,
they are also required to commit themselves to a blameless spiritual lifestyle.
Though the believer may stumble because of the weakness of the flesh, God
still forgives because of Christ's perfection. One does not then approach the
bread and cup in some attempt to prove his or her worthiness but indeed quite
the opposite; because he or she is never worthy save for Christ's own substi-
tutionary atonement, one must approach in response to grace. Christians need

---

[80] *Hubmaier*, 398; *Schriften*, 358.

[81] *Hubmaier*, 398; *Schriften*, 358.

[82] Rempel, 76. To buttress this argument, Hubmaier himself stated: "For just as water
baptism is a public testimony of the Christian faith, so is the Supper a public testimony
of Christian love. Now he who does not want to be baptized or to observe the Supper, he
does not desire to believe in Christ nor to practice Christian love and does not desire to be
a Christian", *Hubmaier*, 399; *Schriften*, 358-59.

[83] *Hubmaier*, 399; *Schriften*, 359.

only prove their sincerity in desire for partaking of communion and come to a full comprehension of the meaning of its symbolism.[84] It was only those regenerate, confessing and baptized Christians in the community who are eligible for participation in communion. Hubmaier reasoned that "without this inner communion in spirit and in truth, the outward breaking of bread is nothing but an Iscariotic and damnable hypocrisy."[85] Moreover, Hubmaier imparted to his Moravian community that God requires not only expressions of commitment and love through words but also that such utterances be exemplified in actions, lest the symbolism of communion be undermined with glib cant and its prolegomenous ceremony diminished to meaningless chatter.[86]

Having completed this time of self-examination, the congregation is called upon by the priest to assume an attitude of prayer as final preparation for the Eucharist. This prayer begins first with a period of "common silence" for the purpose of individual and corporate reflection on Christ's suffering. The prayer is concluded as the congregation together repeats the Lord's Prayer "reverently, and with hearts desirous of grace".[87]

Finally, for those who desired participation in communion, the priest calls upon the congregation to take the pledge. This is the heart of Hubmaier's distinctive sacramental theology in praxis; the sacramental sign is preceded by its true sacrament as pledge. Hubmaier referred to this sacrament as a "pledge of love". This excerpt is arguably the most valuable liturgy in all Anabaptism. With the priest leading the litany, the text of the pledge follows:

> Brothers and sisters, if you will to love God before, in, and above all things, in the power of his holy and living Word, serve him alone, Deut. 5; 6; Exod. 20, honor and adore him and henceforth sanctify his name, subject your carnal and sinful will to his divine will which he has worked in you by his living Word, in life and death, then let each say individually:
> **I will.**
> If you will love your neighbor and serve him with deeds of brotherly love, Matt. 25; Eph. 6; Col. 3; Rom. 13:1; I Pet. 2:13f., lay down and shed for him your life and blood, be obedient to father, mother, and all authorities according to the will of God, and this in the power of our Lord Jesus Christ, who laid down and shed his flesh and blood for us, then let each say individually:
> **I will.**
> If you will practice fraternal admonition toward your brethren and sisters, Matt. 1:15ff.; Luke 6; Matt. 5:44; Rom. 12:10, make

---

[84] Mabry, *Balthasar Hubmaier's Doctrine of the Church*, 174.
[85] *Hubmaier*, 398; *Schriften*, 358.
[86] *Hubmaier*, 402; *Schriften*, 361.
[87] *Hubmaier*, 402; *Schriften*, 361.

peace and unity among them, and reconcile yourselves with all those whom you have offended, abandon all envy, hate and evil will toward everyone, willingly cease all action and behavior which causes harm, disadvantage, or offense to your neighbor, [if you will] also love your enemies and do good to them, and exclude according to the Rule of Christ, Matt. 18, all those who refuse to do so, then let each say individually:

I will.

If you desire publicly to confirm before the church this pledge of love which you have now made, through the Lord's Supper of Christ, by eating bread and drinking wine, and to testify to it in the power of the living memorial of the suffering and death of Jesus Christ our Lord, then let each say individually:

I desire it in the power of God.

So eat and drink with one another in the name of God the Father the Son and the Holy Spirit. May God himself accord to all of us the power and the strength that we may worthily carry it out and bring it to its saving conclusion according to his divine will. May the Lord impart to us his grace. Amen.[88]

The liturgy then commences with a priestly prayer and the basic words of institution as the bread is broken. This preliminary liturgy leading to the Lord's Supper comes as a pledge of self-offering of each congregant to the others. The importance of the meaning of this pledge cannot be exaggerated for its spiritual relationship to the Supper. Indeed, the meal itself, as the liturgy indicates, serves as symbolic confirmation of this pledge of love. Thus, while he reacted against the transubstantiative character of the medieval mass, Hubmaier replaced the notion of the real presence of Christ with that of Christ's body, the congregation, who acts in Jesus' stead during his present earthly absence.[89] Hence, as the believers recollect Christ's sacrifice, they commit to subject themselves to similar sacrifice in Christ's community for one another, to forgive one another, and willingly to receive such offering from the others as they covenant with one another. God communicates divine grace, then, through such communal actions in the spirit of Christ, and not through the bread and cup *ex opere operato*.

The pledge cannot be separated from its subsequent symbolic act of communion. Before the pledge of love begins, Hubmaier directed the priest to explain the simplicity of the Eucharist, that "the bread is bread and the wine wine and not flesh and blood, as has long been believed."[90] Furthermore, the worshipers are then invited to participate in the Supper only if they rise and repeat

---

[88] *Hubmaier*, 403-404; *Schriften*, 361-62.

[89] Rempel, 77.

[90] *Hubmaier*, 403; *Schriften*, 361.

"with heart and mouth" its associated pledge. Any attempt, then, to extricate the litany from the act of communion would be an inappropriate eisegetical act. While Hubmaier intended the pledge to serve as a means to instruct the laity and ensure communion's heartfelt comprehension and acceptance by the worshiping community, it plays an equally integral role for the modern reader today in explicating Hubmaier's mature Eucharistic thought.

This pledge may be delineated into three general categories. First, one pledges to love God above all else and serve God exclusively. This commitment entails obligating oneself to honor and worship God and subjecting one's fleshly, sinful will to God's divine will. This having been stated and the believer having acclaimed his or her agreement, the priest continues by expanding the covenant to encompass one's commitment to neighbor. Implicit in this move is that the Christian serves God and fulfils the initial pledge, at least in part, by serving and sacrificing for others.

This notion is characteristic of Hubmaier's and the general Anabaptist peculiar understanding of Christ's present absence from humanity on earth. While this unusual aspect of Hubmaier's Christology will be outlined in the following section of this chapter, it is, nevertheless, worthy to note at this juncture the ethical implications of one's commitment to exclusive duty to God: the submission of one's self to others through service and self-sacrifice. Additionally, the ready participant pledges to remain obedient to parental and all other authorities through Christ's power.[91]

Yet Hubmaier's third provision in the covenant is perhaps the most surprising: The believer pledges to practice "fraternal admonition" to fellow congregants. This is to say that one promises to chastise any who has not remained faithful in his or her heretofore stated Christian discipline for the purpose of promoting unity and peace in the congregation. This admonition indicates, however, that such discipline be applied to oneself as well, as all believers are also required to promise reconciliatory efforts for all hateful and offensive actions they might have displayed to their neighbor. Lastly, each believer pledges to exclude those who refuse to participate in such rapprochement.[92] Hubmaier deemed these actions as necessary for church order as interpreted through Christ's admonition in Matthew 18.[93]

---

[91] W.J. McGlothlin argued that this clause of submission to authority distinguishes Hubmaier from other Anabaptists in that, though utilized in worship in a free Moravia, it still portrayed a Hubmaier insistent upon the Christian duty to obey the magistracy. W.J. McGlothlin, "An Anabaptist Liturgy of the Lord's Supper", *Baptist Review and Expositor* III (1906), 82-83.

[92] The question as to the ban's relationship to the sacraments will be taken up in the fourth chapter of this book.

[93] Presumably this refers specifically to verses 15 through 20 where Jesus presents the three stages of Christian correction: by individual, small group, and entire congregation. Only if the sinful person does not repent before the church is he or she banned or treated as "a pagan or tax collector" (v. 17).

Only after making such commitments to God and one another through the pledge of love is the Moravian Christian spiritually prepared for communion. Indeed, as Hubmaier outlines for the priest to say at the conclusion of the pledge, the eating of bread and drinking of wine come as public confirmation of the communal pledge as well as memorial to Christ's passion.[94] Thus, one will not encounter traditional sacramental language in the event of the Supper as much as in one's commitment of obedience to the commands of Christ. On this notion of sacramentalism, Hubmaier manifests a clear departure from the medieval and even Lutheran understandings of the ordinances as imparting grace. For Hubmaier, the heartfelt promise of the believer is that which conveys God's grace, and the ethical and covenantal response is liturgically articulated in the communal covenant before bread is ever broken. Sacrament, then, is found not in the Supper itself but in the believer's initial and continual commitment of obedience to God. Only through one's compliance to Christ and implicit acquiescence to one's fellow believers may a person receive the benefits of God's imparted grace. Thus, those who participate in the Supper are not made open to the conveyance of grace through the meal itself but instead through the pledge of love by committing themselves therein to faithful service to God and to one another.[95]

Having led the congregation through the requisite pledge of love, the priest then begins the actual introduction and invitation to the ordinance of communion. The priest begins with a scripted prayer of thanksgiving to God for God's love and Christ's atoning sacrifice for all believers. Then the service proceeds with the traditional words of institution and offering of both elements to the members present.

The service is concluded with a theological summary given by the priest:

> Most dearly beloved brethren and sisters in the Lord. As we now, by thus eating the bread and drinking the drink in memory of the suffering and shed blood of our Lord Jesus Christ for the remission of our sins have had fellowship one with another, I Cor. 10:17; 12:12; Eph. 4:4; Col. 1:3; Eph. 1; 4; 5, and have all become one loaf and one body, and our Head is Christ, we should properly become conformed to our Head and as his members follow after him, love one another, do good, give counsel, and be helpful to one another, each offering up his flesh and blood for the other. Under our Head Christ we should also live, speak, and act honorably and circumspectly, so that we give no offense or provocation to anyone, Matt. 18; Mark 9; Luke 17; I Cor. 8. Rom. 14. So that also those who are outside the church might not have reason to blaspheme our head, our faith, and church, and to say: 'Does your head Christ teach you such an evil life? Is that your faith? Is that your

---

[94] *Hubmaier*, 404; *Schriften*, 362.
[95] Mabry, *Balthasar Hubmaier's Doctrine of the Church*, 169.

baptism? Is that your Christian church, Supper, and gospel, that you should lead such an ungodly and shameful life in gluttony, drunkenness, gambling, dancing, usury, gossip, reviling, cursing, blasphemy, pride, avarice, envy, hate and wrath, unchastity, luxury, laziness, and frivolity? Matt. 18:6. Woe, woe to him who gives offense! It would be better for him that a millstone should be hung around his neck and he should be cast into the depth of the sea. Let us rather take upon ourselves a righteous, honorable, and serious life, through which God our Father who is in heaven may be praised.[96]

From this initial summary one may readily observe the ethical commitment and its consanguinity to the ordinance. The actual act of the Supper as a memorial to Christ's sacrifice for the believer's absolution then takes on the expression of unity of fellowship. Again, the community is reminded that through the communion of one loaf and cup, so they, too, are one body. Yet in this statement, the congregation is not simply unified for the sake of pleasing God but for the purpose of effective Christian witness. The Supper, then, reminds of one's duty to and indeed serves as public proclamation of Christ's transforming power. Hubmaier seemed particularly concerned that such witness was not undermined by worldly actions which outsiders might deem hypocritical to the radical Christian community's view of needful righteousness. Deviations from such moral standards would enervate the teachings of Christ, Christian faith, and one's pledge in baptism, communion, and to the gospel.

In order to maintain this high ethical standard, the priest is called upon to remind the congregation of its duty of fraternal admonition:

Since our brotherly love requires that one member of the body be also concerned for the other, therefore we have the earnest behest of Christ, Matt. 18:14ff., that whenever henceforth a brother sees another erring or sinning, that he once and again should fraternally admonish him in brotherly love. Should he not be willing to reform nor to desist from his sin, he shall be reported to the church. The church shall then exhort him a third time. When this also does no good, she shall exclude him from her fellowship. Unless it should be the case that the sin is quite public and scandalous; then he should be admonished also publicly and before all, so that the others may fear, I Cor. 5:1; I Tim. 5:20; Gal. 2:11.[97]

The ban, then, just as and in connection with the Supper, served as a reminder to the believer to discipline others in the community when need arose. Public

---

[96] *Hubmaier*, 405; *Schriften*, 363.
[97] *Hubmaier*, 406; *Schriften*, 363.

sin required public condemnation not only for the sake of the prodigal but also as deterrent against others who might be tempted waywardly to follow.

Hubmaier directed the priest to conclude:

> Whereupon I pray and exhort you once more, most dearly beloved in Christ, that henceforth as table companions of Christ Jesus, Luke 22:15, you henceforth lead a Christian walk before God and before men. Be mindful of your baptismal commitment and of your pledge of love which you made to God and the church publicly and certainly not unwittingly when receiving the water and in breaking the bread. See to it that you bear fruit worthy of the baptism and the Supper of Christ, that you may in the power of God satisfy your pledge, promise, sacrament, and sworn commitment, Matt. 3:8; Luke 3:8. God sees it and knows your hearts. May our Lord Jesus Christ, ever and eternally praised grant us the same. Amen.[98]

From this conclusion, one may garner an encapsulated version of Hubmaier's sacramentalism. Sacrament is not the ordinance itself but its accompanying pledge and promise to live as Christ directs. Indeed, Hubmaier used "pledge", "promise" and "sworn commitment" here as synonyms to "sacrament". The Hubmaierian priest reminds the congregation that these sacramental commitments are binding because the believer participated in them knowingly and voluntarily. The believer pledges in response to God's grace to live in accordance with God's commands. As such, *Eine Form des Nachtmahls Christi* serves as a consistent practical liturgical implementation and literary culmination of Hubmaier's Eucharistic doctrine.

Theological Reflection on Hubmaier's Eucharistic Thought

Balthasar Hubmaier's Eucharistic thought is emblematic of the compilation of his entire theology. Hubmaier is eclectic in the development of his thought but curiously unique in its appropriation. Clearly Hubmaier's work reflected a theological break from his medieval training, especially regarding the sacraments. As his theology matured, he also articulated differences from other Protestant theologies, namely Lutheran and Zwinglian Eucharistic notions. Hubmaier mainly set out to differentiate his interpretation of the Supper from the Roman mass. Distinctive in this argumentation is Hubmaier's conviction that the ordinance of communion is incapable of conveying grace *ex opere operato*. Instead, the rite became a symbolic ceremony done in remembrance of the once present but now risen Christ.

---

[98] *Hubmaier*, 406; *Schriften*, 363-64.

At the same time, Hubmaier was also quick to distinguish the process of his Eucharistic claims from that of Zwingli, though they inevitably arrived at parallel, characteristically anamnetic conclusions. Hubmaier reached this position by means of a medieval literalism which he paradoxically conveyed through spiritualistic symbolism. For Zwingli, Christ's words of institution, *"Hoc est corpus meum"*, are relegated to the figurative realm. The verb *"est"* is interpreted by the latter to be rendered "signifies" so as to preserve the rite as symbolic and as a memorial. For Hubmaier, such interpretation was not appropriate because it abused any literal rendering of Christ's words. Hubmaier resolved this puzzle by interpreting the subsequent sentence of the scripture text as elucidative and explicatory of the first: "Do this in remembrance of me." As such, the aggregate of Christ's intention for the Supper is interpreted by the Moravian reformer in a unique fashion: "From all these words follows the conclusion that the bread offered, broken, taken and eaten is the body of Christ in remembrance."[99] Consequently, Hubmaier found solace in preserving the literal quality of the predicate while, at least in his mind, achieving the anamnetic spirit of Jesus' and Paul's commands to memorialize Christ in Luke and I Corinthians respectively. It then follows, via Hubmaierian logic, that the second sentence qualifies the first.

Having said all this, the point remains that Hubmaier's Eucharistic conclusion is the same as Zwingli's, differing only in their hermeneutical routes. Vedder notes of this exegetical process that Hubmaier "immediately argues away that for which he has so valiantly contended, in a manner more creditable to his ingenuity than to his good sense and good faith" and that such differences occurred "on Hübmaier's part . . . [as] nothing more than a survival of that subtle, hair-splitting method of debate learned by him in the universities, from which he never completely emancipated himself."[100]

Regardless, Hubmaier came to this position by means, at least in justification, of a biblical interpretive principle: *"Talia sunt subiecta qualia permittuntur ab eorum predicatis*, that is: The preceding words should be understood according to the following words."[101] In Hubmaier's mind, this exegetical tool allowed him to interpret scriptural passages in context. Nevertheless, the application of such an pedantic prescript belies his attempt to render the "right, natural meaning" of a text. The Anabaptist theologian collapsed two separate phrases into one conjoint theological expression in order to placate his own predetermined doctrinal outlook, while hypocritically accusing his detractors of distorting Scripture in order to produce their theological conclusions. Consequently, while Hubmaier's biblical interpretation of these passages is compelling and persuasive, it is not altogether consistent with his supposedly elementary and unbiased approach to reading scripture simply and straightforwardly.

---

[99] *Hubmaier*, 324; *Schriften*, 293.
[100] Vedder, 208-209 and 210.
[101] *Hubmaier*, 324; *Schriften*, 293.

For this the most scholarly of Anabaptists, the Bible should be read with common sense in order to produce a singular and sound interpretation of the written word.[102] Yet as Rempel notes, "the exegetes use the fruit of their labor to give substance to what they believe. At the same time, their doctrinal commitments determine the vantage point from which the text is perceived."[103] In Hubmaier's case, his peculiar Christological presuppositions of the presence of Christ, at least in part, colored his "simple" reading of the Bible.

Although it would be of service to Anabaptist scholarship, an in-depth study of Hubmaier's Christology clearly exceeds the purview of this work. Focus shall instead be limited to this doctrine's relationship to the sacraments in general and the Supper in this particular chapter. Stated succinctly, Hubmaier's Christology in relation to the Supper is based upon his interpretive epigram, "the body of Christ in remembrance". For Hubmaier, the ascension of Christ is essential in understanding God's historic and continual interactions with humanity. Because He rose visibly into heaven and now sits at the right hand of the Father, Christ should be viewed as having completely departed from the plane of history. Thus, His physical presence or absence is inexorably consistent with His spiritual embodiment. Hence, Hubmaier did not get bogged down into the details of the real special presence of Christ in, around and under the bread, or His mysterious presence in the elements.[104] Christ could not be present , Hubmaier reasoned, both in heaven and in the elements simultaneously.

Hubmaier argued this point of Christ's present earthly absence vehemently. Utilizing Isaiah 66:1-2, ("But the Most High does not live in temples made with hands. As he says through the prophet, 'Heaven is my throne and earth my footstool. . . .'"),[105] Hubmaier disputed the use of idols and the concept of transubstantiation, which he interpreted as a form of idolatry. Instead, the breaking of bread and drinking of the cup are human acts that aid the believer's memory of the One no longer present. Additionally, Hubmaier's interpretation of the ascension narrative is essential to understanding his Christology. After Christ disappeared in the clouds in Acts 1:9-11, the angels who appear to the disciples inform them, "This Jesus who has been taken from you into heaven will come

---

[102] See Walter Klaassen, "Speaking in Simplicity: Balthasar Hubmaier", 139-47.

[103] Rempel, 61.

[104] One exception to this pattern comes at the conclusion of Hubmaier's *Einfältiger* where having argued Christ's full absence from the meal through simple interpretation of various passages and logic, Hubmaier surprisingly relegated communion to the realm of mystery: "O you dear good Christians: Since you see that this matter of the Supper is so high and weighty, we can neither comprehend nor grasp it with human reason", *Hubmaier*, 336; *Schriften*, 303. Nevertheless, such a statement should be regarded as an aberrant thought emblematic of Hubmaier's lingering scholasticism and a literary flourish characteristic of concluding authorial humility and not a legitimate or novel element in this thought.

[105] Scripture text here cited from *Hubmaier*, 335. See also *Schriften*, 302.

as you have seen him ascend into heaven." It followed then, in Hubmaier's mind, that the Second Person of the Trinity will return in physical, bodily form only "as you have seen him." "Thus", the Anabaptist theologian wrote, "we do not want to seek him either in the bread or in the wine."[106]

While this may seem awkward or at least peculiar to students of modern and classical theology, this application of these texts was generally representative of early Anabaptism. This notion was occasionally referred to as "the doctrine of the real absence."[107] Here, the crucified Christ is not transmitted into the presence of the congregation but the congregation to the historic presence of the crucified Christ. Consequently, in the breaking of bread and pouring of wine the essence and substance are united and thus are only symbolic elements because Scripture clearly articulates that the Son now resides in heaven.

Such convictions break with general patristic church tradition that perceived the Second Person of the Trinity as omnipresent and thus still working in history, at least spiritually. Indeed, Hubmaier's works make no interaction even with Luther's notion of the ubiquity of Christ: that Christ could be present in heaven and also among the elements simultaneously. Although Hubmaier maintained a medieval dichotomous cosmology, the physical and the spiritual realities of Christ were, at least at times, not as disjointed as many of his contemporaries would have insisted. Hence, his rendering of the phrase, to "sit at the right hand of the Father", was indicative of Christ's physical relation to the First Person of the Godhead. At least in this case, Hubmaier's simplistic approach to biblical exegesis portrayed its foibles in its attempts to decipher consistently and accurately the meaning of the writing. Biblical exegetes have long determined that sitting at the "right hand" is more an expression of power and favor and one not intended to imply a physical dimension or direction.[108] Thus, Hubmaier seemed blinded to a more authentic interpretation through figurative expression because of the dogmatic literalism governing his hermeneutic.

At the same time, his Christological explanation of Christ's accounted absence reveals Hubmaier's understanding of the Trinity as a whole. Hubmaier seemed to perceive the presence of God in three persons as only sequential manifestations of God to humanity.[109] While he avoids the pitfalls of modalism by furnishing concurrent localities of each member of the Godhead, Hubmaier sequestered God to certain forms at particular periods of human history, via the Father to Son to Spirit.

---

[106] *Hubmaier*, 334; *Schriften*, 302.

[107] Mabry, *Balthasar Hubmaier's Doctrine of the Church*, 171.

[108] Mabry argues that "the fact that Christ has a position of favor and power with God would not preclude Him from being also in the sacrament of the Eucharist (if he chooses); rather, it would more likely enhance the possibility that he could do so", *Balthasar Hubmaier's Doctrine of the Church*, 171.

[109] Rempel, 85.

Hubmaier's portrayal of humanity's current status and interactions with God at this point becomes even more curious to the reader. Pneumatologically, the Holy Ghost has replaced Christ Jesus as God's presence in the earthly realm and has been the Person working with and among humanity subsequent to the ascension. Nevertheless, significant to Hubmaier's systematic thought is that the church itself becomes God's representative and surrogate incarnation. Here Hubmaier particularly makes use of the notion of the "power of the keys" (Matt. 16:16-19). On this point, Hubmaier noted that "Christ assigned all his authority to the holy Christian church and hung the promised keys at her side, that she should use the same for the loosing and binding of sins according to his command in his bodily absence, until his second bodily coming."[110] While the ban and the power of the keys will be discussed in chapter four of this work, it is worthy to note briefly at this juncture its relationship to Hubmaier's Eucharistic theology. With Christ currently occupied in the heavenly realm, His Bride acts in His stead in human history through tangible work and witness with the Spirit acting as the guarantor of this authority.[111] Thus, while the Spirit acts as the Person of God currently interacting with the Word, it is the church more than the Spirit which is the present form of Jesus Christ. Of consequence to the Eucharist is that the power of the keys would be nullified if Christ were to return in the elements or as somehow mysteriously present during communion. Instead, for Hubmaier, God is made incarnate *in ecclesia*.

Thus, Hubmaier's appropriation of Christology and its consequent rejection of transubstantiation, partnered with his understanding of Christ bequeathing his "keys" to the church, constitute important theological transitions from the objective to the subjective, from God's action to the individual and corporate human response. The Catholic emphasis on the priest consecrating the elements is transposed to an accentuation of a community's recollection of the Lord. Furthermore, because Luther and even Zwingli also emphasized the divine will in their stances on the ordinances and the church, Hubmaier portrayed some theological distance from their perspectives as well.[112] For Hubmaier, the individual Christian was at liberty to respond to God in obedience and to become a part of the true church of true believers voluntarily gathering to pledge their love for God and one another. Communion was interpreted as that symbolic ceremony which represented and followed that sacramental pledge.

With this in mind, Hubmaier ontologically transferred the *res* which the bread signifies from Christ to Christ's Body, the church. While this ceremony initially conveys the importance of recalling the passion of Jesus on the cross, it also and perhaps more significantly characterizes the promise of love to sacrifice for one another. Thus, communion is as much an ecclesial as a Christological activity, if not more so. "The Supper", Rempel notes of Hubmaier's thought, "is the primal sign that Christians are committed to live in love toward each other and the

---

[110] *Hubmaier*, 415; *Schriften*, 371.
[111] Rempel, 82-83.
[112] Rempel, 44.

world."[113] Hence, Hubmaier's previous language regarding the Supper as memorial was generally negative, stripping away the sacramental import placed therein by Catholic authorities and some magisterial reformers. Yet having reinterpreted the rite in terms of church ethics, Hubmaier added a positive role to the rite: the symbolic response to grace and seal of one's covenant to love the others. Herein communion becomes less the recollection of a divine, erstwhile action and more an ethical human action for contemporary existence.[114]

Hubmaier's final claim as to what the Supper is rather than what it is not perhaps becomes the most unique and original feature of his Eucharistic theology. While other Anabaptists integrate similar arguments regarding Christ's absence, Hubmaier stood apart on the degree to which he emphasized the rite as ethical response beyond memorial. Christians were called to long for communion, in Hubmaier's thought, not to experience Christ in the Eucharistic elements but to experience the heartfelt communion with one another as His Body. Only indirectly and symbolically does the congregation experience Christ. Nevertheless, the Lord's Supper is not existentially sacramental through some mystical transformation of the congregants but sacramental only by human ethic through their willing response to God's grace through their promise to love one another.

Consequently, though he expostulated the notion that sacrament is a medium of grace, Hubmaier did not thereby enervate sacramentalism. Instead, the former Catholic professor and priest reinterpreted the notion of sacramentality. Avoiding the individualistic pitfalls of spiritualism, Hubmaier articulated a theology of communion which transposed "sacrament" from a means to grace to its response; from the divine, objective will to the ethical, anthropological and ecclesial realms. From this position, Rempel argues that Hubmaier elevated the fourth gospel above the synoptics, wherein John's Last Supper makes no mention of bread and wine but only of Jesus' humility and love in ethical action by washing the feet of his disciples. The writer of the gospel concludes by recounting Christ calling on the disciples to do the same for one another. Communion, then, is understood by Hubmaier as emulative of Christ's loving sacrifice and condescending service in human history.[115]

The Lord's Supper then came to the Hubmaierian Anabaptist community not as a literal sacrifice of Christ but as an expression of the community to sacrifice for one another. Communion became a symbolic expression of faith that was emblematically entered into through baptism, continually guarded through the discipline of the ban and reenacted through corporate worship, pledge and Eucharist.

---

[113] Rempel, 63.
[114] Rempel, 63.
[115] Rempel, 86-87.

Hubmaier, then, primarily viewed the Supper as a seal and symbolic confirmation of the sacramental pledge of one's love for the others. It is a communion that encompasses all of one's life and work as a Christian.[116] Thus, while he was in keeping with other Anabaptists in rejecting the notion of grace being conveyed through any physical object, Hubmaier understood the Supper to be a symbolic attestation of one's principled answer to the offer of God's grace through witting and willing righteousness and service for others. Herein one may commune with God through remembrance of God's Son by partaking of Christ's real body and blood in *anamnesis*. Additionally, one may commune with his or her neighbor through one's promise to prolong the earthly presence of Christ by means of the sacrificial service of and for the church.[117] In both senses does one find communion. Through the requisite pledge of love does one find sacrament.

---

[116] Mabry, *Balthasar Hubmaier's Doctrine of the Church*, 168.
[117] Rempel, 79.

CHAPTER 3

Baptism as Sacrament

Balthasar Hubmaier wrote more on the theology and practice of baptism than any other subject. Indeed, one might postulate that Hubmaier's baptismal theology distinguishes him more from both Catholic and magisterial Protestant traditions than any other aspect of his thought. Even though his mature cogitation concerning baptism was inextricably related to the developments in his view of a visible church and a strong anthropological emphasis on human response to God's saving action,[1] baptism, nevertheless, rightly or wrongly, exemplified Hubmaier's unique positioning as countering other reformers and crossing over to Anabaptism. Hubmaier's other writings seem to be eclipsed by the volume of his baptismal works.

The weight of his baptismal attention probably came primarily as a result of Hubmaier's felt need to respond to his critics. In fact, a significant portion of this genre of literature is polemical. Nevertheless, intentionally or unintentionally, baptism's attention in Hubmaier's thought is emblematic of its requisite focus in the life of his congregational praxis. Hubmaier would regard water baptism to be the visible sign or symbol of one's response in faith to God, one's connection and submission to the discipline of the church, and one's public witness both within and without the believing community to God's saving work. Baptism is the visible sign of the believer's sacramental pledge of love to God and the congregation. Its accentuation within the tomes of Hubmaier's writings is at least proportional to its liturgical import within the community of faith. Furthermore, that water baptism serves as the visible sign of one's inner sacramental pledge to God and church in faith upholds its cardinal consideration within this study. Yet, in order to understand more fully the doctrine and practice of Hubmaier's baptismal theology and its distinguishing characteristics, this chapter will first outline the development of his sacramental transitions from Roman Catholic to a distinctly Anabaptist cogitation regarding this rite.

---

[1] In his dissertation on this subject, Eddie Mabry argues that Hubmaier "developed his baptismal theology in harmony with his doctrine of the church, while presupposing an ontological concept of justification and free will." See Eddie Louis Mabry, "The Baptismal Theology of Balthasar Hubmaier" (unpublished dissertation, Princeton Theological Seminary, 1982), iv.

The Development of Hubmaier's Baptismal Thought

This book has previously established that Hubmaier's thought was, at least in his early life, deeply ensconced within medieval Catholicism. Undoubtedly through his early vocation as Cathedral cleric in Regensburg and parish priest in his first few years in Waldshut, Hubmaier baptized at least several infants in accordance with Roman practice and within its theological norms. Herein, baptism was the remedy for original sin. The manifestation of faith in response to this rite was not requisite and as such baptism was appropriately administered to infants. One benefited from the conference of grace *ex opere operato* regardless of faith. Each baptized person would be seen as effected ontologically via this external rite.[2]

Such a view would doubtlessly have been characteristic of Hubmaier's schooling and representative of his early thought and praxis. However, Hubmaier at some point altered his convictions on the rite of baptism radically. Pinpointing the time of this transition, what many regard not only as his subsequent break from Zwingli but also his conversion to Anabaptism, proves more difficult. Though his own (re)baptism and that of three hundred in his Waldshut church came at holy week (or soon thereafter) in 1525, Rollin Armour observes rightly that "so extreme a move did not develop overnight, of course."[3]

Empirical data can, naturally, only be garnered from Hubmaier's correspondence (and the recipients' responses) coupled with his theological writings. The historian then depends upon (and is limited to) extant writings for subjective factuality and may only conjecture thereafter on the events, influences and other pressures which precipitated such thought, particularly through periods of philosophic and theological metamorphosis. Naturally, Hubmaier is no exception to this prescript.

Therefore, this portion of the study shall begin first by analyzing Hubmaier's early letters and records to surmise through them as to the time wherein he became influenced by other people and events which initiated his theological sojourn from Catholic sacramentalist to Anabaptist reformer. All the while, this book will argue, Hubmaier preserved something of his scholastic, medieval past by retaining its sense of sacramentalism, yet transposing the dispensation of grace from the symbol itself to the promise of the believer which the symbol represents and conveys.

Well after his adoption of Anabaptist beliefs, Hubmaier reflected in his *Dialogue with Zwingli's Baptismal Book*, written in 1526:

> For, truly, if I be permitted to boast, *in six years* no subject has been
> opened up which is clearer, brighter, and more publicly testified to

---

[2] Steinmetz, *Reformers in the Wings*, 203.

[3] Armour, *Anabaptist Baptism*, 19.

everywhere in Scriptures than that of water baptism, that one should apply it to believers and not to cradle babies.[4]

From this notation, scholars have logically concluded that Hubmaier's questions regarding the adequacy of pedobaptism may have dated back to 1520 or 1521. This suggestion presents excellent possibilities regarding influences on Hubmaier during that period and shall be discussed later.

Yet, Hubmaier continued to outline the development of his thought through his *Dialogue* by recounting, polemically to Zwingli, their legendary conversation by the moat in Zurich in 1523.[5] In this writing, Hubmaier argued that he and Zwingli at that point both agreed "that one should not baptize children before they had been instructed in the faith" and that Zwingli's own writings questioned the biblical backing for such a practice.[6]

While older Anabaptist scholarship has questioned the accuracy of Hubmaier's account,[7] namely that he and Zwingli would have challenged infant baptism so early, more recent research has affirmed the timeline of Hubmaier's claims.[8] Hubmaier's words are further buttressed both by the possibility of a third party witness[9] and by Zwingli's own admissions to entertaining believer's

---

[4] *Hubmaier*, 177; *Schriften*, 172-73 [italics mine].

[5] *Hubmaier*, 194-95; *Schriften*, 186-87. See also pg. 29 of this present text for details of this historical account.

[6] *Hubmaier*, 195; *Schriften*, 186. See also Zwingli's 18th Article on Confirmation in Zwingli, *Huldreich Zwingli samtlich Werke*, II, 122-25 [hereafter *SW*]; Zwingli, *Huldruch Zwingli: Writings*, II (ed. E.J. Furcha; Allison Park: Pickwick Publications, 1984), II, 11-102 [hereafter *ZW*].

[7] e.g., Wilhelm Mau, *Balthasar Hubmaier* from *Abhandlungen zur mittleren und neueren Geschichte*, XL (eds. Georg von Below, Heinrich Finke and Friedrich Meinecke; Berlin & Leipzig: Walter Rothschild, 1912), 80.

[8] While Bergsten suggested that the bitter debate with Zwingli in 1525-6 "caused him to overemphasize the significance of his early doubts regarding infant baptism as well as his conversation '*auf dem Graben'*", Bergsten, along with Armour, both affirm that problems with pedobaptism were certainly part of this conversation. See Bergsten, *Balthasar Hubmaier: Seine Stellung zu Reformation und Täufertum*, 111-12; Bergsten, *Balthasar Hubmaier: Anabaptist Theologian and Martyr*, 80-81; and Armour, 20. Here Armour states: "there is no identifiable reason for doubting the substance of his claim."

[9] Hubmaier named Sebastian Ruckensperger from St. Gall (formerly the prior at Sion in Klingau), as also being present during the Graben conversation, *Schriften*, 186. Nevertheless, Ruckensperger's own account is, to this writer's knowledge, uncertain. Additionally, historian Johannes Kessler recorded in his *Sabbata* the date of this event [May 1] and some of the discussion of the Zurich moat conversation, all of which coincide with Hubmaier's testimony. This history, while not firsthand, was noted by Bergsten that "without a doubt eyewitnesses related all this to [Kessler]", Bergsten, *Balthasar Hubmaier: Anabaptist Theologian and Martyr*, 79.

baptism.[10] Additionally, Hubmaier might be credited to some degree by the mere fact that he consistently recounted this story at least three times: twice in his written works and then later in 1526 during his trial and public examination in Zurich.[11] These historical details have led Rollin Armour to conclude: "As early then as the spring of 1523, Hubmaier was entertaining questions about the validity of infant baptism."[12]

While it does seem abundantly clear that Hubmaier was examining the issue of baptism by 1523, it seems probable that he had already arrived or was close to arriving at a final position of anti-pedobaptism during this period. This text shall argue that, if we take Hubmaier by his word, this process began even earlier as Hubmaier struggled internally before making his new position public. It seems more conceivable that Hubmaier's doubts concerning the rite actually began, as he himself stated, in 1520, and that such uncertainty originated, curiously, from reading works of Martin Luther.

Luther's Influence

Although Martin Luther seemed always to argue for infant baptism as biblically legitimate and exemplifying God's grace, Hubmaier was moved by Luther's words regarding the place of faith in baptism. Parenthetically, Hubmaier's theological training in medieval Catholic schools paralleled more of Luther's rigorous scholarship than the relatively paltry training Zwingli had received.[13] Regardless, in 1518, Martin Luther responded to Hubmaier's doctor father, Johannes Eck who in his *Obelisci* had articulated the Catholic notion that a sacrament confers grace upon the recipient regardless of the person's spiritual condition. Luther answered by arguing that faith was always necessary on the part of the recipient, for faith and not the sacramental action is that which justifies. The sacrament can only justify because it is believed, not based upon the action in

---

[10] Zwingli admitted: "for some time I myself was deceived by the [Anabaptist] error and thought it better not to baptize children until they came to the age of discretion." Zwingli, "Of Baptism", from *Zwingli and Bullinger* (The Library of Christian Classics XXIV), 139.

[11] *Hubmaier,* 194-95; 257; *Schriften*, 186-87; 234-35; and *ZW* II, 100.

[12] Armour, 20.

[13] Steinmetz attentively observes: "The similarities between Luther and Hubmaier are marked, particularly if one compares Luther with Zwingli, Oecolampadius, Calvin, or even Melanchthon. Both Luther and Hubmaier were born in the early 1480's; both had an old-fashioned scholastic theological education, Luther at Erfurt and Wittenberg, and Hubmaier at Freiburg and Ingolstadt; both earned a theological doctorate in the same year (1512); both made a point of studying Greek and Hebrew; both served as university lecturers . . . ; and both were associated during the early stages of their careers with the *via moderna.*" See Steinmetz, *Luther in Context*, 60.

itself.[14] Again Luther explained this view of requisite faith before participating in the sacraments in his 1519 *Disputatio de lege et fide*: "If indeed we are justified by faith, it follows that the sacraments are not efficacious except by faith in Christ."[15]

While it is uncertain whether Hubmaier encountered these latter two works which exemplify Luther's position on this issue, Hubmaier did relate that he came upon Luther's 1520 *Ein Sermon von dem neuen Testament, das ist von der Heiligen Messe,* in 1521. In this famous tract, Luther again outlined his doctrine of *sola fide* in relation to the sacraments.

Scholars are quick to indicate that Hubmaier probably misunderstood Luther,[16] or at least he had applied Luther's doctrine to an extreme unintended by Luther. For Luther, faith comes as a gift from God. For Hubmaier, faith was not merely divine gift, but, importantly, arose out of human capacity in response to hearing the gospel.[17] Thus, Hubmaier displaced the objective "sacramental" understanding of grace being divinely dispensed through the sacrament with the anthropological relationships established between the baptized and his congregation as with the baptized and the Lord. The covenant of the human pledge in response to God's promise of salvation becomes Hubmaier's new understanding of sacrament. Nevertheless, as one scholar observes: "In the close, indispensable link between faith and sacrament, in which faith may always be seen to arise from the basis of the word, Hubmaier thinks along Lutheran lines."[18] Consequently, while Luther and Hubmaier ultimately diverge dramatically in their sacramental theologies, Luther's works may be the starting point from which Hubmaier began his baptismal reforms. Through his unique gift of theological synthesis, combined with his brilliant education and intellect, Hubmaier probably appropriated Luther's sacramental criticism of medieval scholasticism into his developing baptismal and ecclesiological thought and eventual reforms.[19]

Beyond Luther's works, it becomes more difficult to ascertain which magis-

---

[14] Martin Luther, "A sterisci Lutheri adversus Obeliscos Eckii", *D. Martin Luthers Werke*, I (Weimar: Böhlau, 1883), 286.

[15] See Luther, "Disputatio de lege et fide", *D. Martin Luthers Werke*, VI, 24; cited also in Mabry, *Balthasar Hubmaier's Doctrine of the Church*, 133.

[16] Armour, for instance, indicates that "Luther did not intend what Hubmaier attributed to him", 24.

[17] See Eddie Mabry, *Balthasar Hubmaier's Understanding of Faith*, particularly 19-21.

[18] Christof Windhorst, *Täuferisches Taufverständnis: Balthasar Hubmaiers Lehre zwischen Traditioneller und Reformatorischer Theologie* (Leiden: E.J. Brill, 1976), 102.

[19] For further discussion of Hubmaier's interpretation and appropriation of Luther's notions of sacrament and justification, especially via Zwingli's covenantal theology, see David Steinmetz, *Reformers in the Wings*, 203-208. See also Brian C. Brewer, "Radicalizing Luther: How Balthasar Hubmaier (Mis)Read the 'Father of the Reformation'", *MQR* 84, no. 1 (January 2010), 95-115.

terial reformers, dissident leaders and groups were direct influences upon Hubmaier's theological conversion outside of Zurich. Certainly Hubmaier, while in Waldshut, was well positioned geographically between Basel, Zurich, Schaffhausen, and other major cities which hosted reformation proposals. Whether Thomas Müntzer, the Zwickau Radicals, and other Spiritualists who had intimated disdain for or already outright rejected pedobaptism had a direct impact upon Hubmaier during these formative years is a matter of debate that may never be evidentially resolved.[20]

The Influence from Zurich

Nevertheless, what does seem apparent is the theological influence from Zurich on Hubmaier's baptismal thought in the early to mid 1520s, both from Zwingli and subsequently from his disquieted disciples. This influence became most pronounced as Hubmaier was invited to and participated in the Second Zurich Disputation in 1523, which in itself may be indicative of Zwingli's relationship to and respect for Hubmaier at that juncture.

While the focus of debate was on the issues of images and the Supper, it is telling that Hubmaier sided with and spoke for Zwingli's moderate and circumspect reforms on the former but represented the Grebel circle's more radical and swift reforms on the latter.[21] Consequently, Hubmaier publicly portrayed some knowledge of as well as support and kinship to both camps.

---

[20] For instance, on the matter of Münzter's influence, Johann Loserth argues that Münzter was integral to forming Hubmaier's baptismal thought, but Bergsten writes only that "through literary and, perhaps, personal influence Müntzer could have had the effect of stimulating and strengthening Hubmaier's criticism of infant baptism which he had already expressed . . . earlier." Yet Vedder argues, "It is absurd to attribute the rise of this question [of baptism] in Zurich to the agency of Thomas Münzer. . . and therefore to establish any sort of connection between him and the Anabaptists is to descredit the latter – which is a thing that many writers, from Bullinger to our day, have busily attempted to do." See Loserth, *Doktor Balthasar Hubmaier und die Anfänge der Wiedertaufe in Mähren* (Brünn: R.M. Rohrer, 1893), 73; Bergsten, *Balthasar Hubmaier: Anabaptist Theologian and Martyr*, 151-52; and Vedder, 105,107.

[21] In the case of images, Hubmaier argued: "For there are many persons who mightily adhere to the images. Therefore the clear holy Word of God against images and idols in Old and New Testament must be shown to the people earnestly and often with care and diligence. This will exercise its authority and power and with time will drive all the images out, for it is impossible that the Word of God should be preached and not bring works and fruits in that whereto it was sent from God [Isa. 55:10]." Yet in the latter case of the Supper, Hubmaier urged: "therefore the priest must not preach anything in the mass other than the pure, true, clear Word of God of which they are signs. He who celebrates mass otherwise is not properly holding mass. . . . The follower must be faithful or Christ is pushed aside", *Hubmaier*, 26, 28; *Schriften*, 762, 786-87.

It shall become more clear through the development of Hubmaier's own thought and writings on the subject of baptism how the Waldshut reformer would retain, yet ultimately modify, not only his notion of medieval sacramentalism but also his theological affinity with Zwingli. Indeed, Armour rightly notes that "Zwingli's own thought on baptism had within it some of the seeds which grew into Anabaptism",[22] regardless of whether this reformation gardener intended such crop. Yet, two months after the Second Disputation, Zwingli entrusted the speed and extent of his proposed reforms to the Zurich Council, eliciting further distance between himself and the Grebel circle.

Upon his return to Waldshut, Hubmaier called for a similar disputation to be held in Waldshut and published his first work, *Eighteen Theses*, in early 1524 as the basis for its discussion. Herein, baptism was only broached twice, with neither reference indicative of radical thought yet testifying to some degree of mainstream Protestant thinking. Here he stated:

8.   Since every Christian believes and is baptized for himself every one should see and judge by Scripture, whether he is being rightly fed and watered by his shepherd.

9.   Since Christ alone died for our sin, in whose name alone we are baptized, so shall only he be appealed to as our sole Intercessor and Mediator. Here all pilgrimages fall away.[23]

Scholars are uncertain from these comments of the level of baptismal thought or reform Hubmaier had entertained by this date.[24] One might read into article eight a necessity of belief both from Hubmaier's word order ("believes and is baptized") and an implication for the responsibility of those baptized Christians to discern Scripture individually as to test the priest. Nevertheless, a full admission to and argument for believer's baptism is not altogether noticeable here. It is safe to say, then, that Hubmaier was at least unprepared to make public his radical thought on the subject of baptism, if he had any at that juncture.

What might be more revealing on the subject of baptism than those references which specifically mention the rite are those which speak to the issue of faith:

1.   Faith alone makes us righteous before God.

2.   This faith is the knowledge of God's mercy, which he has shown us by offering his only begotten Son. Here fail those who are Christian in appearance [only], who have only an historical faith in God.

---

[22] Armour, *Anabaptist Baptism*, 26.

[23] *Hubmaier*, 33; *Schriften*, 73.

[24] While Wilhelm Mau argues that these comments indicate a Hubmaier who simply approved of the current practice of baptism, Armour notes that such statements are "too general to justify the claim". See Mau, 81 and Armour, 21.

3.   Such faith cannot be idle, but must break forth in gratitude to-
     ward God and in all sorts of works of brotherly love toward oth-
     ers. This casts down all artifice such as candles, palm branches,
     and *holy water*.[25]

While in no way revealing Hubmaier's fully developed baptismal theology, these
first three articles do portray the soteriological and anthropological emphases in
Hubmaier's over-arching theology, which would also serve as foundational elements of his ecclesiological and baptismal thought.

These three succinct statements demonstrate Hubmaier's idea that faith is
both a merciful and revelatory gift of God and a human response to God's dispensation of mercy. If such faith cannot be embodied on the part of the recipient
"historically" or potentially only, but must also be appropriated kinetically, it
unveils the basis upon which Hubmaier will predicate his sacramental thought.
Herein, the faithful response on the part of the believer is that which exemplifies true Christianity, whereas the mere dispensation of historical knowledge or
even the external power of any artifice on behalf of the believer is diminished
in import. Hubmaier even named "holy water" as an example of such misled
distortions of sacramental ontology. Thus, while his *Eighteen Articles* in general
does not reveal his changing sentiment regarding the rite of baptism outright, it
does at least suggest the direction of his sacramental thought in general and his
baptismal doctrine in particular.

Hubmaier's *Articles* largely parallel Zwingli's, for as Armour states, the
Zurich reformation was "the most important influence of all"[26] on Hubmaier's
own proposals for reform. Thus, Zwingli's questions for the conference regarding grace *ex opere operato* laid the groundwork for Grebel's more radical criticisms of pedobaptism and Hubmaier's eventual reforms. Subsequently, in a letter to Fridolin Lindauer in October 1524, Zwingli questioned: "How could an
incorporeal substance be cleansed by a physical element?"[27] Such a question
demonstrated Zwingli's insistence that inner spiritual action be separated from
its outward symbols. Consequently, for Zwingli the ontological transformation
of the participant in baptism or the Supper cannot be effected through the external rites of the church.

While Zwingli's approach to justification through faith differs little from
Luther's view, the role of the sacraments in that process exposes a significant
break between Luther on one hand and Zwingli and Hubmaier on the other. As
Luther held the more conservative view that God transforms the person internally through external elements to which God has affixed his salvific promise,
Zwingli boldly separated the symbol from the spiritual reality, the outer sign
from the inward actuality. Thus, the baptism of the Spirit was free from water

---

[25] *Hubmaier*, 32 [italics mine]; *"weyhwasser"*, *Schriften*, 72.
[26] Armour, 25.
[27] Zwingli, "Letter to Fridolin Lindauer", (October 20, 1524) *ZW* VIII, 236.

baptism, for God may work if and when God determines.[28]

For Zwingli, the baptism of the Spirit is God's gracious work that instills faith in the Christian. Water baptism is consigned to the church's response to that grace. Yet Zwingli ultimately allowed for the continuation of infant baptism as testimony to a person's anticipation of God's inward work which is always separated from the sign. For Zwingli, God's sovereignty and freedom still must be upheld over a human's faithful response. Thus, one's experience of regeneration is not requisite for the outward sign, merely one's anticipation of it. Children of Christians may unquestionably look forward to God's inner working because of their inheritance of salvation based upon the promise in God's own covenant. Baptism, then, serves as the New Testament continuation of that which was represented through Old Testament circumcision: It is a designation or outer seal of God's covenantal promise of salvific and parental watch-care.[29] Water baptism may then be dispensed before or after the baptism of the Spirit, and baptismal instruction may precede or follow the symbolic action that illustrates it.[30]

In his treatise, *Of Baptism*, Zwingli explicates this position:

> We now examine equally carefully the question of signs in order to expose the mistake which once deceived me as found in certain writers. For some have taught that signs are given for the confirmation of an existing faith in that which we have already learned and to which we are pledged. But this is not so. The danger is that often we are so inclined to accept that which is superficially attractive, and is perhaps attractively presented, that we stumble into it blindly, not paying any heed to the Word of God or the inward man, that is, faith. It is true, of course, that some signs are given the better to confirm faith, or in some sort to reassure the flesh, which does not allow faith any rest. But such signs are not pledges, but miraculous signs, like Moses' rod and Gideon's fleece and innumerable others given to the fathers. At the moment, however, we are not speaking of miracles, but of the seals and pledges which are not miraculous, like circumcision under the old covenant. Circumcision did not confirm the faith of Abraham. For circumcision was given to Abraham when by faith he was already accounted righteous by God and the seed of Abraham. . . . And in Genesis 17 God himself makes it quite clear that circumcision is not a sign for the confirmation of faith but a covenant sign: 'This is my covenant, which ye shall keep, between me and you and thy seed after thee; every man child among you shall be circumcised.'. . . Similarly baptism in the New Testament is

---

[28] Steinmetz, *Reformers in the Wings*, 204.

[29] Steinmetz, *Reformers in the Wings*, 204-205.

[30] G.W. Bromiley, Introduction to "Of Baptism", *Zwingli and Bullinger*, 122.

> a covenant sign. It does not justify the one who is baptized, nor does it confirm his faith, for it is not possible for an external thing to confirm faith. For faith does not proceed from external things. It proceeds only from the God who draws us. Therefore it cannot be grounded in any external thing."[31]

Hubmaier did not disagree with Zwingli that baptism was a covenantal sign and even a spiritual continuation of that represented in circumcision. Instead, the crux of Hubmaier's disagreement with Zwingli on baptism stemmed from the meaning of covenant itself. While Zwingli stressed the importance of God as the instigator of spiritual covenant, that God provides grace and mercy to his elect through the work of the Spirit, Hubmaier emphasized the human response to grace. Baptism then comes as the symbolic representation of a new Christian's commitment to enter into covenant with God.[32] Thus, building upon Zwingli's divorcement of sign from inward reality, combined with Luther's emphasis of faith preceding the rite, Hubmaier harmonized a theology[33] that only adult Christians who have manifested faith may appropriately participate in the rite of baptism. Furthermore, Hubmaier maintained his sacramental understanding of baptism from his medieval Catholic training, yet exchanged the sign of water itself for the human act of pledge and promise as sacrament.

Nevertheless, for a brief time, both Zwingli and Hubmaier were writing on the subject of baptism, sounding similar themes, but implying divergent ends.[34] Zwingli, for instance, wrote in his treatise *Of True and False Religion*: "These ceremonies are external signs which demonstrate to others that the recipient has pledged himself to a new life and will confess Christ even unto death."[35] At the same time, Hubmaier wrote a colleague that baptism is "a sign assuredly also a 'symbol' instituted by Christ . . . (whereby for the sake of the faith and in hope of the resurrection to life eternal one binds oneself to God even unto death). [This meaning] should be valued more seriously than the sign itself."[36] Nevertheless, only Hubmaier would conclude from this that the practice of pedobaptism was unwarranted, for, as he concluded, "infant baptism is a kind of vessel without wine."[37]

---

31 Zwingli, "Of Baptism", from *Zwingli and Bullinger*, 138-39.

32 Steinmetz, *Reformers in the Wings*, 205.

33 Indeed, Carl Sachsse argues that Hubmaier appropriated an ecletic variety into his contemporary theology gradationally as he was exposed to a wider gamut of theological works and life experiences. And yet, Sachsse argues that Hubmaier melded these theologies independently into a unique synthesis. His doctrine of baptism is no exception. See Sachsee, *D. Balthasar Hubmaier als Theologe*, esp. 117-63; 192-94.

34 Armour, *Anabaptist Baptism*, 26.

35 Originally cited in *ZW* III, 773; here cited in Armour, *Anabaptist Baptism*, 26.

36 *Hubmaier*, 70.

37 *Hubmaier*, 70.

Possible Influence of Humanism

For Hubmaier, baptism signified the Christian's pledge of love in response to God's grace. This is not to say that Hubmaier would deny the sovereignty of God, but only that he saw a place and particularly emphasized the need for a person's retroaction to such a grace for faith to be genuine and valid. That Hubmaier would stress the importance of anthropology in the *ordo salutis* might give rise to the question of the influence of humanism in general and Erasmus in particular on his thought. Certainly Erasmus was a contemporary of Hubmaier whose writings were read widely, probably even by the Waldshut priest himself. Some scholars believe that Eramus convinced both Hubmaier and Zwingli of the distinction between inner and outer baptism and Hubmaier of the importance of teaching to accompany the rite in order for its meaning to be authentic.

It is abundantly clear that Erasmus touched upon various subjects important to Anabaptism, particularly regarding the necessity of faith and human response.[38] At one point, for instance, Erasmus wrote:

> Do you really think that the ceremony of itself makes you a Christian? If your mind is preoccupied with the affairs of the world, you may be a Christian on the surface, but inwardly you are a Gentile of the Gentiles. Why is this? It is simply because you have grasped the body of the sacrament, not the spirit. The ceremony consists of washing the body with water, but for you this is not a cleansing of the soul. Salt is placed upon your tongue, but your mind remains uncured. The body is anointed with oil, but the soul remains unanointed. You have been sprinkled with holy water, but this accomplishes nothing unless you cleanse the inner filth of your mind.[39]

Elsewhere, Erasmus wrote:

> Do you think that Christ is found in ceremonies, in doctrines kept after a fashion, and in constitutions of the church? Who is truly Christian? Not he who is baptized or anointed, or who attends church. It is rather the man who has embraced Christ in the innermost feelings of his heart, and who emulates Him in pious deeds.[40]

Though such examples might display this humanist's influence upon Hubmaier's sacramental thought, it is more easily established that what many theo-

---

[38] Much of this subject is outlined in chapter 1 of this book.

[39] From Erasmus' *Enchiridion*, 66; here cited in Friesen, 31.

[40] Originaly cited from Erasmus, *The Education of a Christian Prince* (ed. Lester K. Born; New York: Norton, 1968), 153; here cited in Friesen, 31.

logical historians have mistaken exclusively as humanism is, instead, at least in large part, Hubmaier's lingering medieval Catholicism. That Hubmaier's extensive theological training, which led him to a doctorate in theology at the University of Ingolstadt under the tutelage of Johannes Eck, was grounded in uncritical nominalism should bring greater evidence to the emphasis he placed upon the human will and response to God as integral to salvation and, hence, to his understanding of sacrament.[41] Perhaps, then, it would be more circumspect and sagacious to suggest that any influence on the part of Erasmus or other humanists came as a way of complementing and confirming Hubmaier's already long-held beliefs. Hubmaier certainly reinterpreted and altered these Catholic beliefs, but they were nevertheless convictions from which he would never completely depart.[42]

Hubmaier's Correspondence

Regardless of such influences, Hubmaier's correspondence at that time attested to his desire to remain close, both in terms of camaraderie and theological reflection, with Zwingli and the Basel reformer, Oecolampadius. From late 1524 to early 1525, Hubmaier had been in some dialogue with these reformer counterparts, particularly testing with them his growing conviction of anti-pedobaptism through their own theological reforms. Whether these magisterial reformers ignored Hubmaier's requests for discussion or they simply did not find his questions on baptism of material interest to their reform work at that juncture has been a matter of scholarly debate.[43]

Such correspondence from Hubmaier's pen is extant today only because it was kept by its recipients and its subsequent rival traditions to Anabaptism.

---

[41] David Steinmetz makes this argument. See his "Scholastic and Radical Reform: Nominalist Motifs in the Theology of Balthasar Hubmaier", *MQR* 45, No. 2 (April 1971), 130. Additionally, Alvin J. Beachy has argued that some elements of Hubmaier's theology, particularly his doctrine of justification in connection to anthropology, actually displays elements of medieval mysticism and not merely nominalism. For example, Beachy holds that Hubmaier's concept of the human *geyst* remaining uncorrupted by the fall and still holding inclinations toward God was something which paralleled this mysticism. Hubmaier's trichotomous anthropology, Beachy points out, held great affinity with mystic John Gerson's thought. See Alvin J. Beachy, *The Concept of Grace in the Radical Reformation* (Nieuwkoop: B.D. Graaf, 1977), 201.

[42] See Eddie Mabry, *The Baptismal Theology of Balthasar Hubmaier,* 196-215; and David Steinmetz, "Scholastic and Radical Reform: Nominalist Motifs in the Theology of Balthasar Hubmaier", 130-31.

[43] John Howard Yoder has argued the former while Old has suggested the latter. See Yoder, *Täufertum und Reformation in der Schweiz*, Part 1, *Die Gespräche zwischen Täufern und Reformatoren*, 1523-1538 (Karlsruhe: H. Schneider, 1962), 13-39; and Old, 95.

These letters would have been ultimately marked as heretical or, at least, as among non-magisterial thinking by his more mainstream peers to even remain safe within the stacks of a magisterial owner.[44] At the same time, given the comments Hubmaier made in some of his existing letters, it seems that some correspondence from his hand has been lost. For example, in one undated letter which experts believe must have been written sometime in late 1524, Hubmaier appeared to be reemphasizing his uncertainty regarding the practice of infant baptism.[45] This letter asked Zwingli to respond at last to Hubmaier's previous request as well as this present letter on this issue "for God's sake".[46] Unfortunately, the initial letter to Zwingli has been lost.

Regardless, such correspondence suggests that Hubmaier undoubtedly felt a theological kinship with Zwingli, Sebastian Hofmiester and Oecolampadius on many issues. Hubmaier continued to hope, even after he became resolute in his anti-pedobaptism and began to implement baptismal reforms, that the reformers all might "arrive at a good peace".[47] At one point, all three of these latter magisterial reformers apparently also doubted the practice of infant baptism, though more privately perhaps than Hubmaier, but all save Hubmaier also eventually relented and returned to more conservative justifications for the established custom.[48]

For his part, Hubmaier continued to stress his discomfort with continuing the practice. Finally in January 1525, Hubmaier wrote Oecolampadius of his now settled theological conviction:

> But now the time has come to speak out openly and to everyone concerned what earlier we whispered only among ourselves. May God 'the best and greatest' be blessed, for along with this new atmosphere of freedom to speak out he has also given us at the same time receptive listeners. . . .
>
> We ourselves have indeed earlier taught as well that according to the ordinance of Christ, the very young should by no means receive baptism. As a matter of fact, who instituted baptism? Of course, Christ. When? Late in Matthew's account. In what words? (Matt. 28:19): 'As you go forth, teach all nations, baptizing them in the

---

[44] Pipkin and Yoder, 67.

[45] Yoder argues of this letter that "this doubt is, however, not an indication of direct contact between Hubmaier and the Zurich circle of 'radicals'". See Yoder, "Balthasar Hubmaier and the Beginnings of Swiss Anabaptism", 6.

[46] Originally cited in *ZW* VIII, no. 353, pg. 344; here cited in Yoder, "Balthasar Hubmaier and the Beginnings of Swiss Anabaptism", 6.

[47] *Hubmaier*, "Letter to the Zurich Council", 91.

[48] albeit a forced change of theology by the Schaffhausen government for Hofmeister. See Heinold Fast, *Quellen zur Geschichte der Täufer in der Scweiz, Zweiter Band, Ostschweiz* (Zurich: Theologischer Verlag, 1957), 13-20.

> name of the Father and of the Son and of the Holy Spirit.' Quite right.
> Why, then, do we baptize the very young? Baptism, the saying goes,
> is a naked sign. Why is it that we dispute so fiercely over this 'sign'?
> The sign is assuredly also a 'symbol' instituted by Christ with words
> significant and solemn to the highest degree: 'In the name of the
> Father and the Son and the Holy Spirit.' Anyone who weakens this
> sign or abuses it gives offense to the words with which Jesus inaugu-
> rated the sign, though of course the bonding signified by that sign and
> symbol (whereby for the sake of the faith and in hope of the resurrec-
> tion to life eternal one binds oneself to God even unto death) should
> be valued more seriously than the sign itself. . . . But it is not possible
> that this significance should fit the very young.[49]

While obviously very early in his public commitment to believer's baptism,[50] Hubmaier already manifested in this letter not only a biblical justification for his stance but, more important to this work, a theological description of to what the ordinance points: the participant's commitment to God "even unto death". Herein Hubmaier's concept of covenant becomes apparent. It is the response of faith on the part of the believer to God, enacted by the believer's promise. The act of water baptism is merely a "sign and symbol" to that bond, though to Hubmaier this was not an unimportant gesture.

The heartfelt commitment or bond is what underlies Hubmaier's reforma-tion thought and his attempt at baptismal reform in Waldshut. In his letter to Oecolampadius, Hubmaier continued this thought:

> In baptism there is made a bond with God, to which now the Apostolic
> Creed attests, showing forth verily the apostolic majesty and a renun-
> ciation of Satan and all his pretentiousness even unto the water, i.e.
> unto death. The bond in the Lord's Supper is like it, whereby I com-
> mit myself to lay down my body and blood for his sake, as Christ did
> for me. And so we have the laws and the prophets. Whence I think,
> indeed I know, that a return to true Christianity will never be effected
> unless baptism and the Lord's Supper are brought back to their nature
> and genuine purity.[51]

Thus, Hubmaier saw a need to reform baptism and the Supper as conditions to renew the church. For these symbols to reconstitute their true meaning, the church must restore their connection to a believer's heartfelt pledge to God (in

---

[49] *Hubmaier*, 69-70.

[50] In fact, Armour observes this letter to be the "first express denial of infant baptism from Hubmaier's hand", 22.

[51] *Hubmaier*, 70.

baptism) and to one another (in the Supper).

As important as such statements are to understanding his early radical thought, perhaps more significant still are Hubmaier's comments in the postscript to Oecolampadius. Herein he explained his somewhat conservative application of his baptismal principles in the context of corporate worship:

> I like to assemble the congregation in the place of baptism, bringing in the child. I exposit in the native tongue the gospel text: "Children were brought. . ." (Matt. 19:13). As soon as his name has been given to him, the whole congregation on bended knee prays for the child, entrusting him to the hands of Christ, that he may be ever closer to the child and pray on his behalf. If there are parents of a sick child at a given time, who most earnestly wish the child to be baptized, I baptize it. In this matter, I take on the sickness myself along with the sickly little ones, but only for a time, until better instructed. But as for interpreting the Word, I do not give ground in the least respect.[52]

This statement, which might be the earliest form of an infant dedication of its era, showed, if not a consistency of liturgy with his theology, at least a pastoral sensitivity to the families in his charge. Whether Hubmaier's reluctance to enforce *in toto* his new theology came as pastoral capriciousness or exposed some lingering doubts regarding his radical thought is uncertain.[53] While remaining an independent thinker and reformer, Hubmaier, at this juncture, had hoped to stay in good standing with both magisterial and radical reformers. From the level and character of his correspondence with Oecolampadius in particular, Hubmaier remained encouraged.

Oecolampadius, at least for a brief time, shared with Hubmaier an honest uncertainty as to the proper timing and interpretation of baptism within Scripture. As such, he was more open to Hubmaier in such discussions than were their other reformer counterparts in Zwingli, Bucer and Capito. Nevertheless, Oecolampadius initially responded to Hubmaier's letter by stating his own fidelity to the traditional baptismal practice. Presumably basing his resistance to Hubmaier's reforms upon the promise of I Corinthians 7:14 (that children are made holy through their parents), Oecolampadius held that infant children of

---

[52] *Hubmaier*, 72. It is important to note that while Oecolampadius would answer Hubmaier's writing with a first letter arguing for the continuation of infant baptism, in a second letter he commended Hubmaier and strongly encouraged the latter's new infant dedication in lieu of pedobaptism. Oecolampadius, *Briefe und Akten zum Leben Oekolampads* I (ed. Ernst Staehelin; Leipzig: M. Heinsius Nachfolger, 1927), 344, 357; here taken from Pipkin and Yoder, p. 72, n. 18.

[53] Pipkin and Yoder note that at this point Hubmaier had begun to share the basic convictions of the developing "left wing" of the Zurich Reformation, "yet without participating in their meetings or in the psychological dynamics of the coming to birth of Zurich Anabaptism", 79.

Christian parents would then be saved from the punishment of original sin. Baptism for Oecolampadius served as the symbolic embodiment of such a covenantal understanding.[54]

In that same month, indeed nearly to the day of the writing of Hubmaier's letter,[55] Zwingli had begun to speak out publicly against his former disciples and new radicals in Zurich's First Baptismal Disputation. Not surprisingly, Zwingli dominated the disputation and argued against the radicals' antipedobaptism. Also predictably, the Zurich City Council ruled in favor of Zwingli and took measures to stamp out the Grebel circle's movement, forcing out and subsequently imprisoning the Anabaptist leaders in that region.[56]

While Hubmaier had been in correspondence with both Oecolampadius and Zwingli for over a year prior to the implementation of the Waldshut reformer's relatively conservative baptismal innovations, Hughes Old observes that "these [latter] two Reformers did not give Hubmaier's questions anything like the attention they deserved, or anything like the attention he demanded."[57] It seems unlikely, however, that Hubmaier would have remained a mainstream reformer had he received more "guidance". In fact, two weeks following Hubmaier's letter to Oecolampadius and Zwingli's public remarks regarding Hubmaier's and the radicals' new practices, Oecolampadius wrote Hubmaier again. In this second letter, the Basel reformer conceded the equivocal character of the Scriptures regarding baptism and that the propriety of the now traditional practice of infant baptism was unclear. Significantly, Oecolampadius now applauded Hubmaier's conservative practice of infant dedication and baptism to the sick and expressed sanguine hope that such practice would spread *omnibus*.[58]

Hubmaier's Baptismal Writings

Oecolampadius' words were somewhat prophetic as Zurich was simultaneously dispersing its radical "heretics" by banishing them from the capitol city. Although rendered as unorthodox by the Zurich council, the newly (re)baptized Grebel circle came as a source of great encouragement to Hubmaier. Scholars

---

[54] Oecolampadius, 344-45.

[55] The Council was held January 17, 1525. Hubmaier's letter to Oecolampadius is usually dated January 18, but Armour dates it January 16. See Armour, *Anabaptist Baptism*, 22.

[56] Bergsten, *Balthasar Hubmaier: Anabaptist Theologian and Martyr*, 228.

[57] Old, 95.

[58] Oecolampadius, 345. Rollin Armour observes that Oecolampadius continually struggled with the issue of baptism as late as 1527, when he wrote that the timing and manner of the rite were *adiaphora* (indifferent). Thus, the Basel reformer allowed unwilling parents of newborns to wait until their child was three years old before administering water baptism. See Armour, *Anabaptist Baptism*, 23; cf. "Letter to Zwingli", Aug. 20, 1527, *ZW* IX, No. 644, 195-96.

now believe that Conrad Grebel, the earliest of Anabaptism's leaders, visited Hubmaier and Waldshut following his dismissal from Switzerland in February, shortly after Reublen's first visit.[59] Regardless of the extent of Reublen's possible influence and effect over Grebel, the fact that Hubmaier's affinity to Anabaptism exceeded a typological and entered into a direct relationship at least at this juncture is widely accepted. That other Christians had undergone an adult or confessor's baptism strengthened Hubmaier's resolve towards Anabaptism. Regardless, as MacGregor has observed, Hubmaier was still reluctant at this point to join the nabaptists by receiving rebaptism himself.[60]

The Grebel circle had already experienced friendly relations with Sebastian Hofmeister and at least sensed Hubmaier's sympathies. Having retreated from Zurich to the then safe wings of Hofmeister's Schaffhausen, the former Zwingli disciples encouraged a city debate on the rite of baptism. But Zurich pressured its cancellation.[61] Subsequently, the new Anabaptists sent Reublin and Grebel as emissaries to Waldshut. Hubmaier, heartened by the Zurich radicals and in response to Zwingli's declared victory in Zurich, issued *A Public Challenge to All Believers* on February 2, 1525.

Though still considered publicly as a friend to Zurich, Hubmaier's declaration called for debate on baptism and issued a challenge in his own name. While his *Public Challenge* was printed in full previously in chapter 1 of this book, it is important to note Hubmaier's stress here that any pedobaptist challenger must use "with German, plain, clear, and unambiguous Scriptures that deal only with baptism", while Hubmaier promised to hold himself to the same standard.[62] Additionally, the Bible to be used needed to be "fifty or one hundred years old" in order to serve as "the right, proper, and true arbiter" of the dispute.[63]

That the *Challenge* came without a set date or time for debate suggests the probability that it was as a *pro forma* challenge for the purpose of rhetoric and public precedence for liturgical reform.[64] This supposed call for dialogue came as a means for Hubmaier's contesting the outcome of the previous debates and the sources from which the Zurich debate (and perhaps the Wittenberg debate) were based, namely more recent and, in Hubmaier's mind, less reliable translations of the Bible.[65] Such a public divorce from more recent translations and the preference for ones "fifty or one hundred years old" are indicative of Hubmaier's movement toward Anabaptism. Hubmaier still maintained a Protestant approach to interpretation through *sola scriptura*, but he emphasized the need for an older and more reliable text for argumentation. His approach to biblical

---

[59] See Bergsten, *Balthasar Hubmaier: Anabaptist Theologian and Martyr*, 229.
[60] MacGregor, *A Central European Synthesis*, 129.
[61] Pipkin and Yoder, 78.
[62] *Hubmaier*, 80.
[63] *Hubmaier*, 80.
[64] Pipkin and Yoder, 79, particularly n. 6.
[65] Armour, *Anabaptist Baptism*, 24.

hermeneutics which led him to both this interpretation and dependable source shall be discussed later in this chapter.

Though records indicate that a few townspeople in Waldshut were baptized by Reublin on his January visit, Hubmaier and most of his parish would wait until Holy Week of that year before marking themselves as Anabaptists through (re)baptism.[66] While the details of the (re)baptisms were outlined previously in the first chapter, what is significant to note at this juncture is the extent to which Hubmaier went to convince at least some in his parish to accept the new baptism. Several sources claim Hubmaier possibly manipulated many of the townspeople to be rebaptized. Even though these testimonials all come from opponents of Hubmaier, their combined accounts must be taken seriously. For instance, later that year, Zwingli wrote that in his drive to be reelected as pastor by his entire, previously Catholic, flock, Hubmaier had "divided the pious folk and brought them into danger."[67] Additionally, Kessler chronicled in his *Sabbata* that when Hubmaier observed some uneasiness and indisposition among his membership for rebaptism, he threatened to leave the Waldshut church since the Scriptures had produced little fruit in them. Thus, out of their devotion to their spiritual leader and in order to not be rebuked as weak believers, the congregation apparently reluctantly consented to rebaptism. Lastly, Abbot Caspar of St. Blasien reported that those who did not acquiesce were banished from their homes.[68]

If these accounts are even partially accurate, they reveal an incongruous theological hypocrisy on the part of Hubmaier. If Hubmaier was building a theology of confessor's baptism, maintaining that such a rite is symbolic of a genuine sacramental response to God's grace on the part of the recipient, then every effort at compulsory or compelled baptism diminished, disregarded and contradicted Hubmaier's own newfound convictions regarding the subjects of baptism, covenant, sacrament and the morphology of his soteriology. Regardless of the potential for such Machiavellism and theological hypocrisy, Hubmaier's entire congregation and the Waldshut town council became Anabaptist.

Having finally affiliated with Anabaptism through his liturgical reforms, Hubmaier resolved to defend his reforms theologically. Though distinctly Anabaptist, Hubmaier still perceived himself as a colleague of Zwingli,[69] probably due to Hubmaier's distance from Zurich, his non-participation in the baptismal disputations, and the continued magisterial supervision of his radical reforms. Thus, upon the advent of publishing a treatise in response to Zwingli's first demonstrative defense of pedobaptism, Hubmaier wrote the Zurich Council on July 10, 1525:

---

[66] MacGregor, *A Central European Synthesis*, 123.

[67] From Zwingli's *An Answer to Doctor Balthasar's Booklet on Baptism*, here cited from Bergsten, *Balthasar Hubmaier: Anabaptist Theologian and Martyr*, 230.

[68] Bergsten, *Balthasar Hubmaier: Anabaptist Theologian and Martyr*, 231.

[69] Pipkin and Yoder, 90.

> I recently read a booklet by Master Ulrich Zwingli concerning baptism, in which he is of the opinion that he has adequately demonstrated that young children should be baptized. Just last Friday I began one of my own and should if God wills be done by tomorrow, in which I thoroughly demonstrate that they should not be baptized.[70]

Hubmaier then requested the Council to grant him safe passage to Zurich to discuss this matter of difference with Zwingli and to do so "secretly or publicly, alone or before the entire honorable Council of Zürich. . . . so that, whether quietly or publicly, as God wills, we might arrive at a good peace."[71]

The following day, Hubmaier completed his tract, *On the Christian Baptism of Believers* (hereafter *On Baptism*). Apparently written in only five days, the book has been touted by scholars as "Hubmaier's best and most significant writing", "his best and most complete theological work", and "the most serious attempt of any Anabaptist writer to give us a systematic presentation of his understanding of baptism".[72] Published in Strausburg on July 11 of that year, *On Baptism* serves as Hubmaier's response to Zwingli's preceding defense of infant baptism, *On Baptism, Rebaptism and Infant Baptism*, though Zwingli's name is never mentioned in Hubmaier's treatise. The text begins, whether as rhetorical modesty or revealing genuine humility, with Hubmaier confessing his reluctance to step forward publicly to write such a polemical treatise:

> I know and must confess with the prophet Jeremiah that the way of the human being does not lie in his own power; nor does it lie in the power of man to govern his own steps [Jer. 10:23]. The human heart undertakes also to do something for itself, but God directs and controls according to his pleasure. For I had always intended to remain alone in my barrel and cave and not at all to creep out into the light, not that I feared the light, but in order that I might remain in peace. But God ordained differently and has pulled me out against my will to give account to anybody who requests it concerning my faith as it is in me, namely in the matter of infant baptism and the true baptism of Christ. Until now I had hoped that someone else would have done such.[73]

Hubmaier believed that there were many others who could have taken up this

---

[70] *Hubmaier*, 90.

[71] *Hubmaier*, 91.

[72] Pipkin and Yoder, 95; Carl M. Leth, "Balthasar Hubmaier's 'Catholic' Exegesis", in *Biblical Interpretation in the Era of the Reformation* (eds. Richard A. Muller and John L. Thompson; Grand Rapids: Eerdmans, 1996), 105; and Old, 93; respectively.

[73] *Hubmaier*, 97; *Schriften*, 119.

defense, but he was compelled to bear the weight of this responsibility of safe-guarding the "true baptism" against the "child washers".[74] Indicating that those in his camp were experiencing the same criticisms as Christ, Jeremiah and Paul, Hubmaier insisted he and his colleagues who were "orthodox and goodhearted" Christians were in no way forming a new sect, and he decried the rumormongers as distorting Anabaptism's core beliefs and obscuring and darkening the "clear, bright, and plain baptismal Scriptures".[75]

From the outset, then, Hubmaier indicated his intention to demonstrate that those who had recently undergone adult baptisms had not been "rebaptized" (as Zwingli had charged). Instead, Hubmaier proposed to prove that their original infant baptisms were not valid baptisms at all since pedobaptism was inconsistent with a simple understanding and straightforward interpretation of the Scriptures. Thus, the reader is exposed not only to a highly developed defense of confessor's baptism, but also to Hubmaier's unfolding hermeneutical principles. Such interpretive rules are integral to understanding Hubmaier's theology of baptism.

Keen observers of Hubmaier's theology have noted a shift in the Waldshut reformer's approach to and use of the Bible. Armour observes three distinct stages of Protestant hermeneutics during Hubmaier's sojourn to radicalism.[76] First, Hubmaier aligned himself with Zwingli against the radicals during the Second Zurich Disputation on the subject of the roles of Scripture in the church. During this conference, Hubmaier stated: "For in all divisive questions and controversies only Scripture, canonized and sanctified by God himself, should and must be the judge, no one else: or heaven and earth must fall", and that "holy Scripture alone is the true light and lantern through which all human argument, darkness, and objections can be recognized".[77] Such statements certainly reveal a high view of Scriptural authority. Nevertheless, Hubmaier was more moderating in his proposals for reform and biblical conformity, especially on the careful removal of images from the church, than were Grebel and his eager colleagues.

Yet by the following year, Hubmaier would write against his former teacher, Johannes Eck: "Search in Scripture, not in papal law, not councils, not fathers, not schools; for it is the discourse which Christ spoke which shall judge all things."[78] Hubmaier limited the church's authority in "matters as concern offense and brotherly love" but confined all matters of faith and practice exclusively to the Bible.[79]

Lastly, by 1525, Hubmaier argued against any human practice unless specifi-

---

[74] *Hubmaier*, 97; *Schriften*, 119.

[75] *Hubmaier*, 98; *Schriften*, 120.

[76] Armour, *Anabaptist Baptism*, 28.

[77] *Hubmaier*, 23; *Schriften*, 717.

[78] *Hubmaier*, 53; *Schriften*, 88.

[79] *Hubmaier*, 54; *Schriften*, 89.

cally mandated by Scripture. Applying this standard to the sacrament of baptism, he concluded his treatise *On Baptism* by reasoning: "The first question: Whether infant baptism is forbidden in the Word of God. Answer: Yes. For baptizing believers is commanded. So by this it is already forbidden to baptize those who do not yet believe."[80] While this interpretive method might appear too strict and overbearing for church practice, Hubmaier softened his argument by giving a humorous example:

> You say: But nowhere in Scripture is there written a clear word that one should not baptize [children]. Answer: It is written clearly enough. He who has eyes, let him see it. But that it is not written explicitly: 'Do not baptize them,' to this I answer: Then I may also baptize my dog and my donkey, circumcise little girls, mumble prayers and hold vigils for the dead, call wooden idols St. Peter, or St. Peter and St. Paul, take infants to the Lord's Supper, bless palm branches, herbs, salt, butterfat, and water, sell the mass as a sacrifice. For it is not prohibited anywhere in explicit words that we do these things. Realize what a nice double popery we would set up again if it were acceptable to juggle outside the Word of God in those matters which concern God and the souls.[81]

Thus, both Zwingli and Hubmaier maintained high views of Scripture, yet their differing interpretations of the nexus of implicit versus explicit material from the Bible would be a hermeneutical *cul-de-sac* between them.[82]

Beyond his denunciation of implicit assumptions from Scripture for church practice, Hubmaier sought to take seriously the word order of biblical passages. Though his treatise attempted to exegete (or at least cite) a number of Scripture texts, none comes to the fore more readily in this debate than Christ's Great Commission in Matthew 28 and Mark 16. Utilizing these and other supporting New Testament texts, Hubmaier deduced an *ordo salutis* which he overlaid numerically within each representative text. His stated sequence was: (1) word, (2) hearing, (3) faith, (4) baptism, (5) work. From this structure, Hubmaier demonstrated its application on the commission passages. For instance, Hubmaier pointed out that Jesus states in the Gospel of Mark: "Go therefore into all the world and preach the gospel (*word*) to all creatures (*hearing*). He who be-

---

[80] *Hubmaier*, 136; *Schriften*, 151.

[81] *Hubmaier*, 136; *Schriften*, 152.

[82] Wayne Pipkin observes that Hubmaier did not reject implicit biblical interpretation "because it was from Zwingli, but because it would open the door once again to papalism. . . . It is not only a question of hermeneutic, but of soteriology. A radical and stringent hermeneutic is necessary to insure salvation." See H. Wayne Pipkin, "The Baptismal Theology of Balthasar Hubmaier", *MQR* 65 (Jan. 1991), 41.

lieves (*faith*) and is baptized (*baptism*) will be saved (*work*)."[83] Hubmaier continued: "I do not find, however, any passage which says: Go forth into all the world and baptize young infants and teach them some years later."[84]

These Great Commission texts are significant in order to grasp the theological differences between Zurich and Waldshut. Though other Anabaptists had utilized these passages in the past in defense of their cause, Hubmaier recognized the need to be more forcefully lucid. His strong argument came to refute Zwingli's treatise where the Zurich reformer attempted to utilize word sequence to his own advantage. In his own treatise, *On Baptism, Rebaptism and Infant Baptism*, Zwingli claimed that in the Matthean passage, both "baptize" and "teach" are gerundives from the main verb clause "make disciples". It then followed, according to Zwingli, that the word order would imply baptism before teaching as requisite for true discipleship.[85] With his careful reply, utilizing nine other New Testament passages,[86] Hubmaier systematically discounted Zwingli's argument via word order and further buttressed his position that Scripture never explicitly endorsed pedobaptism and thus its long-held practice was based on nothing but church tradition.

To further support this reasoning, Hubmaier presented a biblical parry to Zwingli's and other covenantal reformers' claims that children were saved through the faith of their parents:

> Dear friends, [such an argument] is nothing. For it often happens that father and mother bring forth both good and bad fruit. Take, for example, Abel and Cain, Esau and Jacob. It is up to God, not to father and mother, for before they were born, God said, 'Jacob I loved, but Esau I hated,' Mal. 1:2f; Rom. 9:13. It would also often grieve a child to the heart and lead him to eternal damnation if his salvation were to depend upon the faith of his father or mother, godfather or godmother.[87]

Zwingli, in Hubmaier's mind, had dissociated baptism from personal faith. If baptism could be made acceptable by parental proxy, Hubmaier wondered, how could one ascertain the genuineness of a father's or mother's Christianity? If such faith were not valid, parental dependency would not be the child's means to salvation but rather the means to his condemnation. Instead, Hubmaier saw

---

[83] *Hubmaier*, 130 [parenthetical adaptations mine]; *Schriften*, 146.

[84] Armour's translation. See Armour, *Anabaptist Baptism*, 28. Cf. *Hubmaier*, 130; *Schriften*, 146.

[85] Zwingli, *ZW* IV, 231-34. Armour also makes this point. See Armour, *Anabaptist Baptism*, 28.

[86] Acts 2:36-47 8:4-13; 10:44-48; 16:33-40;18:8-11 19:1-10, I Corinthians 1:13-25; I Peter 3:20-22; and Hebrews 10:22-25.

[87] *Hubmaier*, 141; *Schriften*, 156.

the Scriptures as arguing simply for individual faith and individual responsibility. Zwingli would ultimately counter with the collective and objective faith of the believing community which spiritually nurtures the child's salvific safety. Thus, Zwingli and Hubmaier departed from one another soteriologically between the objective divine work and the subjective human response to salvation, and between demands corporate and individual in the faith, respectively.

Additionally, Hubmaier and Zwingli separated on one general interpretive principle: the explicit and implicit understandings of Scripture. As outlined earlier, Hubmaier required that Scripture explicitly allow infant baptism in order for such practice to be justified. Since his "simple reading" of related passages did not result in such an understanding, pedobaptism must then be discarded. It then follows that if one were to accept Hubmaier's mature biblical hermeneutic, then one would be hard-pressed to make an argument against the Waldshut reformer's baptismal logic. At the same time, Hubmaier's biblical interpretation is overly simplistic in its argument that Zwingli should "strive for the clear, plain and pure Word of God" and in its sophomoric conclusion that Zwingli must then concede. Second, Hubmaier himself violated his own simplistic rubric for interpretation from time to time, drawing from patristic and other historic sources of church tradition when they seemed to aid his point. At the same time he denounced them as spurious when they were used by his enemies or were not helpful to his arguments. Indeed, Hubmaier clearly took advantage of his extensive education as a doctor of theology, bringing any church father or conciliar statement to his defense when he so desired. Armour notes of this that "he did not intend to provide added authority for his beliefs – Scripture was all-sufficient for that, he said – but he did hope to prove to his opponents that believer's baptism has been the early practice of the church."[88] Nevertheless, Hubmaier's criticism of Zwingli's understanding of covenant and of Catholic overtones of *ex opere operato* remain basically consistent in his writings throughout his brief Anabaptist life.

At the same time, what has not been consistently emphasized regarding Hubmaier's baptismal thought and, more generally, his sacramental theology, is the great emphasis he placed on the issue of faith and response to covenantal grace. In his *On Baptism,* in the context of refuting pedobaptismal justifications, Hubmaier attempted to grant the reader another glimpse of this facet of his theological position. Having maintained that pouring water over children in the name of the Father, Son and Holy Spirit did not affect the faith of children but only moistened their skin, Hubmaier argued the following point:

> But baptizing in the name of the Father, and the Son, and the Holy Spirit takes place when a person *first confesses* that he is a sinner and guilty, when he then believes in the forgiveness of sins through Jesus Christ and therefore resolves henceforth to live according to

---

[88] Armour, *Anabaptist Baptism,* 49.

> the Rule of Christ as far as God the Father, and the Son, and the Holy Spirit will give him grace and strength, *and* when he *now* testifies all such publicly before people with the reception of the outward water: *that* is *water baptism.*[89]

This statement encompassed the heart of Hubmaier's baptismal theology. Baptism is first and foremost one's confession of faith and one's subjective entrance into the covenant of God. Grace is then not conferred by water, infused by Christ, received via parental proxy or upon promise of future faith. Grace is only appropriated in the heart of a responsive believer, and this, for Hubmaier, is one's baptism. In Lutheran fashion, the symbol is separated from the object itself. Yet diverging from Lutheranism, Hubmaier's notion of sacrament takes place through one's personal response, not through the element. Water baptism, then, is secondary, serving as symbolic means of proclamation of the person having already received the sacrament through faith. On this point, Hubmaier is nonpareil not only as a reformer but as a first generation Anabaptist,[90] representing his theological sojourn from Catholicism, Lutheranism, and Zwinglianism to radicalism. Hubmaier never completely abandoned his theological past but merely synthesized it into an eclectic new system. At the same time, Hubmaier was convinced that this novelty was, in fact, the biblical intent. Thus, while Zwingli and Hubmaier debated the proper placement and timing of the outward sign of baptism, their disagreement originated primarily from their divergent concepts of faith.

Objective and Subjective Faith

Zwingli's and Hubmaier's views of baptism are marked by each reformer's distinct understanding of faith. Both men separated faith from its corresponding sign in baptism (i.e., the Spirit of God is that which saves and not the element of water itself). Yet, Zwingli stressed the objective working of God while Hubmaier underscored the subjective, spontaneous response to God's grace on the part of the believer. The two reformers, in turn, would each gravitate to scriptural passages that appeared, at least to them, to support their own presuppositions.

Zwingli's objective spiritual regeneration placed salvation completely in God's hands. To demand the manifestation of faith within the human would be to undercut or at least diminish God's gracious action. God works sovereignly whenever and in whomever God pleases.[91] Correspondingly, Zwingli adopted a doctrine of election as a soteriological basis for pedobaptism's continued prac-

---

[89] *Hubmaier*, 142 [all italics mine (save for final *that* which is Pipkin & Yoder's)]; *Schriften*, 156-57.

[90] Pilgram Marpeck, Dirk Philips, and Menno Simons would all articulate similar sacramental ideas a few years after Hubmaier's death.

[91] Zwingli, *ZW* IV, 221.

tice.[92]

Hubmaier, on the other hand, in no way denied God as the initiator of grace,[93] yet the Anabaptist leader equally heralded the need for human response to that grace for the salvific transaction to be made complete. Rollin Armour rightly observes: "Without that brief moment of personal commitment following the hearing of the Gospel and preceding the full regenerating gift of grace, there could be, in Hubmaier's view, neither personal conversion nor objective grounds for baptism."[94]

This is not to imply that Hubmaier was without nuance as a humanist, for he continued in his *On Baptism*, stating:

> Fourth, since therefore the human being knows and confesses that he
> is by nature an evil, worm-eaten, and poisoned tree, who neither can
> nor wants to bring forth good fruit out of himself, thus this pledge,
> promise, and public testimony does not happen out of human powers
> or capacities, for that would be presumptuousness. But it takes place
> in the name of God, the Father, and the Son, and the Holy Spirit, or in
> the name of our Lord Jesus Christ. . . .[95]

This inward change must be substantiated by means of the outward reception of water baptism.[96] While the timing and sequence is central to Hubmaier's de-

---

[92] Zwingli, "Refutation of Baptist Tricks", *Selected Works of Huldreich Zwingli* [hereafter, *SW*] (Philadelphia: University of Pennsylvania, 1901), 237-47.

[93] Hubmaier would, in fact, compare Christ to the Samaritan who brings wine and oil to heal the sick person. The wine, in Hubmaier's allegorical interpretation, is that which leads the sinner to repentance and the oil the soothing command to believe the gospel. "Through such words of comfort", Hubmaier argued, "the sinner is enlivened again, comes to himself, becomes joyful and henceforth surrenders himself entirely to this physician Christ", *Hubmaier*, 144; *Schriften*, 159.

[94] Armour, *Anabaptist Baptism*, 31.

[95] *Hubmaier*, 146; *Schriften*, 160.

[96] Hubmaier stresses: ". . . when a person now confesses himself to be a sinner, believes on the forgiveness of sins, and has committed himself to a new life, then he professes this also outwardly and publicly before the Christian church, into whose fellowship he lets himself be registered and counted according to the order and institution of Christ. Therefore he professes to the Christian church, that is, to all the brothers and sisters who live in faith, that in his heart he has been thus inwardly instructed in the Word of Christ . . . . Then he lets himself be baptized with outward water in which he professes publicly his faith and his intention, namely, that he believes that he has a gracious, kind and merciful God and Father in heaven through Jesus Christ, with whom he is well off and satisfied", *Hubmaier*, 145-46; *Schriften*, 160.

bates with Zwingli and, later, with other reformers, the necessity of faith on the part of the individual is primary for Hubmaier to its symbol in the reception of water baptism.

Hence, Hubmaier and Zwingli's theological disagreement may be located on this objective/subjective intersection. Both men would argue a separation of salvation from the element of water itself from I Peter 3:21 ("and this water symbolizes baptism that now saves you also – not the removal of dirt from the body but the pledge of a good conscience toward God"). From this passage, Hubmaier posited the notion that the baptizand must already have appropriated such a "good conscience".[97] For Zwingli, it was merely the "promise" of a good conscience that was necessary.[98] Thus, the necessity of whether faith must be personally appropriated before baptism and, in turn, the understanding of humanity's role and capacity within the *ordo salutis* embodied this argument.

Variations on Covenant

The theological separation on the basis of objective and subjective realities between Zwingli and Hubmaier is inextricably related to their developing concepts of "covenant". Although Zwingli may have held the Old Testament as more pertinent to baptismal theology (particularly circumcision) than did his Waldshut counterpart,[99] both utilized Hebrew Scripture and its covenantal language as grounds for their respective soteriological understandings.

Circumcision served, for Zwingli, as the clear, biblical precedent and type to water baptism. The Hebrew Scriptures included the children and descendents in God's covenant with the nation of Israel. Children, along with their parents, enjoyed the promises and blessings of God bestowed upon them.[100] The sign of

---

[97] Hubmaier is then moved to define baptism in water as "nothing other than a public confession and testimony of internal faith and commitment by which the person also testifies outwardly and declares before everyone that he is a sinner. . . . He has committed himself and is determined henceforth to live according to the Word and the command of Christ. . . .", *Hubmaier*, 100; *Schriften*, 122.

[98] Armour develops this point of contention based upon I Peter. See Armour, *Anabaptist Baptism*, 31. Cf. *Hubmaier*, 117; *Schriften*, 136; Zwingli, *Taufe und Wiedertaufe*, ZW, IV, 248.

[99] Zwingli would argue against the Anabaptists: "Further, since you reject the Old Testament for the reason that you cannot endure what is deduced from it in reference to infant baptism, you clearly evince that you make of no account of him who is God both of the Old Testament and the New", "Refutation of Baptist Tricks", *SW*, 152. While the visceral nature of Zwingli's argument led to some inaccuracy regarding the Anabaptists' views of canonical authority, it nevertheless suggests the potential that Zwingli held a higher view of the Hebrew texts than did the Anabaptists.

[100] Here Zwingli maintained: "I might adduce numberless examples, for the Hebrews use almost no figure more extensively, but I think a taste has been given by which you will easily tell all the rest. 'Israel my inheritance'. To whom was this said, if not to the Israelitic posterity? But children can not receive this. It does not follow therefore they did

these promises came through circumcision, which was primarily performed on Hebrew boys in infancy (though adult men also participated). If the sign of New Testament covenant was baptism, Zwingli reasoned, it should likewise be made available to children of the believing community. Here Zwingli argued:

> I. The children of Christians are no less sons of God than the parents, just as in the Old Testament. Hence, since they are sons of God, who will forbid their baptism?

> Circumcision among the ancients (so far as it was sacramental) was the same as baptism with us. As that was given to infants so ought baptism to be administered to infants.[101]

Armour observes that "of all Zwingli's arguments for infant baptism this was the strongest, for it found support in the very structural principles of the Reformed covenant theology already taking shape in his own hands."[102] Thus, just as the case with the sons of the ancient Hebrews in circumcision, Zwingli maintained, children of Christian parents belong to the new covenant of God. Circumcision and baptism represent the outer seals of their respective covenants. In circumcision, Hebrew infants could not respond to God but only anticipate their own acceptance of God's provision; so too Christian babies were appropriate and fitting baptizands to receive God's sovereign grace and covenant. Since God works independently from the physical sign (as opposed to both the Catholic and Lutheran connection of inner to outer baptism), Zwingli maintained that the Holy Spirit would act freely and sovereignly, unbound to the creaturely elements and earthly signs. It follows for Zwingli, then, that the sign might just as easily precede as follow the saving action of the Spirit in both circumcision and baptism.[103]

Hubmaier in no way disavowed baptism's connection to the covenant. Antithetically, such a notion was at the heart of his baptismal theology. However, Hubmaier did not see in New Testament baptism an inescapable tie to Old Tes-

---

not belong to the inheritance or the peculiar people", *SW*, 162.

[101] Zwingli, "Refutation of Baptist Tricks", *SW*, 139.

[102] Armour, *Anabaptist Baptism*, 36.

[103] On this point, Armour argues that Zwingli actually developed this typological concept of sacrament from various theological precedents in Melanchthon and Gabriel Biel in order to justify pedobaptism against Hubmaier. "If Catholic theology, which usually spoke of the redemptive power of sacraments as deriving from the incarnation, could produce a minority wing capable of identifying circumcision and baptism", Armour writes, "it was relatively easy for Zwingli to make such an identification, particularly when pressure from the Anabaptists gave him added need for Biblically supported bases for infant baptism", *Anabaptist Baptism*, 36-37.

tament circumcision as did Zwingli. Instead, Hubmaier understood God's new covenant sealed through baptism as the sign of one's spiritual appropriation of belief and willing participation in the new Israel of the church.

Even though he was accused of overlooking the authoritative precedence of the Old Testament, Hubmaier found antecedent passages from the Hebrew Scriptures to support his own claims regarding baptism. Integral to this Anabaptist's argument was I Peter 3:20-21: ". . . In [the ark of Noah] only a few people, eight in all, were saved through water, and this water symbolizes baptism that now saves you also – not the removal of dirt from the body but the pledge of a good conscience toward God. It saves you by the resurrection of Jesus Christ." Hubmaier maintained that this passage clearly portrays the ark as the "shadow of baptism" and that those who entered the ark did so only because they first believed.[104] Later, Hubmaier added that "Whoever believes the Word of God now enters the ark of Noah, which is a proper figure [or type] of water baptism, so that he not drown outside of this ark in the flood of sins, I Pet. 3:21."[105] Thus, the ark becomes an Old Testament typological precedent for entry into God's protective covenant through water baptism in the New. When a person confesses belief and receives baptism, this believer voluntarily enters the true ship of salvation through which he or she might escape the floods of sin by God's grace.

Zwingli and Hubmaier differed primarily then on the cardinal participant in covenant. Zwingli saw God as not only the initiator of the covenantal promise but also as the sole actor in the salvific process. The Christian believer or child plays a passive role in experiencing God's election through Christ's grace. The Holy Spirit, in accordance with divine timing, enters the person to instill faith. Baptism, then, serves as a sign of this action having taken place for the believer or in anticipation of this action for the children of Christians.[106]

On the other hand, the response of the individual to God's initiatory promise was integral to Hubmaier's understanding of covenant. While God still inaugurates the covenant of salvation, such an offer demands human answer. Individual believers, then, become central actors by their response to God's grace through their submission to God's covenant, sealed in water baptism.[107] Baptism served, for Hubmaier, as the sign of one's previous inner confession of faith and as seal of one's public promise to live obediently in Christ and with His church. On this point, Hubmaier wrote:

> Third, when a person now confesses himself to be a sinner, believes
> on the forgiveness of sins, and has committed himself to a new life,
> then he professes this outwardly and publicly before the Christian

---

[104] *Hubmaier*, 134; *Schriften*, 150.
[105] *Hubmaier*, 371; *Schriften*, 336.
[106] Steinmetz, *Reformers in the Wings*, 205.
[107] Steinmetz, *Reformers in the Wings*, 205.

church, into whose fellowship he lets himself be registered and counted according to the order and institution of Christ. Therefore he professes to the Christian church, that is, to all brothers and sisters who
live in faith, that in his heart he has been thus inwardly instructed in
the Word of Christ and so minded that he has surrendered himself
already to live according to the Word, will and Rule of Christ, to ar-
range and direct his doing and not doing according to him, and also to
fight and strive under his banner until death. Then he lets himself be
baptized with outward water in which he professes publicly his faith
and his intention, namely, that he believes that he has a gracious, kind,
and merciful God and Father in heaven through Jesus Christ, with
whom he is well off and satisfied. He also has expressed his intention to him and committed himself already in his heart henceforth to
change and amend his life. This he testifies publicly with the reception of water.[108]

Even as Hubmaier placed the human as the central figure in baptism, it is erroneous to conclude from this that he himself was a pure humanist. The individual was
capable of responding to God only because of God's initial action. Yet, humanity plays the leading role, nonetheless. While in Zwingli's covenantal theology,
God is the sole actor, Hubmaier's understanding is a two-sided covenant, where
God and humanity each agree to take on mutual obligations. Without the free response of humanity, the covenant would be incomplete. Thus, when held against
Zwingli's theory, Hubmaier's covenantal definition appears deeply anthropological. While departing from Augustinian notions of divine sovereignty and prede-
terminism, Hubmaier nevertheless insisted that he in no way undermined God's
authority even in salvation. Instead, as outlined previously, Hubmaier saw God
choosing to work within an ordained process rather than by exercising his absolute potential. Here Steinmetz explains further:

By making use of their limited human freedom, sinners dispose their
wills for the reception of grace, which cannot be given to them without their free and uncoerced consent. When sinners respond to the
offer of the gospel, God *must* regenerate them, not because of the
quality of their response but because God has bound himself by his
promises to justify everyone who responds to the gospel. God is a
captive of his own covenant; the freedom of the absolute will has
been imprisoned by his ordained will.[109]

---

[108] *Hubmaier*, 145-46; *Schriften*, 160.
[109] Steinmetz, *Luther in Context* (Grand Rapids: Baker Book House, 2002), 69 [italics
his]. See also Kirk MacGregor, "Hubmaier's Concord of Predestination with Free Will",
Direction 35, no. 2 (Fall 2006), 279-99.

Pertinent to Hubmaier's and Zwingli's debate on the covenant was the written recantation Hubmaier penned in Zurich, renouncing his Anabaptist theology. With
the hope of freedom from imprisonment and relief from torture in return for this
retraction,[110] probably by early January 1526 the Waldshut reformer temporarily
acquiesced:

> I, Baldasar Huebmor from Fridberg, confess publicly in my own hand
> that [in the past] I could only understand all the Scriptures which deal
> with water baptism as saying that first one should preach, then one be-
> lieves, and then one is baptized. I finally settled upon that conviction.
> Now, however, I have been shown by Master Huldrych Zwingli how
> the covenant of God, made with Abraham and his seed and [shown]
> circumcision as a covenant sign, and how baptism takes the place of
> circumcision. I have not been able to refute this.[111]

Regardless, after his arrival in Nikolsburg several months later, Hubmaier again
began publishing treatises denouncing Zwingli's baptismal views.

The Baptism of John

The fascinating differences between Hubmaier and Zwingli in their covenantal
debates on baptism become most distinct in their discussion on the Scripture passages which describe the baptisms performed by John the Baptist in light of those
subsequently done in Christ's name. This apparently idiosyncratic topic actually
helps outline the development of both theologians' covenantal thought.

Zwingli challenged the medieval tradition that gave little significance to
John's baptisms. Late medieval theologians had argued that John's baptisms
must have been enacted without the proper triune form and, as such, did not
carry the *ex opere operato* characteristic to make them sacramentally efficacious. Since Zwingli had already discounted the *ex opere operato* quality of
baptism, relegating baptism to the symbolic realm, John's baptisms could be
seen as the equivalent as those later performed in Jesus' name by the apostles.

---

[110] Zwingli would later write in a letter to Gynoräus: "When [Hubmaier] saw that this
course [of debate and tactics] did not succeed . . . and after many crafty tricks, he came to
the point of saying that he would recant. The Council did not compel this, except in case
he were unwilling to depart from the city. For it had made not severer provision against
those who do not wish to desert the cause of catabaptism than they should leave the city",
here cited in *Hubmaier*, 157-58; cf. *Schriften*, 704. Nevertheless, upon his public retraction of this recantation in the Abbey, Hubmaier was taken to the torture rack.

[111] *Hubmaier*, 151; *Schriften*, 148.

This was especially true, Zwingli argued, since John taught his followers to place their hope in the coming Christ. Because baptism is a covenantal sign which should never be confused with the thing signified, rebaptism for the followers of John, then, would be superfluous. Thus, anyone who continues to argue for the sign to convey grace is guilty of idolatry.[112]

Although he had also departed from the *ex opere operato* sacramentalism, Hubmaier was much more extensively trained in medieval scholasticism than his Zurich counterpart, and he maintained the Catholic dichotomy. While such an argument revealed Hubmaier's continued medieval conservatism, indeed even a lingering sacramentalism (though transposed from the signs to their corresponding theological and liturgical confessions), it justified the Anabaptist practice of rebaptism.

Steinmetz rightly notes that this controversy was "far more significant than the limited nature of its subject matter might suggest. John stands between the two testaments and a number of crucial issues intersect in him."[113] For Hubmaier, John's preaching and baptisms were merely prologues to the new covenant subsequently instituted by Christ. For Zwingli, they were virtually one and the same, as John pointed to the coming Christ just as the apostles pointed to the resurrected Lord. Here, Zwingli argued:

> John pointed to Jesus with his finger and testified that He was the Son
> of God, saying, 'Whoever believes in him shall have everlasting life.
> . . .' Is that not the whole Gospel, clear and plain? Away then you
> who divide baptism. . . ! For the Gospel began with the preaching of
> John.[114]

Zwingli saw baptism serving as one's initiation into faith both for John and for the apostles of Christ.[115] He pushed the Lutheran point of the separation of *res* and *signum* to the furthest extreme short of spiritualism. Still relying upon Augustinian and Lutheran theological perspectives, Zwingli demonstrated that the disciples had no more power over the inner baptism of the Spirit than did John, and God was free to work in accordance with divine sovereignty.

While basing his theological case on the spirit of this Lutheran dichotomy, Zwingli conceded that there was no historical precedent for his argument. Thus, from this weakness, Hubmaier excitedly found great theological allies in the patristics: "God be praised that we [Anabaptists] are not the only crazy stub-

---

[112] Steinmetz, "The Baptism of John and the Baptism of Jesus in Huldrych Zwingli, Balthasar Hubmaier and Late Medieval Theology", in *Studies in the History of Christian Thought*, XIX (ed. Heiko A. Oberman; Leiden: E.J. Brill, 1979), 173, 175.

[113] Steinmetz, "The Baptism of John and the Baptism of Jesus", 169.

[114] Originally cited in *ZW*, IV, 265; here cited from Armour, *Anabaptist Baptism*, 38.

[115] Old, 97.

born heads, as you call us, but all theologians with us, except for you."[116] Ironically delighting in support from the likes of Origen, Cyril, Theophylact, Chrysostom and Jerome,[117] Hubmaier hypocritically betrayed his previous ostensible aversion to scholasticism, its church tradition and ancient thinkers. So overwhelming was this temptation of returning to the church fathers that Hubmaier could not yield to his previous convictions.

Hubmaier argued that the baptism of John was not even a baptism of forgiveness but merely of repentance:

> Therefore John says, John 1:23, "I am a voice of one crying in the wilderness: 'Prepare the way of the Lord.'". . . Recognition of sins and not the pouring of water leads to Christ who is the way, the truth, and life, John 14:6; Matt. 9:12. Now, however, the sick and not the healthy need the doctor. John points to this doctor and says, 'Now, then, I have led you into the recognition of sins and into hell. If you would then now rid yourself of the same, then behold the lamb of God who takes away the sin of the world, John 1:36. Run to him, beseech him, your sins will be forgiven and you will be led back out into heaven.'[118]

Hubmaier posited that John was still working out of the paradigm of the Law and could not have been working from Christ's grace, which would be inaugurated through his passion and resurrection. Only Christ could forgive sins before Calvary. As such, the authority given to the disciples by the risen Christ in the Great Commission allowed for baptism to carry with it the meaning of forgiveness.

Here, Hubmaier positioned his argument as a divine mandate, insisting upon the reception of the sign following the inner reception of grace:

> From this [Great Commission] we realize once again the seriousness with which Christ wills that those who have been instructed in faith should be baptized. For a serious command demands serious obedience and fulfillment. Truly, truly I say to you, Christ did not use such precious words in vain as something which we might do or leave undone.[119]

---

[116] *Hubmaier*, 208; *Schriften*, 196.

[117] *Hubmaier*, 210; *Schriften*, 197.

[118] *Hubmaier*, 209; *Schriften*, 196.

[119] *Hubmaier*, 122; *Schriften*, 140-41. Steinmetz goes as far here as to say that Hubmaier insisted that "water baptism was necessary to salvation as an expression of obedience to Christ". See Steinmetz, "The Baptism of John and the Baptism of Jesus", 177. While Hubmaier clearly comes very close to this in this citation, Steinmetz may be slightly overstating Hubmaier's point. Hubmaier nonetheless placed a much higher value on the earthly signs in connection to the inner spiritual work they represent than did Zwingli.

John's preaching and baptism, then, were merely introductory and incomplete to the coming gospel of grace. The new baptism represented the new covenant, which came only through the mercy of the risen Christ.

In his swiftness to justify rebaptism, though, Hubmaier might be accused of undercutting the significance of John the Baptist's biblical and theological contributions. John's work was merely limited to preparing humanity for the consolation of Christ's grace in Hubmaier's thought and is otherwise diminished to the realm of Hebrew legalism.[120] Here Hubmaier wrote:

> From this it follows that the water baptism of John is nothing but a public testimony which the person receives and gives because he confesses and recognizes that he is a miserable sinner, who cannot help himself nor give himself counsel, who does nothing good but that all his righteousness is corrupt and reproachable. . . . His awareness and conscience learned from the law, which is knowledge of sin, show this to him. Now John is there and points him to Christ, that in him he will find discharge of his sins, rest, peace and security so that he not remain in despair and thus be lost eternally. In summary, God leads through John downward into hell and through Christ upward again.[121]

Because Hubmaier recognized the theological implications of conceding to Zwingli John's baptism as acceptable for the reception of faith, Hubmaier then enervated the import of John's baptismal work by negating it as a form of new covenant baptism. Rebaptism was thus required of all those who were baptized by John to be truly baptized in Christ. Consequently, Hubmaier believed that infants in his day must also be later rebaptized as confessing adults because faith in Christ was not present in them either, although he would quickly add that the baptism of infants was no baptism at all. Thus, technically, the rebaptism of John's disciples in Acts 19 was the only true case of rebaptism in Hubmaier's mind. Through the diminution of John, Hubmaier simultaneously distinguished the work of Christ from the tomb as *sine qua non* in salvation, the great commission as central to authoritative baptism in His name.[122]

Therefore, Hubmaier maintained his medieval reliance upon Matthew 28

---

[120] Steinmetz, "The Baptism of John and the Baptism of Jesus", 177-78.

[121] *Hubmaier*, 106; *Schriften*, 127.

[122] Ironically, Hubmaier waters down this distinction by portraying how John's ministry followed the same sequence (preaching, hearing, confession, baptism and repentance) as would the *ordo salutis* through Christ. This, nevertheless, served as further support against infant baptism. See *Hubmaier*, 106-11; *Schriften*, 127-31.

and scholasticism's distancing of John's baptism from that of Christ. Hubmaier merely pressed the point of medieval tendencies as a reformer instead of rejecting them, as had Zwingli. Indeed, Hubmaier viewed John as not even the transitional figure between the testaments, as late medieval theologians had moderated. John was still in the world of sin, hell, and death.[123] Additionally, while he, at least in most places, separated the sign of water from the salvation event itself, Hubmaier maintained a sense of medieval sacramentalism. Yet Hubmaier departed from his medieval past by relocating the conveyance of grace in outward baptism from the physical element of water to the act of inner conversion and submission:

> But the outward water baptism of Christ signifies an inward comfort which precedes the water in faith through the recognition of the forgiveness of sins. . . . The water baptism of Christ in this sense means heating, quickening, comforting, making alive, leading again out of hell.[124]

In categorizing the two testaments separately as law and grace and consigning John the Baptizer to the former, Hubmaier was able to formulate a new covenantal theology based exclusively upon the conversion of the responsive adult.[125] He even alluded to such confessional sacramentalism as paralleling the vows of ordination:

> On the other hand, the baptism of Christ is a public and outward confession or oath of faith, that is, that the person inwardly believes the forgiveness of his sins through Christ, for which reason he lets himself be enrolled and outwardly dedicated among Christians, and that he wants to live according to the Rule of Christ.[126]

Hubmaier's understanding that the Anabaptist baptismal pledge would replicate the Catholic vows of ordination may stem from the influence of Martin Luther, who argued for a priesthood made up of all Christians in his *Babylonian Cap-*

---

[123] *Hubmaier*, 209-10; *Schriften*, 197.

[124] *Hubmaier*, 209; *Schriften*, 197.

[125] Armour points out, nevertheless, that Hubmaier would later refer to only one covenant. See Armour, *Anabaptist Baptism*, esp. 40-44. Hubmaier would write in May of 1527 that "there is only one marriage and only one church of the only bridegroom and Head, Christ Jesus,. . . . This marriage is just the mystery of which Paul wrote: 'The mystery is great. (We have till now called it a sacrament.) I speak, however, of Christ and the church,' Eph. 5:23", *Hubmaier*, 454-55; *Schriften*, 403. Here, the Old Testament was viewed as a prologue to the saving work of Christ in the New. See Steinmetz, "The Baptism of John and the Baptism of Jesus", 180-81.

[126] *Hubmaier*, 209; *Schriften*, 196.

tivity of the Church and in other writings.[127] In support of this link to Luther, one may readily see that the Wittenberg reformer connected baptism to a sort of universal ordination when he wrote, "Now we, who have been baptized, are all uniformly priests in virtue of that very fact".[128] Thus Hubmaier may have been applying liturgically what Luther had developed theologically, connecting the vows of baptism to the long-practiced vows of ordination. However, it is worth noting at this juncture that Kirk MacGregor perceives the influence on Hubmaier's use of ordination language for baptism as having a point of origin older than his German Protestant contemporary. MacGregor posits that "Hubmaier [initially had] embraced Bernard [of Clairvaux]'s doctrine of ordination, according to which ordination serves as a 'second baptism'".[129] It would follow, then, that as he became an Anabaptist pastor, revoking his vow to the Catholic priesthood, Hubmaier would apply the sacramental vow of ordination to the universal priesthood of all true believers through their baptisms.

Regardless, the baptism in Christ became for Hubmaier an outward symbol of the internal "yes" to God made in the heart of the converted. "Not that [baptism] cleanses the soul", Hubmaier contended, "but rather the 'yes' of a good conscience toward God which preceded inwardly in faith."[130] This role of baptism in relation to the divine call for human response is central to Hubmaier's notion of mutual covenant and his general meaning of sacrament. At the same time, Hubmaier's insistence on the inward "yes" for the remission of sins reveals his continued reliance upon late medieval nominalism where human action is requisite.[131]

Thus, Zwingli understood the place of baptism as a gift of God and as functioning within the corporate community of faith. Hubmaier, on the other hand, believed that baptism was based upon the response of an individual as an expression of personal faith and as an oath of submission to God and the Christian community.

In fact, early in the course of his baptismal writings and rebuttals, Zwingli appeared to argue upon Anabaptist lines: "Baptism is the sign of a pledge", he said, "which indicates that whoever receives it is committed to amend his life and follow after Christ. . . . The man who receives the sign of baptism designates himself as one who wants to hear what God says to him, learn His precepts, and live according to them."[132] Such statements seem to imply the volun-

---

[127] See Luther, "The Babylonian Captivity of the Church", *LW* 36, 112-13.

[128] Luther, "The Pagan Servitude of the Church", *Martin Luther: Selections from his Writings* (ed. John Dillenberger; New York: Anchor Books/Doubleday, 1962), 345. Cf. Luther, "The Babylonian Captivity of the Church", *LW* 36, 112.

[129] See Kirk R. MacGregor, *A Central European Synthesis*, 124. For further development of this concept, see also Todd E. Johnson, "Initiation or Ordination?: Balthasar Hubmaier's Rite of Baptism", *Studia Liturgica* 25 (1995), 68-85.

[130] *Hubmaier*, 118; *Schriften*, 137.

[131] Hughes O. Old also makes this observation. See Old, 99.

[132] Zwingli, "Taufe und Wiedertaufe", *ZW* IV, 231, 218 ; (trans. G. Bromiley), 141.

tary affirmation of faith on the part of the baptizand as requisite for the baptismal rite.

Hubmaier could hardly contain his excitement at such a rhetorical vulnerability:

> *Deo gratias* [Thanks be to God]. The truth must once again come to light. If baptism is truly a sign of commitment, then one must have expressed the commitment before the sign is attached to him. Likewise, before someone expresses the commitment one should teach him beforehand with words or in Scripture. Or it would be a blind commitment, which would mean nothing. He must also agree to it with express words or one does not attach the sign to him. Now tell us something without any addition, my Zwinngle: Where, when, and how does the cradle baby express such commitment? You say the father and mother, the godmothers and godfathers do that for the child. Did you not just say that baptism is a sign of commitment by which the one who takes it shows that he wants to improve his life and follow Christ? Pay attention. You said: the one who takes it, *he*, not another on his behalf. For it is not a secret to you that it would be an addition not grounded in the Word of God. Look, my Zwingle, how your self-confessed truth has taken away the ground from children's baptism.[133]

It is evident that Hubmaier clearly articulated a different form and function for baptismal commitment than did Zwingli. The pledge must be agreed upon by the willing party, not on behalf of an unwitting baptizand. The understanding of salvation as a two-sided covenant undergirded Hubmaier's baptismal theology at this point.

At a later time, however, Hubmaier seemed to lessen his use of covenantal language to describe the oath in baptism. In his *On Infant Baptism Against Oecolampad*, written in Nikolsburg in 1527, Hubmaier responded to the Basel reformer's critique of Anabaptist language. Through the use of dialogue treatise, Hubmaier quoted Oecolampadius as arguing that baptism is more of a testimony than a covenant between Christians. Through baptism, Hubmaier understood Oecolampadius to say that Christians testify that they are bound to Christ. Hubmaier responded that such a critique is well taken, yet even this understanding of baptismal testimony should then lead one to reject infants as candidates: "Can a cradle baby give such witness and unite itself thus to Christ?", Hubmaier rhetorically asked.[134] Thus, the apprehension of the sacrament as a meaningful and heartfelt pledge or oath to God enacted before the believing congregation as one's witness to faith was integral to Hubmaier's thought.

---

[133] *Hubmaier*, 196; *Schriften*, 187.
[134] *Hubmaier*, 290; *Schriften*, 267.

That this pledge was both horizontal and vertical was significant in Hubmaier's theology. A baptizand pledges not only to yield himself according to the "rule of Christ" but also to submit himself to the church for discipline to that end, "so that when he transgresses they now have the authority to admonish, punish, ban and reaccept him. . . . Where does this authority come from, if not from the pledge of baptism?"[135]

Thus, the vow taken in baptism, just as the pledge taken before the Supper, instills in the believer the authority of both Christ and the church as spiritual guardians. Acceptance and utterance of such oaths convey grace as they complete the salvific covenant. Consequently, the pledge serves as the sacrament with which the elemental signs of water, bread and wine confer.

Infant Salvation, Children and Original Sin

Debates concerning pedobaptism versus adult baptism often led to discussions on the spiritual status of children. The writings of Zwingli and Hubmaier were no exception. Zwingli viewed the burden of original sin as having no effect on those who carry it until acted upon by the individual in conscious sin, and, Zwingli added, "one can do that only if he knows the law."[136] Interestingly, the infant now seems to benefit from its lack of comprehension. This being the case, Zwingli opened the door to the potential of even children of non-Christians to be saved. Nevertheless, Zwingli was certain Christian children were secure within the fellowship of the church and with the promise of salvation:

> Not only believers then are of the church and people of God, but their children. And when the Catabaptists admit that sons of Abraham according to the flesh were within the people of God, but suppose that our own sons according to the flesh are not, they commit a great wrong. . . . Is Christ less kind to us than to the Hebrews? God forbid![137]

While Zwingli revealed possible ignorance only in the case with children of unbelievers, Hubmaier portrayed complete benightedness in this facet of soteriology:

---

[135] *Hubmaier*, 127; *Schriften*, 145. This concept of church discipline and authority will be developed more thoroughly in the following chapter under the topic of the "power of the keys".

[136] Originally cited in Zwingli, "Taufe und Wiedertaufe", *ZW* IV, 307-309; here cited in Armour, *Anabaptist Baptism*, 35.

[137] Zwingli, *SW*, 236.

> . . . I confess here publicly my ignorance. I am not ashamed not to
> know what God did not want to reveal to us with a clear and plain
> word. He said to me as he said to Peter, 'What business is it of yours,
> as to what I will do with infants? Follow me, look to my word and
> will,' John 21:22. But yet I will humbly and earnestly beseech him that
> he be a merciful Father to them. I commit this into his hands. His will
> be done. With this I will leave it. For if he does not want it to be done,
> then even if one were to throw them into the water a thousand times, it
> would still not help because water does not save.[138]

Hubmaier applied his "simple" reading of the biblical text at this juncture with
apparent humility. He would subsequently deny the possibility of confession
through parental proxy with the example of those parents in biblical accounts
who bore both "good and bad fruit": Cain and Abel, Esau and Jacob, etc. "It is up
to God, not to father and mother", Hubmaier argued, "for before they were born,
God said, 'Jacob I loved, but Esau I hated,' Mal. 1:2f; Rom. 9:13."[139] Surprisingly,
then, Hubmaier and Zwingli now reversed roles somewhat as Zwingli argued
for the importance of human response, albeit through a parental substitute, while
Hubmaier left this issue to the mystery and sovereignty of God.

Furthermore, Hubmaier would question the interpretation of those who utilized the popular saying of Jesus ["Let the little children come to me, . . . For
the kingdom of heaven belongs to such as these" (Matt. 19:14; Mark 10:14;
Luke 18:16)] as grounds for infant salvation. In January 1525, Hubmaier wrote
a letter to Oecolampadius which, in conclusion, asked the Basel reformer his
understanding of this passage. Hubmaier expressed his own opinion, emphasizing the word "such" as intimating his understanding of it as spiritual allegory.[140]
Oecolampadius did not respond to this particular question in subsequent letters,
only later informing Hubmaier of his agreement with Zwingli on the baptismal
matter.

Hubmaier later wrote with greater certainty in defense of his position, emphatically denouncing those who utilized this pericope from the gospels to justify pedobaptism and pedosalvation: "That is wrong! They are doing violence
and injustice to Scripture. It is written: For 'of such' is the kingdom of heaven.
Christ wants to teach us humility here. . . ."[141] The Anabaptist theologian continued by pointing out that Paul admonished the church to cease thinking like
little children: "In regard to evil be infants, but in your thinking be adult (I Cor.
14:20)". Additionally, Hubmaier argued, Paul said Christians should "not be infants" in their capricious understanding (Eph. 4:14). Consequently, Hubmaier

---

[138] *Hubmaier*, 140-41; *Schriften*, 155.

[139] *Hubmaier*, 141; *Schriften*, 156.

[140] *Hubmaier*, 71.

[141] *Hubmaier*, 141; *Schriften*, 155.

portrayed Christ as taking a "physical parable and [leading] it to a spiritual meaning."[142] Thus for Hubmaier the believing community does not include even the children of believing parents (though parents carry the responsibility of teaching them), and the Anabaptist reformer admitted uncertainty regarding the inclusion of children in the Kingdom of God.[143]

The question then arises within Hubmaier's theological framework as to when a person is of appropriate age to understand and participate in the initiatory covenant of baptism. Thus, when Zwingli criticized Hubmaier's position, arguing that baptism dedicates a child to live according to the Word of God, Hubmaier quickly retorted:

> Does such a child who is one hour old have such a will? You must confess: No. Why do you baptize it then? You say: The will only comes seven years later. Well said. So should one also put off baptism, until the time that the will is now here. . . . Yes, the one who is baptized should know and believe beforehand the will and ordinance of Christ, Matt. 28:19-20 and Mark 16:15-16, and promise in water baptism to keep the same afterward.[144]

By age seven a child may then be prepared for baptism, contingent upon his or her readiness to hear and respond to God's Word. Before this time, apparently, such faith is not yet developed satisfactorily since Hubmaier's threshold for salvation required both one's understanding and acceptance of the Gospel and one's ethical response to the grace of God.

The Role of Free Will

Hubmaier's call for human response to God's grace as the fulfillment of sacrament and the necessary answer to God's salvific offer seems to highlight a sense of voluntarism within his theology. While faith requires this human response, Hubmaier emphasized that it is still a gift of God, leading modern

---

[142] *Hubmaier* 141; *Schriften*, 156.

[143] On this point, Armour opines that "there would seem to have been no reason why Hubmaier could not have successfully and profitably taken Zwingli's views and adapted them to his own framework", 35. Such a view, though, overlooks the vulnerability this would have developed for the place of children within the church. Either they were part of the church through covenant faith, as Zwingli believed and employed through parental proxy, or they were not, as Hubmaier had heretofore seemed to imply. Because faith and the efficaciousness of the sacraments were reliant upon adult comprehension and response, ambiguity and divine mystery may well have been Hubmaier's best defense in the matter of child salvation.

[144] *Hubmaier*, 188; *Schriften*, 181.

scholars to characterize Hubmaier anywhere from pelagian to a proto-modified Calvinist.[145] Against the new Protestant backdrop of the likes of Luther, Oecolampadius, Bucer and Zwingli, Hubmaier's anthropomorphic tendencies are relatively distinguished. Yet against Gabriel Biel, Erasmus and other optimistic humanists, Hubmaier's anthropocentrism seems more subdued. Consequently, one scholar has sagely observed: "Labels tend to blur finer distinctions without which it is impossible to understand the uniqueness of Hubmaier's theological contribution."[146] While both Luther's and Erasmus' influences upon Hubmaier have been previously outlined in this book,[147] the focus of free will and justification will now be explored in regards to the baptismal pledge and its accompanying symbol of water baptism.

Since one must first receive inner baptism through a conscious reception of faith and the manifestation of belief before water baptism was administered in Hubmaier's church, Hubmaier portrays the *ordo salutis* as a condition in which God and humanity cooperate. God may act sovereignly and absolutely, but God nevertheless chooses to act within certain ways. The spirit in each person wills to do good but must battle against the corruption of the body and the neutrality of the soul.[148] Thus, within their range of this limited freedom, when humans respond to the gospel, God must save them:

> So great and mightiful is the power and dignity of the prophecies of God who has become human and revealed through his Word, who cannot deny himself, or heaven and earth must first fall into pieces, Luke 21:33. Not that our will, word, or work are so high and valuable in themselves, but so powerful and forceful are the divine prophesies in all the believers.[149]

Thus, God recognizes the human reaction to the free and universal divine offer. God initiates as humanity affirmatively responds to fulfill the covenant. For Hubmaier, God draws humans to be saved if they are willing, or God permits them to be damned if they refuse God's offer. But ultimately, God sovereignly ordains human choice as determinative to retroact and complete salvation. This capacity of response must be exercised, in Hubmaier's ethics, for water baptism to be rightly and meaningfully administered.

The conscious positive response of the believer to the salvific proposal was integral for Hubmaier in returning the church to a believing, voluntary communi-

---

[145] See Johann Loserth, "Balthasar Hubmaier", *The Mennonite Encyclopedia* 2, p. 52, for the former, and Robert Macoskey, "The Contemporary Relevance of Balthasar Hubmaier's Concept of the Church", *Foundations* 6 (April 1963), 99-122, for the latter.

[146] Estep, "The Anabaptist View of Salvation", *Southwestern Journal of Theology* 20 (Spring 1978), 34.

147 See chapter 1 of this work.

[148] *Hubmaier*, 433-39; *Schriften*, 385-89.

[149] *Hubmaier*, 474; *Schriften*, 417-18.

ty. Like his Anabaptist counterparts, Hubmaier was concerned about the decline of genuine belief and practice within the church. Thus, a believer's commitment of faith, testified to through heartfelt confession and emblemized through the reception of water, ostensibly served as the means through which one's authentic faith might be made known.

From this juncture, the soteriological cleavage between Zwingli, Luther and Staupitz on one hand and Hubmaier on the other becomes most pronounced. Hubmaier's reliance upon his late medieval past comes to the fore, particularly his affinity with the Occamist concept of *synderersis* (human longing for God's goodness) and the medieval theological axiom: *facientibus quod in se est Deus non denegat gratiam* ("to those who do what is in them God does not deny his grace").[150] This is not to say that Hubmaier manifested here Biel's optimistic anthropology based on James 4:8 ("Draw near to God, and he will draw near to you"). The Word of God must still be preached as well as appropriated positively by the individual conscience. Because the faculty of human reason has been corrupted by the fall, humans must have their comprehension restored by the Spirit of God. As their minds then join with their inexorably willing spirits, humans may overcome their sinful flesh only through God's grace. Since it has not been damaged by the fall, once empowered by this new knowledge of the gospel through God's Spirit, the human spirit may find its way back to God. The soul is repaired because of the action of God's Spirit through the proclaimed Word. The preaching of the Word gives opportunity for the soul to learn good and evil once again and thereby be restored to freedom. But the soul is altered as it unites with the spirit as the person reaches out to God in faith. All this, nevertheless, is a result of God's gracious proclamation of the Word. Subsequently, God regenerates those who respond positively[151] in accordance with the two-sided covenant outlined earlier. Hubmaier explained this mutuality by noting:

> Here, however, an equating and mixing of the wills is going on
> . . . . As soon as now God turns to us, calls, and admonishes us to
> follow after him, and we leave wife and child, ship and tools, also

---

[150] See Gabriel Biel, *Epitome et collectorium ex Occamo circa quatuar Sententiarum libros,* II (Tübingen, n.p. 1501/Frankfurt: Minerva, 1965), for several citations of this theme. See also Denis R. Janz, "Late Medieval Theology", in *The Cambridge Companion to Reformation Theology* (eds. David Bagchi and David C. Steinmetz; Cambridge: Cambridge University Press, 2004), 12.

[151] Even after returning to free will, the soul may turn from God and not enter into covenant with God. In an interesting analogy, Hubmaier stated: "The soul stands between the spirit and the flesh, as Adam stood between God, who tells him he should not eat of the tree of knowledge of good and evil, and his Eve, who tells him he should eat of the tree, Gen. 2; 3. The soul is now free and may follow the spirit or the flesh. However, if it follows Eve, that is, the flesh, then it becomes an Eve and flesh. If it is obedient to the spirit, then it becomes a spirit", *Hubmaier*, 440; *Schriften*, 391.

everything that hinders us on the way to him, we are already helped, John 1:35ff. That is called his facing and drawing will with which he wants and draws all people so that they be saved. Nevertheless, the choice lies with them for God wants them, unpressed, unforced, and without coercion.

Whichever people do not accept, hear, or follow after him, the same he turns himself away from and withdraws from and lets them remain as they themselves want to be. That is now called the withdrawing will of God. . . .

Not that there are two wills in God, . . . for there is one single will in God, but one must speak about God humanly and with human words, as if he had eyes and ears, face and back, turned to and away from, and that because of our small understanding. . . .

The hidden will of God still remains upright and omnipotent, according to which he can do what he wants and no one need question, 'Why do you do that?' Rom. 9:20. His facing will is a will of mercy. His withdrawing will is a will of his justice and punishments, of which we are guilty with our vices, and not God.[152]

Humanity then contained a freedom of the will, but a limited freedom. Salvation was only possible by a grace mediated by the consent of the believer. At the same time, humanity is inept in its ability to choose goodness without the regeneration by the Holy Spirit. Thus, Hubmaier held neither a strict doctrine of election nor an overwhelming humanism, leading one scholar to observe that Hubmaier

. . . is [attempting] to blend what are in fact two different concepts of faith. On the one hand he seems to want to hold on to some of the Anabaptist idea of faith as somehow arising out of human capacity, and maintain the importance of human free will and the ability of human beings to cooperate with God in the salvation process. On the other hand, at the same time, Hubmaier seems to want to keep certain elements of faith as understood by Luther, Zwingli and other magisterial reformers, as entirely a gift of God, apart from, and unmerited by, any acts on the part of human beings.[153]

---

[152] *Hubmaier*, 474-76; *Schriften*, 418-19.

[153] Mabry, *Balthasar Hubmaier's Understanding of Faith*, 74. Rollin Armour likewise notes: "At the same time, it must be admitted that it is to a degree illegitimate to call Hubmaier's thought 'Catholic,' for he wholly repudiated the Catholic sacramental theology which was interwoven with all other aspects of Catholic thought, anthropology included. On the other hand, Hubmaier was not 'Protestant' in the classical and normative sense either, for he understood faith to be a human action of belief which brought divine grace rather than, as in Luther and Zwingli, a more passive trust created within man's

Irrespective of this theological dialectic, human freedom is requisite for spiritual regeneration to take place. Because faith must precede the sign, a concept Hubmaier adopted ironically through Luther,[154] regeneration is an indispensable prerequisite to the administration of water baptism.[155] Water baptism serves, for Hubmaier, as "an outward and public testimony of the inner baptism in the Spirit".[156] It follows that for Hubmaier infant baptism was then unwarranted.

Three Baptisms

Throughout his writings, Hubmaier distinguished between various kinds of baptism. Early in his disputes with Zwingli, Hubmaier identified five types of baptism:

1. "Baptism in water", by which Hubmaier meant the outward form.
2. "Baptism in water, for or unto change in life." Here baptism contains both outward symbol and inner meaning as the baptizand commits to live within the discipline of Christ and his church.
3. "Baptism in the Spirit and fire." This concept distinguishes itself from the mere outward symbol. Spiritual baptism refers to the conversion of the heart through the Holy Ghost.
4. "To be reborn out of water and Spirit." Here Hubmaier seemed to imply a sense of spiritual security "to help the sinner out of fear and dread".
5. "Baptism in water in the name of the Father, Son and Holy Spirit, or in the name of our Lord Jesus Christ." Here, Hubmaier meant the actual public confession and commitment to

---

heart *sola gratia*", *Anabaptist Baptism*, 34.

[154] See chapter 1 of this text.

[155] Steinmetz, *Luther in Context*, 70. Steinmetz elsewhere notes that "Hubmaier faces in two directions. His view of baptism and of the voluntary church represents a break with the past and the anticipation of new currents which gained in significance after his death. But his views of grace and free will represent a continuation into the sixteenth century of conservative theological motifs from the later Middle Ages over against the radical theological insights from Luther", *Reformers in the Wings*, 207. Thus, Hubmaier's eclectic syntheses exemplify his unique assimilation of thought and praxis which resulted in the Anabaptist sacramentalism that this book develops.

[156] *Hubmaier*, 349; *Schriften*, 313.

the faith before God and the congregation.[157]

Initially this breakdown came in answer to Zwingli's four types.[158] However, Hubmaier's five kinds of baptism were ultimately streamlined in his later writings to a more readily comprehensible three: Spirit, water and blood.

Written in Nikolsburg in 1526, Hubmaier's *A Christian Catechism* succinctly describes these three types in dialogical format between Leonhart, the tutor, and Hans, the catechumen:[159]

> *Leonhart:* After faith what do you desire?
> *Hans:* Water baptism.
> *Leonhart:* How many kinds of baptism are there?
> *Hans:* Three kinds.
> *Leonhart:* What are they?
> *Hans:* A baptism of the Spirit, a baptism of water, and a baptism of blood.
> *Leonhart:* What is the baptism of the Spirit?
> *Hans:* It is an inner illumination of our hearts that takes place by the Holy Spirit through the living Word of God.
> *Leonhart:* What is water baptism?
> *Hans:* It is an outward and public testimony of the inner baptism in the Spirit, which a person gives by receiving water, with which one confesses one's sins before all people. One also testifies thereby that one believes in the forgiveness of his sins through the death and resurrection of our Lord Jesus Christ. Thereupon one also has himself outwardly enrolled, inscribed, and by water baptism incorporated into the fellowship of the church according to the institution of Christ, before which church the person also publicly and orally vows to God and agrees in the strength of God the Father, Son, and Holy Spirit that he will henceforth believe and live according to his divine Word. . . .
> *Leonhart:* What is the baptism of blood?
> *Hans:* It is a daily mortification of the flesh until death.
> *Leonhart:* Where did Christ mention these baptisms?
> *Hans:* Concerning Spirit baptism in John 3:5, concerning water bap-

---

[157] *Hubmaier*, 99-101; *Schriften*, 121-22.

[158] See Zwingli, "Of Baptism", *Zwingli and Bullinger*. The Library of Christian Classics, XXIV (ed. G.W. Bromiley; Philadelphia: Westminster Press, 1953), 132. Here Zwingli defined baptism as immersion in water, inward enlightenment, external teaching combined with external immersion, and external baptism combined with internal faith.

[159] Hubmaier did not choose these names at random but in honor of "the noble and Christian Lords", Lord Leonhart and Lord Hans von Liechtenstein at Nikolsburg. *Hubmaier*, 344; *Schriften*, 310.

tism in Matt. 28:18ff; Mark 16:15f, and concerning the baptism of blood in Luke 12:50.[160]

The development of these three types can neither be attributed to Hubmaier's originality nor to an overt biblical witness, albeit I John 5:6-8 intimates these three as the means by which Christ came.[161] Much of Hubmaier's writings, outside of his five-part and three-part descriptions, distinguished between inner and outer baptism, baptism by the Spirit and by water. That Hubmaier still added a baptism by blood is significant. Here again, we see in Hubmaier a lingering reliance upon his medieval upbringing and training. Other than the passage from I John, there is meager scriptural support for the concept of baptism by blood. Hubmaier, though, cited Luke 12:50, where Christ says, "But I have a baptism to undergo, and how distressed I am until it is completed!" Hubmaier saw Christ's anxious anticipation for the passion on the cross in this passage to exemplify this third baptismal genre. Nevertheless, it is debatable whether this scriptural intimation should be rightly interpreted as explicit prescription for a new form of baptism to be practiced by the saints of Christianity into perpetuity. Thus, Hubmaier once again appears to violate his rule requiring scriptural explicitness in biblical hermeneutics for church praxis, a concept he had hypocritically argued so vehemently for previously in response to Zwingli's writings.

This chapter has already developed Hubmaier's differentiation between water and spirit baptisms, particularly under the rubric "inner and outer" baptisms. But the concept of baptism by blood has yet to be developed in this work. The notion of the baptism by blood found its origins in the development of the early church during a period when unbaptized Christians were being arrested and martyred. Rollin Armour notes that both Tertullian and Cyprian permitted this event to serve as one's testimony and baptism in the faith. Tertullian maintained: "This is the baptism which stands in lieu of the fontal bathing when that has not been received, and restores it when lost."[162] Thus, throughout the early centuries of Christianity, martyrdom was esteemed as a high honor, and, for at least Cyprian, was loftier than baptism by water, "having the distinct advantage of taking one beyond the possibility of sin."[163] Here, patristic thought had as-

---

[160] *Hubmaier*, 349-50; *Schriften*, 313-14.

[161] "This is the one who came by water and blood – Jesus Christ. He did not come by water only, but by water and blood. And it is the Spirit who testifies, because the Spirit is the truth. For there are three that testify: the Spirit, the water and the blood: and the three are in agreement", vs. 6-8.

[162] Tertullian, *On Baptism,* chap. xvi, from *The Ante-Nicene Fathers* (eds. Alexander Roberts & James Donaldson; Peabody: Hendrickson Publishers, 1995) [hereafter *ANF*], 677.

[163] Though, interestingly, Cyprian would also argue that heretics who come to faith at the last moment but before confession within the Church do not benefit from their baptism in blood unless the church declares them to be martyrs. Cyprian, *Epistle LXXXII. ANF* 5, 384. See also Cyprian, "Epistola ad Fortunatum de exhortatione martyrii", *Patrologiae Cursus Completus: Series Latina* IV, col. 654 (ed. J.P. Migne; Paris: Garnier Frères, 1844). Tertullian wrote: "We have indeed, likewise, a second font . . . of blood, to wit;

sumed that God would surely have allowed the requirement of water baptism to be waived because of such an exigency. Thus, Hubmaier's concept emerged from centuries of theological development.

Although spawned from the evolutions in Catholic theology over the centuries, Hubmaier's view of the third baptism is not altogether traditionally medieval. Since Catholic notions of sacrament necessitated water baptism for salvation based on its *ex opere operato* character, baptism by blood became its essential surrogate during periods in which water was not as readily available.[164] Hubmaier also utilized language which at times seemed to indicate the necessity of water baptism, but for the Anabaptist theologian, the purpose of the rite was an act of obedience through the public profession of faith. Essentially, faith is that which saves. But for such faith to be genuine, it must produce confession of one's beliefs. Here Hubmaier passionately argued:

> Secretly believing is something, but not enough. For although one believes with the heart unto righteousness, one must confess with the mouth unto salvation, Rom. 10:10. . . . [Other Christian sects] thought it was enough to believe with the heart and thought it was unnecessary to confess such with the mouth and by fruits. But their opinion is against Scripture, Rom. 10:10; Matt. 10:32: "Whoever confesses me before people, etc."[165]

Hubmaier turned repeatedly to Mark 16:16 ("Whoever believes and is baptized is saved") and added: "Here one must always leave faith and baptism together."[166] Thus, baptism and other acts of obedience are not discretionary. The believer is saved, then, not because of his or her baptism but by virtue of the believer's obedience in proclamation. Conversely, Hubmaier continued, "if he does not do it, however, then he is not condemned because of his non-baptism, but because of his unfaith, from which his disobedience proceeds, Matt.

---

concerning which the Lord said, 'I have to be baptized with a baptism,' when He had been baptized already. For He had come 'by means of water and blood,' just as John has written", Tertullian, *On Baptism*, 677. Thus, Tertullian wrote here more in the context of baptism by blood in lieu of those who did not receive water baptisms. Cyprian typically wrote in the context of a second baptism which followed baptism by water.

[164] Armour, *Anabaptist Baptism*, 53.

[165] *Hubmaier*, 193; *Schriften*, 185.

[166] *Hubmaier*, 193-94; *Schriften*, 185.

7:26."[167] Thus, Hubmaier maintained the Catholic requirement of baptism for the Christian while transposing its salvific quality from the rite *ex opere operato* to the confession and pledge of the believer. His sacramental shift can be understood as transferring its power from the physical elements to the expression of faith and ethical response of the believer.

Having clarified this new meaning, Hubmaier then proceeded to outline his understanding of the third baptism, the baptism of blood, in relation to the inner and outer baptisms of Spirit and water, respectively. So significant was ethical behavior incumbent upon the Christian that Hubmaier held that all three baptisms were necessary for salvation as they were all necessary fruits of authentic faith.[168] While he joined church tradition in interpreting the baptism of blood as culminating in martyrdom, Hubmaier added to this meaning an inexorable process, "the daily mortification of the flesh until death."[169] This entailed the perpetual struggle of continually killing the old Adam (the sinful person or sinful flesh) on one's deathbed.[170] Since through salvation the soul is rehabilitated in knowledge to join with the spirit but the flesh remains condemned, any action leading to the denial and destruction of the flesh would be aidful to the human condition in salvation. Thus, Hubmaier's writings on this third baptism encompass both the daily struggle of Christian discipline in the midst of human temptation as well as the ultimate suffering and persecution for Christian (and Anabaptist) convictions in this life.[171]

Hubmaier, like many other Anabaptists, had come to recognize that persecution, imprisonment, torture and death were the tragic consequences for many who confessed Anabaptist beliefs. Thus, contextually, Hubmaier believed himself to be reforming the church to its historical roots of early Christianity, perceiving the prevalence of Anabaptist persecution as paralleling that of first generation Christians. Consequently, the Anabaptist theologian preserved the ancient concept of baptism by blood, seeing in it a contiguous relationship to the ethical response of Christians to God's grace in baptism by water:

For whoever wants to cry with Christ to God: 'Abba, pater, dear Fa-

---

[167] *Hubmaier*, 191; *Schriften*, 183.

[168] Catholic theology saw the need for only one of the three to take place. See Armour, *Anabaptist Baptism*, 53.

[169] *Hubmaier*, 350; *Schriften*, 314.

[170] Windhorst, *Täuferisches Taufverständnis*, 156-57. Windhorst elaborates by comparing the "old Adam" to the sick Samaritan in Jesus' parable. The sickness (sin) of the Samaritan (the sinful person) is healed by the Good Samaritan (Christ) by pouring the oil (the Word of God) on his wounds. Thus, Windhorst believes Hubmaier saw the parable as the daily battle of fleshly temptation and the killing of sin.

[171] The battle then is both inward and outward as sinful impulses exist both within the world and within the sinner. Because the inner and outer battle is against a common enemy, namely sin, it encompasses the same battle. Winhorst, *Täuferisches Taufverständnis*, 160.

ther,' must do so in faith, and must also be cobaptized in water with Christ and suffer jointly with him in blood. Then he will be a son and heir of God, fellow heir with Christ, and will be jointly glorified with Christ, Rom. 8:17. Therefore no one should be terrified of persecution or suffering, for Christ had to suffer and thus enter into his glory, Luke 24:26. And also Paul writes: 'All who desire to live so devoutly in Christ Jesus will be persecuted,' 2 Tim. 3:12. This is indeed precisely the third baptism or last baptism in which people should indeed be anointed with the oil of the holy and comforting gospel (in order that we may be meek and ready to suffer). Thus the illness is lightened for us, and we receive forgiveness of sins, James 5:14ff.[172]

Here again we might see the transposition of Catholic ritual sacrament to Anabaptist ethical sacrament. This third baptism served as spiritual oil or "last unction"; the latter term Hubmaier himself used interchangeably with this kind of baptism:

Extreme unction, or as it is called in some countries, 'last baptism,' I consider not only a mockery, yea also an idolatry, for to it is ascribed forgiveness for sins; . . . However, the spiritual anointing which Christ announced to us, Luke 10:34 and also James 5:14, I esteem highly and am quite satisfied to have it called the last baptism.[173]

The forgiveness of sins comes through Hubmaier's sacramental act of confession of faith and public pledge to God. One's martyrdom exemplifies such faith actions and thus qualifies as a type of baptism that faithful Christians undoubtedly would ultimately experience. Therefore, unlike his manifold Anabaptist and magisterial counterparts, Hubmaier did not completely eliminate extreme unction as sacrament in the church through his polemical writings but instead replaced it with the third baptism, the baptism of blood.

Faithful Christians, then, are not to attempt to avoid suffering on earth. Instead, they should expect persecution and recognize such experiences as spiritual joy. Suffering, which culminates in martyrdom, serves as the greatest experience in identifying with Christ, taking up one's cross and following Him. Likened unto Christ's passion, human suffering is no sign of defeat but rather of victory, for endurance in persecution exemplifies Christian discipleship. As the Christian now suffers with Christ, so too will the Christian ultimately reign with Him.[174]

---

[172] *Hubmaier*, 301; *Schriften*, 275.
[173] *Hubmaier*, 300-301; *Schriften*, 274-75.
[174] Mabry, *The Baptismal Theology of Balthasar Hubmaier*, 126-27.

Patristic Support for Believer's Baptism

Throughout his polemical writings, Hubmaier attempted, at least in his mind, to find biblical support for his position on baptism, particularly his stance against infant baptism and for confessor's baptism. While he may not have gone through this exercise to find in these "old teachers" a sense of divine authority, Hubmaier did want, as scholars have previously stated, "to make the point that [he] was either schismatic nor heretical".[175] Thus, Hubmaier's *Old and New Teachers on Believers Baptism*, written in Nikolsburg in the summer of 1526, served to buttress his previous theological arguments and biblical exegesis.

This writing was unfortunate on at least two fronts. First, it seemed to violate Hubmaier's anti-scholastic approach to church reform. If the church fathers did not serve as a source of authority for Hubmaier, then his heretofore sporadic citations of them, at most, were more effective than devoting an entire treatise to them. Secondly, Hubmaier set out to prove through proof-texting, often terribly out of context, that numerous patristic sources supported the baptisms of adult believers. Yet, as Armour rightly points out, "his argument was at best a weak one, for not only is his evidence poorly chosen at times . . . , but the argument tends toward a *non sequitur*, as follows: since the early church baptized believers, it did not baptize infants."[176]

At the same time, Hubmaier's second point, an argument based on theology and not church praxis, may have made greater gains. Utilizing the works of Ambrose, Theophylact and even Pope Boniface's canon "On Consecration", Hubmaier established some evidence for the necessity of faith preceding the sign in baptism.[177] On the latter work, Hubmaier wrote:

> The pope says that godparents, when they bring the child to baptism, may not truthfully answer in place of the child that it renounces the devil or that it believes. For they do not know whether that child will be chaste or not, pious or a thief. . . . Likewise, the canon *Prima* [First] points to the article of faith about which one should question before one baptizes a person. The canons *baptizandi* [those being baptized] and *ante baptismum* [before baptism] teach how those who are to be baptized should present themselves several days before to their bishop. Also they should hold themselves back several days from wine and meat. All this cannot apply to children. For water baptism, one's own confession of faith is necessary and foreign faith is not sufficient.[178]

---

[175] Pipkin and Yoder, 245.

[176] Armour, *Anabaptist Baptism*, 50-51.

[177] *Hubmaier*, 253-55; *Schriften*, 231-32.

[178] *Hubmaier*, 254; *Schriften*, 232.

While other scholars have given extensive treatment to Hubmaier's treatise,[179] paying particular attention to Hubmaier's errors and decontextualizations, this chapter will simply summarily note that Hubmaier's work is significant in comprehending his understanding of early church sources. In it, Hubmaier attempted to establish an historical precedent to accompany the biblical interpretation for believer's baptism. Andrew Klager maintains that Hubmaier "used the fathers for apologetic purposes as historical allies in his defense of credobaptism and free will. Clearly, he viewed the fathers favorably, not merely by giving cognitive assent to their teachings, but by accepting them as co-affiliates in the universal church as he understood it."[180] Hubmaier, who undoubtedly distorted the words of past and contemporary theologians to make his point, nevertheless manifested his longing for church reform and his view of early church practice. The foundation of the church, Hubmaier argued, was confession of faith: "the church is built on our faith and confession, and not our faith on the church, but on the preached Word of God, which is God himself and which has become human."[181] To that end, all of Hubmaier's efforts were forged to restore the church's "original purity" as a community of saints.[182] Confession of faith followed by water baptism became its hallmarks.

Baptism in Hubmaier's Liturgical Practice

Like his liturgy for the Lord's Supper, Hubmaier's *A Form for Water Baptism* is a gift for all students of theology, worship and Anabaptism. No other Anabaptist theologian provided such an extensive outline of the contemporary ecclesiastical practice as did Hubmaier. Given the importance of the rite of baptism to Anabaptism in general and to Hubmaier in particular, this worship model is strikingly important, especially with the added knowledge that the work had evolved from Hubmaier's initial liturgical reform in Waldshut to his fully

---

[179] Torsten Bergsten and Rollin Armour provide excellent overviews of this subject, the former focusing particularly on Hubmaier's analysis of Jerome and Augustine, the latter presenting and classifying each of Hubmaier's patristic references. See Bergsten, *Balthasar Hubmaier: Anabaptist Theologian and Martyr*, 280-84, and Armour, *Anabaptist Baptism*, 49-52. Additionally, in his classic study of Hubmaier, Carl Sachsee provides an invaluable service to any scholar who wishes to locate the original primary sources from which Hubmaier summarized each theologian's or canon's arguments for further analysis. See Sachsee, 33-40. Finally, Andrew P. Klager analyzes Hubmaier's use of patristic sources in light of manuscripts from Byzantium to Italy which seemed to support Hubmaier's credobaptist convictions. See Klager, "Balthasar Hubmaier's Use of the Church Fathers: Availability, Access and Interaction", *MQR* 84, no. 1 (January 2010), 5-65.

[180] Klager, 9.

[181] *Hubmaier*, 248; *Schriften*, 228.

[182] Bergsten, *Balthasar Hubmaier: Anabaptist Theologian and Martyr*, 326.

developed liturgical thinking in his final years in Nikolsburg. What is left unknown is the degree to which Hubmaier elaborated his baptismal practice and
the degree to which this document describes something close to the early administration in Waldshut.[183] Regardless, Hubmaier's *Form* is a liturgical gem which
correlates well to the reformer's developed, mature Anabaptist theology.

Under the temporary protected freedoms enjoyed in Moravia, Hubmaier's
Nikolsburg church grew rapidly. The expansion of Anabaptist influence elicited
the need for church teaching (catechesis) and worship order.[184] Thus, from this
brief time of respite and liberty, Hubmaier recorded instructions for church practice.

Revealing his tenuous political circumstance and his own sage diplomacy,
Hubmaier dedicated the baptismal liturgy to Jan Dubcansky, a nobleman of that
region who, while personally inclined toward Zwinglianism, was interested in
unifying the various evangelical splinter reforms.[185] Hubmaier may well have
been attempting to win the nobleman over to Anabaptist causes, or at least to
greater understanding, as he appealed to Dubcansky to consult clerical coun-
sel and come to "see that we [Anabaptists] have thus far not been running in
vain, and that our deeds have been right, appropriate, and fitting, by virtue of
Scripture."[186]

Following this dedicatory preface, the liturgy begins by calling upon the newly
converted to present himself or herself before the congregation and its bishop
to determine whether the neophyte is "sufficiently instructed in the articles of
the law, gospel, faith and the doctrines which concern a new Christian life".[187]
The candidate must portray the ability to pray and demonstrate Christian faith
and understanding. If the candidate completes this catechesis satisfactorily, the
bishop then entreats the congregation to kneel and pray for the new inductee that
God might "graciously impart to this person the grace and the power of his Holy
Spirit and complete in him what he has begun through his Holy Spirit and divine
Word".[188] Thus, the confession of faith and Christian proclamation via episcopal examination are the initial elements of the human response to God's grace.
Nevertheless, such salvific response is not fully realized until the baptismal vow
is taken and the neophyte submits himself or herself to water baptism and the
discipline of the church.

---

[183] Armour believes that this Nikolsburg liturgy at least "preserves the general structure of the later, more formal baptismal services in Waldshut, even if it does not reveal the
method of the first baptism", *Anabaptist Baptism*, 54.

[184] Bergsten, *Balthasar Hubmaier: Anabaptist Theologian and Martyr*, 325.

[185] Bergsten provides further information regarding Hubmaier's relationship to
Dubcansky. See Bergsten, *Balthasar Hubmaier: Anabaptist Theologian and Martyr*, esp.
316-20 and 339-42. Additionally, Zeman outlines Hubmaier's intentions in dedicating this
treatise and several other works to noblemen. See Zeman, 165-72.

[186] *Hubmaier*, 387; *Schriften*, 349.

[187] *Hubmaier*, 387; *Schriften*, 349.

[188] *Hubmaier*, 388; *Schriften*, 349.

Subsequently, the bishop prays for the indwelling of the Holy Spirit in the heart of the new believer and then proceeds with the liturgy of the baptismal pledge. For Hubmaier, this pledge is of weighty importance in order for the legitimacy of the Christian church to be restored and for genuine Christianity to be sponsored.

The sacramental pledge thus follows:

> 'Do you believe in God the Father Almighty, Creator of heaven and earth? If so, speak publicly':
> **'I believe.'**
> 'Do you believe in Jesus Christ his only begotten Son our Lord, who was conceived of the Holy Spirit, born of the Virgin Mary, suffered under Pontius Pilate, crucified, dead and buried, that he went in the Spirit and preached the gospel to the spirits which were in prison, I Pet. 3:19; 4:6, that on the third day he again united with the body in the grave and powerfully arose from the dead, I Cor. 15:4; Acts 2:32, and after forty days ascended into heaven. There he sits at the right hand of his almighty Father, whence he will come to judge the living and the dead? if so speak':
> **'I believe.'**
> 'Do you also believe in the Holy Spirit, and do you believe a holy universal Christian church, a fellowship of the saints, that the same possesses the keys for the remission of sins.[?] Do you believe also the resurrection of the flesh and eternal life? If so, speak':
> **'I believe.'**
> 'Will you in the power of Christ renounce the devil, all his works, machinations, and vanities, then speak':
> **'I will.'**
> 'Will you henceforth lead your life and walk according to the Word of Christ, as he gives you grace: So speak':
> **'I will.'**
> 'If now you should sin and your brother knows it, will you let him admonish you once, twice and a third time before the church, and willingly and obediently accept fraternal admonition, if so speak':
> **'I will.'**
> 'Do you desire now upon this faith and pledge to be baptized in water according to the institution of Christ, incorporated and thereby counted in the visible Christian church, for the forgiveness of your sins, if so speak':
> **'I desire it in the power of God.'**[189]

The bishop then directly administers water baptism in Trinitarian fashion

---

[189] *Hubmaier*, 388-89 [bold mine]; *Schriften*, 349-50.

"for the forgiveness of [the candidate's] sins, Matt. 18:19; Acts 2:38."[190] The congregation is subsequently exhorted to again pray for the baptized believer, that
he or she, along with all those present, would persist in Christian faith through
the strength and constancy God might provide. Thus, like other Anabaptists,
Hubmaier held onto Catholic notions of the potential of apostasy for a believer,
a concept that provided the theological foundation for church discipline and the
ban from fellowship for the wayward church member.

The baptismal pledge is significant beyond its value as an example of
Anabaptist liturgical practice, as important as this might be. Hubmaier elevated
the baptismal pledge to that of sacramental entrance into the church. Having
testified to one's beliefs publicly (through a variation of the Apostles' Creed)
and having committed oneself to the covenant of faith to God and the gathered
congregation, the neophyte is finally granted the full benefits of Christian membership: "participating in the use of her keys, breaking bread, and praying with
other Christian sisters and brothers".[191]

One intriguing aspect of Hubmaier's thought at this juncture is that prayer
and the use of the "keys" seem to be elevated as equivalent ecclesial acts to the
Eucharist. As such, the question of other possible sacramental acts in addition
to baptism and the Supper in Hubmaier's theology will be explored in the next
chapter. For the purpose of this present subject, however, Hubmaier viewed the
pledge and reception of water as allowing one to participate fully in the work of
the church.

Previous scholarship has observed something significantly distinct about
Hubmaier's baptismal practice: It is not an exclusively personal event isolated
from the context of the church and its congregation. Unlike other Anabaptists,
Hubmaier did not seem to accept informal, spontaneous or "roadside" baptisms.
Rollin Armour observes of this that "it seems that Hubmaier practiced baptism
in this general fashion from the beginning of his Anabaptist career, for, in spite
of the alleged indignity of his first baptisms, they were performed within the
church building and, presumably, with the approval of the congregation for the
occasion."[192] Armour's point is not peripheral. This initiatory action involved the
entire witnessing Anabaptist congregation and served as a reminder of or recommitment to each Christian's own previous baptismal vow.

Following the episcopal blessing upon the new believer and statements of
commencement into the believing community, Hubmaier concluded his *Form
for Water Baptism* with a discussion of three common errors that he saw the
Catholic Church enact in the ordinances of baptism and the Supper. First, the
Roman Church had allowed for a distortion of God's Word by practicing infant
baptism. Second, the Supper was distributed to those who had not committed
themselves to God and to one another. As Hubmaier saw it, the church had sold

---

[190] *Hubmaier*, 389; *Schriften*, 350.
[191] *Hubmaier*, 389; *Schriften*, 350.
[192] Armour, *Anabaptist Baptism*, 55.

its theological birthright on behalf of the weak and ignorant. He maintained that church discipline and better biblical instruction should be established in order to correct such problems.

Yet Hubmaier's view of the church's third error in his *Form* is most important-to this present work: that water baptism and the breaking of bread are called "sacraments". Instead, Hubmaier articulated well his unique understanding of sacrament: that the elements of water, bread and wine are not sacraments, "but in the fact that the baptismal commitment or the pledge of love is really and truly 'sacrament'. . . ."[193] This former priest, trained in nominalism, then argued philologically that the word "sacrament" from the Latin *sacramentum* means "a commitment by oath and a pledge given by the hand . . . ."[194] Therefore, sacraments for Hubmaier involved voluntary pledges by the believer to Christ and His church. This is the heart of Hubmaier's theology on this subject.

The *Apologia*

Hubmaier's Moravian tranquility was short-lived as Nikolsburg, just as Waldshut before it, proved to be only a brief refuge. In July 1527, he was arrested by King Ferdinand's soldiers and ultimately imprisoned at Kreuzenstein Castle north of Vienna. Unlike his experience in Zurich several years earlier, Hubmaier this time did not recant his beliefs in order to receive freedom or avoid execution. While attempting to appease Catholic authorities to the best of his ability, Hubmaier in no way diminished his Anabaptist convictions regarding the sacraments. In his *Apologia* written shortly before his death, Hubmaier wrote:

> For I have taught nothing else regarding baptism except that it is a public and oral confession of the Christian faith, and a renunciation that one must address to the devil and his works, so that a person, in the power of God the Father and the Son and the Holy Spirit, may yield himself in such surrender that he is willing with Christ to suffer, die and be buried, in the faith that he will arise with him to everlasting life, Rom. 6:4; this he testifies by receiving water baptism. But concerning the Lord's Supper I have taught that it is a testimonial of brotherly love, that as Christ loved us unto death so we should also love one another and each perform toward one an-

---

[193] *Hubmaier*, 391; *Schriften*, 352.

[194] *Hubmaier*, 391; *Schriften*, 352. Wayne Pipkin notes of these remarks that "Hubmaier affirmed a sacrament of obedience, one that creates and is the basis of a new, alternative, prophetic community, enrolled under Christ and liable always to correction and encouragement to discipleship", H. Wayne Pipkin, "The Baptismal Theology of Balthasar Hubmaier", 52.

> other the works of mercy, concerning which Christ will demand an
> account on the judgment day, Matt. 25:40. . . . This witness of love
> occurs through the breaking of bread, which is eaten in memory of
> Christ's suffering which he endured for us out of love, for the remis-
> sion of our sins . . . .[195]

While he obsequiously proposed postponing this article of belief in deference to
the Catholic king's wishes, at least until such time that a church council could be
held on this matter, Hubmaier nonetheless did not surrender his Anabaptist beliefs. The sacraments of confession through baptism and pledge of love through
the Supper were integral to his vision of church renewal and biblical restoration.

Conclusion

In summary, as was the case with communion, baptism for Hubmaier was sacramental only as it involves a pledge to God and to the congregation. Baptism
is a voluntary, personal pledge in which the individual promises to follow Christ
and God's teachings all his or her days but also agrees to submit oneself to the
discipline and order of the church. Because of the continued potential of apostasy even after such a covenant is completed, the new believer (or at least new
Anabaptist) is reminded of life's inexorable battle with iniquity. The neophyte
"breaks out into word and deed" in the midst of the isolating traps of "tribulation,
temptation, persecution, the cross, and all the sorrow in the world".[196] Clinging to
the Word of God, the new believer is sheltered from the devil's and the world's
"fiery arrows".[197] Thus, while supported by the congregation, the new Anabaptist
would see the road of true Christianity to likely be a relatively solitary one.

However, the significance of the local congregation in that same promise
should not be overlooked. The baptismal pledge and its symbolic action in water
enroll the believer into the community of faith. The private nature of faith then is
secondary to its corporate obligation. Water baptism, which concludes the public
proclamation of genuine faith and submission to discipline, safeguards the in-
tegrity and authenticity of the believing community. This corporate trajectory of
Hubmaier's baptismal understanding effectuated his bold proclamation:

> Where there is no water baptism, there is no church nor minister, nei-
> ther brother nor sister, nor brotherly admonition, excommunication,

---

[195] *Hubmaier*, 556-57; *Schriften*, 487.

[196] *Hubmaier*, 101; *Schriften*, 122.

[197] *Hubmaier*, 101; *Schriften*, 122.

> or reacceptance. I am speaking here of the visible church as Christ did
> in Matthew 18:15ff. There must also exist an outward confession or
> testimony through which visible brothers and sisters can know each
> other, since faith exists only in the heart. But when he receives the
> baptism of water the one who is baptized testifies publicly that he has
> pledged himself henceforth to live according to the Rule of Christ. By
> virtue of this pledge he has submitted himself to sisters, brothers, and
> to the church so that when he transgresses they now have the author-
> ity to admonish, punish, ban, and reaccept him. . . . Where does this
> authority come from, if not from the pledge of baptism?[198]

Baptism, the initiatory guardian of the believing community, is also the *sine qua non* of the disciplined church. Faith is then not something merely accepted but also proclaimed through the pledge of water baptism. The Anabaptist participates in such a pledge in order to complete the salvific covenant with God and submits to the symbol of the pouring of water through obedience. It follows then that the sacrament of baptism is both one's promise to God and one's public oath to God's church to live within the discipline of the faith.

Baptism is salvific, but not in a transubstantiative sense through the element of water. Instead, it is called a baptism *in remissionem peccatorum*, "by the power of the internal 'Yes' in the heart, which the person proclaims publicly in the reception of water baptism, that he believes and is already sure in his heart of the remission of sins through Jesus Christ."[199] Thus, for Hubmaier, the water does not cleanse the soul, but the "yes" of a good conscience in faith is that which saves, an affirmation professed publicly and sealed covenantally through baptism.

In addition to its corporate and individual natures, as a commitment between God and the congregation, Hubmaier's concept of baptism, as we have seen previously, was comprehended in three forms:

> Baptism is sometimes taken for the internal baptism of the Spirit,
> John 3:5-6, sometimes for the outward water baptism, Matt. 28:19.
> In the third place, sometimes it is taken for the subsequent suffering,
> when Christ says, 'I must let myself be baptized beforehand with a
> baptism, and I am anxious until it has been completed,' Luke 12:50.[200]

While the third type, as discussed previously, portrayed the difficult path of Anabaptist faith and discipline, the first two types appear as most significant in

---

[198] *Hubmaier*, 127; *Schriften*, 145.
[199] *Hubmaier*, 118; *Schriften*, 137.
[200] *Hubmaier*, 189; *Schriften*, 182.

Hubmaier's sacramental theology.

Hubmaier's continually stressed that the act of pouring of water is not the whole of baptism. This symbolic function is the completion and seal of the requisite act of entering God's covenant of faith through an oath of love, agreeing to live within God's ways and within the discipline of the church. That this Anabaptist thinker specified "water baptism" is indicative of his understanding of baptism as inclusive of other expressions than simply the dispensation of water itself. The baptism of the Spirit is that which always must precede water baptism for a genuine believer's baptism to take place. Spiritual baptism involves the "inner illumination of our hearts that takes place by the Holy Spirit through the living Word of God".[201] This initial act of God is that which saves. Nevertheless, the true believer would be compelled to respond to God's action through a retroaction of public profession of this gift of faith. "Water baptism", that second form of baptism, serves as the "outward and public testimony of the inner baptism in the Spirit".[202] Herein, the new believers not only receive water, but also confess their sins and voluntarily agree to be "outwardly enrolled, inscribed, and by water baptism incorporated into the fellowship of the church" in accordance with Christ and before the local congregation. Lastly, each candidate "vows to God and agrees in the strength of God the Father, Son and Holy Spirit that he will henceforth believe and live according to his divine Word".[203] Thus, while Hubmaier distinguished "water baptism" from the other two, we might also see that baptism by water is also inclusive of this public vow of faith and compliance to the rule of Christ within the church.

The baptism by water is integral to the induction into the believing community and instruction in the faith. Yet Hubmaier was clear that such an act is not salvific in itself. God remains sovereign, safeguarding salvation to the internal work of the Holy Spirit. Therefore, Hubmaier was able to maintain a demand for Christian ethics while avoiding radically synergistic tendencies. At the same time, he reasoned that water baptism was a compulsory response to God's saving action. On this point Hubmaier explained:

> Accordingly, if one wants to be a Christian and if he has a baptizer and water at hand, then he lets himself be baptized by virtue of the institution of Christ. If he does not do it, however, then he is not condemned because of his non-baptism, but because of his unfaith, from which his disobedience proceeds, Matt. 7:26. If he had been a true believer, then he would have taken the sign of Christ-believing onto himself, as Christ had instituted it. . . .[204]

---

[201] *Hubmaier*, 349; *Schriften*, 313.
[202] *Hubmaier*, 349; *Schriften*, 313.
[203] *Hubmaier*, 349; *Schriften*, 314.
[204] *Hubmaier*, 191; *Schriften*, 183.

Thus, baptism by water is not salvific, yet it serves as the compulsory anthropological response of God's previous saving action through faith. One's faith, which is a gift of God, is that which saves. The human is condemned only because he or she lacks this faith. Regardless, the fruits of faith, starting with baptism, testify to the existence of God's inner work.

Baptism is then inclusive of both God's saving intervention and humanity's necessary response through proclamation, oath, confession and symbolic seal by the use of water. Consequently, the sacrament of baptism, just as in the case of the Lord's Supper, serves as a believer's response to God's grace. Hubmaier therefore manifested a sacramental shift from his Catholic past of the transubstantive concept of the elements themselves *ex opere operato* to the voluntary human response of the sincere Christian before the community of faith. Hubmaier did not conceive such a radical proposal *ex nihilo* but through the explicit words of Scripture, which he interpreted literally and prescriptively for continuous church practice. Thus, Hubmaier's sacramental theology of baptism was not intended to reform the church *per se* but restore the church to what he understood was its apostolic heritage.

Conceiving the congregations described in the New Testament as containing only enthusiastic and eager Christians, who manifest their beliefs in Christ-like humility, service and witness, Hubmaier understood the practice of baptism as the guardian of such ecclesial purity. Therefore, this sacrament must include one's public confession to God, agreement to live within God's covenantal provision and acquiescence to serve within the church's established and biblical rules of faith. Accordingly, baptism is not only inseparably linked to the pure, believing church, but also acts as its custodian.

Finally, baptism served for Hubmaier as the public profession of faith and commitment to the faith for life. While the believer was still capable of falling away from this faith, the oath, along with the subsequent baptismal vows of those to follow, serves to remind the Christian of the necessity of continual discipline and missional duty, even to martyrdom, if necessary. Thus, Hubmaier's sacrament is not an end but merely the beginning of Christian proclamation and instruction to a life of faith. Through such a sacramental redirection, the Anabaptist theologian hoped to realize the renewal of what he saw as ancient biblical, confessional and ecclesial praxis.

CHAPTER 4

Other Possible Sacramental Practices

This study, to this point, has described the retention of not only the term but also the theology of "sacrament" within the Anabaptist writings of Balthasar Hubmaier. In reviewing his life and work, especially those matters dealing with the Lord's Supper and baptism, one may readily comprehend the importance Hubmaier placed on the vows of faith of each believer to one another in the Eucharist and commitment to God and the church in baptism. Such vows, followed by their representative symbols in bread, wine and water, constitute "sacrament" in Hubmaier's theological writings.

Hubmaier was uniquely positioned as the most outspoken, prolific and educated of the first generation of Anabaptists. Steeped in a staunchly Catholic upbringing and educated in some of its finest European schools, Hubmaier was early in his adult life a favorite son, professor and priest within the Roman sacramental tradition. Arguably, then, while he was subsequently exposed to various Protestant and dissident influences, Hubmaier never completely divorced himself from certain Catholic principles, in opposition to many of his Anabaptist contemporaries.

Hubmaier's Roman Catholic Church had understood and appropriated the sacraments as the objective working of God *ex opere operato*. Through the actions of the priest with the recipient(s), the Christian might experience the salvation, forgiveness and restoration of a good standing with God. The elements themselves carried such power as God's designated gifts to the church. Thus the church became the means by which the Christian found and maintained salvation.

The Anabaptist Hubmaier never completely abandoned his previous Catholic self. In particular, Hubmaier continued to locate the power of the sacraments within the church. Nevertheless, the elements themselves no longer conveyed grace. Instead, the act of pledging oneself to the others in love, devotion and service through the Supper and pledging oneself to God's ways in baptism sustained this sacramental meaning. Thus, while the cleric still presided over such rites, the sacraments were now performed in correspondence with the entire congregation. Nevertheless, Hubmaier did not radicalize his sacramental thought to the degree of reducing it down to mere individualistic work. The sacraments, while now responses to God's salvation rather than conveyers of it, and while now assigned to the realm of subjective retroaction instead of objective and divine gifts, were nonetheless still centered in and administered by the church.

In addition to continuing to emphasize the role of the sacraments, Hubmaier seemed to retain much of his stance on free will which he inherited from his medieval training. Moreover, this doctor of theology characteristically demonstrated a unique stance within the first generation of the left-wing movement of the Reformation beyond his sacramentality: rejecting non-resistant pacifism and denying church-state separation by accepting magisterial reform. These characteristics, when combined with Hubmaier's sacramentalism, manifest the unicity of his theological appropriations of Catholic principles among the first Anabaptists. Given these distinctive qualities, Balthasar Hubmaier's theology was possibly the most conservative among any of the so-called "radicals".

Consequently, it seems a worthy undertaking, while studying Hubmaier's sacramental theology, to explore whether the former priest might have retained or suggested the existence of other sacraments at the church's disposal. Though Luther, Zwingli and many of their magisterial counterparts in the Protestant wing of Reformation had reduced the sacraments down to the two heretofore outlined, one may question whether Hubmaier, given his strikingly unique redefinition and re-appropriation of "sacrament", might have preserved other sacraments traditional to Catholicism or even created others.

Some scholars of Anabaptism have suggested as much. For instance, in one of his most provocative studies of this figure, James W. McClendon argues that "Hubmaier rebelled but at no time in his life did he ever turn away from [his] central emphasis upon the principal Catholic rites – the administration of baptism, the celebration of the mass, and the exercise of salvific discipline (the sacrament of confession)."[1] McClendon then developed Hubmaier's concepts of the former two rites but, unfortunately, never took up the third. As such, while others scholars have trod the fields of baptism and the Supper in Hubmaier's rich theological vale, they have relatively left unexplored other sacramental possibilities.

After reviewing the extensive works of Hubmaier, one might easily observe that this vacuum in exploring further sacramental options in Hubmaier would come as little surprise. Hubmaier devoted much of his writings to the issues of baptism and the Supper but precious little on other aspects of church practice.

---

[1] James William McClendon, Jr., "Balthasar Hubmaier, Catholic Anabaptist", 22. Likewise in their book, *Baptist Roots*, McClendon and two other historians argue that "Hubmaier's churchly ministry was undergirded by a deep sense of the sacraments of medieval Christianity, and especially of baptism, the Lord's Supper, and confession – each of which he sought to reshape into powerful signs of Christian life within the radical movement." See Curtis Freeman, James Wm. McClendon, Jr, and C. Rosalee Velloso da Silva (eds), *Baptist Roots: A Reader in the Theology of a Christian People* (Valley Forge: Judson Press, 1999), 32. Unfortunately, just as in the case with McClendon's solo piece, this latter work did not pursue the development of what McClendon interpreted as Hubmaier's tri-fold sacramentalism.

William Estep rightly observes the reason for this doctrinal imbalance:

> Admittedly, Hubmaier was not a systematic theologian. There was
> not enough time for that. In the brief span of four years he produced
> all his known works. Often written in haste, at times in prison, and
> always to meet an existential need, it is not surprising that there was
> an unevenness in his works, some errors, and not a few ragged edges.
> Nevertheless, he is doubtless the most influential theologian that six-
> teenth-century Anabaptism produced.[2]

Regardless, the aggregate of Hubmaier's works may provide some trajectory
of thought and at least partial answers to his sacramental intensions and demar-
cations. This chapter will take up the subject first of McClendon's intimation
of a third sacrament and then explore other possibilities for sacraments within
Hubmaier's writings. Given that the Waldshut theologian transformed the act of
sacrament from mediums which dispense grace to liturgically enacted ethical responses or pledges of love and obedience, the possibility of other such responses
seems plausible.

Penance and the Power of the Keys

This study has already established several characteristics within Hubmaier's
theology that portray his close association to his Catholic heritage. While radical in his implications, Hubmaier, unlike any other first generation Anabaptist,
still retained much of the language of his former Roman sacramentalism. Yet
Hubmaier articulately revealed his divergence from medieval Catholicism in
the new roles he assigned to such traditional language. However, Hubmaier, it
seems, also redefined traditional terminology in the case of penance (confession)
and the power of the keys.

Integral to this portion of the study is the notion that Hubmaier, like Catholic
theologians, placed a great deal of stress upon the meaning and power of the
"keys" as chronicled in Matthew 16:19 where Jesus is recorded as saying: "'I
will give you the keys of the kingdom of heaven, and whatever you bind on
earth shall be bound in heaven, and whatever you loose on earth shall be loosed
in heaven.'" Like much of his sacramental theology, this Anabaptist leader
maintained the importance of this statement but reinterpreted its meaning and
praxis. In this case, Hubmaier insisted on translating the second person "you"
in the plural instead of the traditional singular. More precisely, the singular

---

[2] W.R. Estep, "The Anabaptist View of Salvation", 49. While Estep's latter accolade
might be debatable in view particularly of Menno Simons' later contributions to Anabaptism, Estep's understanding of Hubmaier's pressures of time and setting for the development of his practical theology is undoubtedly accurate.

"you" (*Dir*) refers to the unity of the church, even though Peter was directly addressed, while the plural usage (*jr*), for Hubmaier, refers to the many people gathered within the community.³ Consequently, Christ was no longer speaking exclusively to Peter, upon which the Catholic tradition had largely based its concept of apostolic succession, but instead to all who were there gathered and who then comprised the church. Hubmaier expounded:

> When Christ says, 'To you,' [*Dir, dir*] he signifies the unity of the church. But when he says, 'You,' [*Jr, jr*] he indicates that many men shall be gathered together in this unity of faith and Christian love. This same power and these keys Christ gave and commanded to the church after his blessed resurrection, Matt. 28:19ff; Mark 16:15f. Namely, to preach the gospel, thereby to create a believing congregation, to baptize the same in water, thus with the first key opening to her the door the portals of the Christian church, admitting her to the forgiveness of sins, John 20:22f.⁴

For Hubmaier, not only was it sensible that such words of distribution of authority in Matthew 16 and commission in Matthew 28 be applied to the church itself, but also that it seemed cogent that Christ had to be raised and thus was now absent from the earth in order for such authority to need to be transferred.⁵ Before this time, prior to the incarnation, God the Father exercised this power. That authority was transferred to Christ and Christ alone during his life on earth, and he exercised it "in teaching and in deed, as he walked among us bodily".⁶ Subsequently, the ascending Savior had granted this spiritual capacity to the human jurisdiction of the gathered community of believers, "just then he hung this power and these keys at the side of his most beloved spouse and bride".⁷ The church retains this authority and may use its powers freely until the return of Christ who will render a final judgment. At this later juncture, the Son

---

³ Mabry summarily notes that "the point is, that for Hubmaier, the 'you' was always to be understood in this particular passage as referring to the whole church", *Balthasar Hubmaier's Doctrine of the Church*, 78.

⁴ *Hubmaier*, 412; *Schriften*, 368.

⁵ That Christ is risen is also Hubmaier's greatest argument against transubstantiation, as has previously been outlined. Jesus, Hubmaier reasoned, could not be present at the right hand of the Father and also in the elements of the Supper. On this notion, Rempel observes of Hubmaier: "The heavenly Christ remains an abstraction who is never brought to bear on Hubmaier's theological system. Hubmaier has no Christology explicitly set in a Trinitarian framework, in which the ongoing work of the heavenly Christ is as necessary to the salvation of the world as was his historical mission", Rempel, 69. Thus, the active and present Christ serves no practical purpose either in Hubmaier's Eucharistic thought or in his ecclesiology.

⁶ *Hubmaier*, 411; *Schriften*, 368.

⁷ *Hubmaier*, 411; *Schriften*, 368.

will return the authority and its keys back to the Father.[8] For the present interim time, then, the church, both local and universal, contains and sustains this authority. Thus, while he maintained the Catholic interest in the "power of the keys", Hubmaier radically altered its theological rendering: the keys are not held by the clergy on behalf of God for the world; they are instead enjoyed by the church for all of its members.[9]

On first blush, a significant argument might be built for penance to be considered as a sacramental equivalent to baptism and communion. Indeed, both baptism and the Supper contain elements of penitential confession as integral to Hubmaier's understanding of sacramental response. In baptism, for instance, the neophyte is both admitted to the membership of the church and granted power to forgive sin within the community (based upon John 20:22f: "And when he had said this, [the Lord] breathed on them, and said to them, 'Receive the Holy Spirit. If you forgive the sins of any, they are forgiven; if you retain the sins of any, they are retained").[10] Additionally, Hubmaier's liturgy of the Supper also employed language of penitence, which, Hubmaier reasoned, was undoubtedly associated with Christ's transference of the power of the keys to the community of faith. In this latter case, the entire congregation is led by the priest to its knees to pray penitentially before partaking of the elements.[11]

Repentance then grants to the believing congregation the appropriate attitude and spirit to receive God's grace. Indeed, such is reflective of Hubmaier's *ordo salutis* in which the human is led to conviction and then repentance as the initial steps to salvation, a salvation which culminates within the church granted with the power of the keys. In fact, Hubmaier is quick to point out, God is the one who leads each person to such doubts and crises in order for repentance to take place. Additionally, Hubmaier seemed to stress continually that dominical ceremonies were not salvific. Instead, the Anabaptist reformer placed significance in the inward workings of God on the individual. Penitence, it seems, would characterize this internal exercise. Thus, penitence likely would rise to the mark of a human response to God's grace, which, in other contexts, Hubmaier had adopted as his new definition of sacrament.

Nevertheless, one cannot be quick to presume a third sacrament in Hubmaier's liturgical theology. Upon closer inspection, the student of Hubmaier might find penitence as a qualifier for baptism for initial belief and for communion for sustaining one's faith and continuing one's Christian practice of the faith. The power of the keys allows for the church to grant such forgiveness by making in it the place where the Word is heard, shared and responded to, to

---

[8] See *Hubmaier*, 414-16; *Schriften*, 370-71; and Leth, 113.

[9] Carl M. Leth observes that "Hubmaier assumes a community of baptized believers, committed to the Rule of Christ and guided by the Holy Spirit, . . . will exercise the power of the keys correctly", 114.

[10] *Hubmaier*, 412; *Schriften*, 368.

[11] *Hubmaier*, 394; *Schriften*, 355.

bind and loose on earth that which is in heaven. Penitence, while significant for Hubmaier, still seemed to be the preparatory step for participating in "sacrament" and was not a sacrament unto itself. As cited above, Hubmaier required repentance as each candidate enters into baptism, but the latter act constitutes the first "key" into the portals of salvation viz. the church. Instead, during the response and liturgy of baptism, the first exercise of the key of forgiveness of sins was bestowed upon a believer. Thus, the sacrament of baptism included this key to open the door to the church, its bearer. Second, penitence does not carry an independent outward sign conveying its inward quality. Instead, it serves and depends upon the sacraments of baptism and communion as such representative signs.

The power of keys is then not effectually a "sacrament" but instead grants to the church the ability to carry out such sacraments through the dispensation of God's grace.[12] In its place, the heartfelt confession of a believer enables the "sacrament" to be effective. On the other hand, if one's preliminary penitence is disingenuous, he or she could not depend on an *ex opere operato* character of the rite. As Mabry noted, "the inner experience validated the outer".[13] Thus, the act of confession enables sacrament but is not in itself sacramental. Penance, though spiritually restorative in nature, only partially comprises the sacramental act of a response to God's grace. It prepares the individual for a heartfelt pledge

---

[12] How this actually played out in Hubmaier's theology is not altogether clear. While the church has been given the actual power to forgive sins in principle, Hubmaier typically used language of individual confession before God in Hubmaier's own liturgies. Consequently, the result is obscure and perhaps incongruous. On this point, Hubmaier's Catholic-Anabaptist synthesis probably transcends the dialectical to a full-fledged contradiction. See Mabry, *Balthasar Hubmaier's Doctrine of the Church*, 80-81. The best attempt at marrying these concepts in Hubmaier was in Mabry's later work, *Balthasar Hubmaier's Understanding of Faith*, where Mabry concludes that "Hubmaier believes that Christ did not give to the church the power to forgive sins, but only to announce, or confirm, the pardoning of mercies of God's grace for sin. It will be remembered that God by His grace has already decided to forgive human sins before humans even receive the knowledge that they are sinners, and of their pardoning", 101. While this synthesis is appealing, it does not follow Hubmaier's straightforward declaration: "It follows that the Christian church now has this authority to forgive and to retain sins here on earth until the second coming of the Lord, just as the same Christ also possessed when bodily upon earth", *Hubmaier*, 414; *Schriften*, 370.

[13] Mabry, *Balthasar Hubmaier's Doctrine of the Church*, 79. Interestingly, Mabry also points out the weakness in attempting to apply such a principle to enforce a "believers'" church: "However, if the inner experience could not be validated, the church had no way of knowing whether or not the outer experience was valid, and hence no way of knowing who was really a saint, or who was really in the Kingdom of God", Mabry, *Balthasar Hubmaier's Doctrine of the Church*, 79. This point portrays the difficulty not only of Anabaptism's challenge to reform the church to its purity in the sixteenth century but also the same continued difficulty left to its contemporary free church descendants.

of love which is the true sacrament according to Hubmaier. One might argue for Hubmaier that baptism and the Supper still act as the visible signs of repentance as his liturgy called on each believer to confess his or her sins before participating in either sacrament. If the church is indeed acting as the surrogate authority on earth for Christ who is now in heaven, then the great act of initiation in baptism and the rite and symbol of full participation in the church in the Lord's Supper serve as the culmination of one's true confession. As such, Hubmaier, as Carl Leth has noted, insisted that while not sacramental in itself, the power of the keys is "foundational to the proper understanding and practice of the sacraments."[14]

The Ban

Hubmaier desired for the church to be a disciplined community, a congregation made up of true believers, its entrance safeguarded by the initiation of baptism based only upon one's confession of faith and obligation to lead a life in Christian purity. His Anabaptist church community is continually reminded of its dual obligations to God and congregation before partaking of the Supper through the vows of love (based upon Christ's *mandatum novum* in John 13:34). These two "sacraments" have been outlined extensively in the previous chapters. Yet, the necessity of such positive actions suggests a corollary question as to the course of action for apostatic Christians when they do falter in the faith. From this point, Hubmaier developed a theology of the Christian ban. Here he defined the ban as "a public separation and exclusion of a person from the fellowship of the Christian church because of an offensive sin, from which the person will not refrain, recognized according to the earnest and express command of Christ, decided by a Christian congregation, and publicly proclaimed."[15] Interestingly, he saw a need to outline an orderly instruction for dismissing the unrepentant congregant

> so that the Word of God and the whole Christian church might not be shamed, calumnied and despised, and so that the novices and the weak might not be caused to stumble by [one's] evil example or to be corrupted, be startled, afraid, and might know henceforth better how to protect themselves from sins and vices.[16]

The ban does not take place arbitrarily. Hubmaier saw in Scripture the mandate for Christian discipline based largely upon Matthew 18:15-22. Here, one Christian may admonish a fellow, but wayward, believer initially in private, then in

---

[14] Leth, 114.

[15] *Hubmaier*, 410-11; *Schriften*, 367.

[16] *Hubmaier*, 411; *Schriften*, 367-68.

the presence of two or three witnesses, and finally may bring the apostate before the entire church for reproof and correction. If in all these cases the sinner does not repent or portray a desire to "better his life", then he or she is excluded from the fellowship, worship, and life of the congregation.[17] The ban, then, is not enforced by the community because of sin but because of one's persistence in sin and unwillingness to reconcile with the fellowship of the church.[18]

To the point of this present work, Hubmaier saw such an "orderly and earnest command" as finding its prerogative once again in the power of the keys. These keys, as heretofore outlined, provided the church's authority to forgive sins and brought significantly greater meaning to both sacraments of the Lord's Supper and baptism. On this point, Hubmaier wrote:

> Whoever then understands correctly and fully the authority of the use of the Christian keys, the same will also know well and properly how to speak and write of water baptism and the Supper of Christ, namely, that the water does not save us, nor is Christ bodily inside the bread or the wine. But hitherto we had for a long time lost the keys, the belt, the church, water, wine and bread. Then, when we read in the Bible, our Christian house got a roof over it.[19]

From such a statement, one might readily see the importance of the keys in understanding Hubmaier's approach to church reform. Hubmaier's interpretation of the sacraments was integrally related to his understanding of the church and its potential need for renewal. Here the reader comes to understand more fully the importance Hubmaier placed on the subjective openness of the congregant in responding to God than to any special objective grace dispensed in the elements themselves. It is not Christ's real presence but, antithetically, his real absence which gives the sacraments their proper focus and perspective. The basis for receiving forgiveness comes from the temporal authority of the church, granted by Christ in his ascension. It seems to follow, then, that the proper use of the keys has an association with the sacramental, for, as Leth has said for Hubmaier, the "remission of sins and, ultimately, salvation are necessarily linked to incorporation into this community."[20]

For Hubmaier, the first of the two keys is tied to the baptismal pledge in which the baptizand promises to live within the discipline of the community wherein remission of sins and salvation is found. Thus, baptism serves as the first key, the key of initiation into the covenant community of faith, forgiveness and grace. Yet, while it holds in one hand the key of initiation, the church also always holds fast to the second, the key of excommunication, if it must be em-

---

[17] *Hubmaier*, 410; *Schriften*, 367.

[18] Mabry, *Balthasar Hubmaier's Doctrine of the Church*, 82.

[19] *Hubmaier*, 413; *Schriften*, 369-70.

[20] Leth, 115.

ployed. Hubmaier explained:

> Christ, rather, gives to his church a second key, namely the authority
> to exclude again persons who had been received and admitted into the
> Christian congregation if they should not will to behave in a right and
> Christian way, and to close her doors before them, as he says, 'Whose
> sins you retain, to them they shall stand retained," Matt. 18:18. This
> command and authority Christ strengthened with an oath which he
> spoke in his own name as he said, 'Verily I say to you, all that you
> will bind on earth shall be bound in heaven, and what you will loose
> on earth shall be loosed in heaven.' It follows then that the Christian
> church now has this authority to forgive and to retain sins here on
> earth until the second coming of the Lord.[21]

Christ then granted not only to Peter but also to Christ's bride, the church, the
authority to open and close the portals of heaven. This is accomplished by use
of the two keys, namely forgiveness and fraternal discipline.[22] Yet, the inclusion
or exclusion is never solely by the whims of the church but also and more importantly enacted in accordance with the response of the candidate. If a Christian
genuinely repents, then he or she is eligible for church induction. If a congregant,
in turn, refuses to repent, the church retains the power to exclude. Therefore,
Hubmaier associated not only baptism but also the ban with the covenant of God.
The church constitutes the faithful band of genuine believers who are bound
together and reliant upon one another by their pledge of discipline. This filial
dependence is both supportive and corrective in nature.[23] Such an expression may
precipitate the question of whether Hubmaier would have considered the ban
as a sacrament, or more precisely, as a counter-sacrament. This is particularly
propitious given that both the Lord's Supper and baptism before it also utilized
the divinely granted power of the keys. If the act of binding serves and buttresses
the sacraments previously discussed, would not the work of loosing also qualify
for such status?

To bring further support to this claim, Hubmaier's treatise, *On the Christian
Ban,* not only uses the terminology of the power of the keys coterminously with
how he defines "sacrament" in his other writings, but this instruction for dis-
fellowship was also written simultaneously with his sacramental liturgies for
baptism and the Supper in 1527. It then follows, given all of these details, that
an exploration into the ban's relationship to the sacraments is a worthy endeavor.

One helpful passage in Hubmaier's writings on this subject is from his

---

[21] *Hubmaier,* 414; *Schriften,* 370.

[22] Mabry, *Balthasar Hubmaier's Understanding of Faith,* 101.

[23] Armour observes that Hubmaier's covenantal understanding of the ban transcend-
ed both Luther and Zwingli in its association with the baptismal vow, 44.

Christian Catechism. Herein, Leonhart the tutor asks Hans the student various questions of the faith. At one point, Leonhart inquires by what authority the aforementioned fraternal admonition is performed, and Hans replies that the church "calls him forward and admonishes [the sinner] a third time".[24] Then the two characters have the following exchange:

> *Leonhart*: What if the admonished sinner refused to reform?
> *Hans*: In that case the church has the power and the right to excommunicate and ban him as a perjurer and perfidious.
> *Leonhart*: What is the ban?
> *Hans*: It is an exclusion and separation of such a nature that henceforth Christians may have no fellowship with such a person, either in word, eating, drinking, grinding, baking, or any other form, but treat him as a heathen and publican, i.e., as an offensive, disorderly, and poisonous person, who is shunned so that the whole outward church may not be ill spoken of, shamed, and disgraced by fellowship with him or be corrupted by his evil example, but rather that it will be frightened and filled with fear by this punishment and henceforth die to sin. For as truly as God lives, what the church admits or excludes on earth is also admitted, or excluded from heaven.[25]

Thus, while it serves to aid the straying member to perceive the gravity of sin and amend his or her ways and return to the fold, the ban is also exercised as a deterrent for the sake of strengthening its own fellowship and to protect it from slander or shame.[26] Herein, each congregant is reminded that one is saved in conformity to God's will and by the discipline of the church. Thus, as Hubmaier stated previously, one person's omission serves to strengthen the community against perdition and encourage its desire for absolution, which function as the divine purposes for the keys.

At the same time, however, Hubmaier never himself labeled this observance as "sacramental" as he had with communion and baptism. Instead, the ban simply served as the disciplined response of the church community to one's failure to uphold the principles found in Hubmaier's concept of sacrament: a pledge of love to God and to the community of faith to live righteously in accordance with the Rule of Christ. Hubmaier then powerfully stated the ban's relationship to the sacraments:

> . . . evil persons should be promptly excluded and banned [from the church]: those who become unfaithful, who dishonor the sacraments and perjure, who have not held to their pledge, duty, faithfulness,

---

24 *Hubmaier*, 353; *Schriften*, 316.
25 *Hubmaier*, 353; *Schriften*, 316-17.
26 Mabry, *Balthasar Hubmaier's Doctrine of the Church*, 83.

honor and faith in the Almighty God and his only begotten Son, our
Lord Jesus Christ, also to his most beloved bride the holy general and
Christian church, but have made shipwreck of their faith. . . . All, all,
all of them shall be expelled, writes Paul, who counter to the rule of
Christ, Gal. 6:12, to which they had pledged themselves are leading a
disorderly life.[27]

The ban, then, is placed upon those who did not keep their sacramental vows.
The congregation, which holds the power of the keys in its discipline, actually
exercises part of its sacramental pledge by disciplining the members in order
to maintain the purity of the church. Noted Hubmaier, "Thus once again you
see full well that the admonition and ban does not take place out of hatred, nor
to harm anyone, but out of Christian love".[28] Counter-intuitively, one way the
church maintains its "pledge of love" corporately is to exact its discipline on
wayward members through its divinely-borrowed power of the keys. However,
the role of the keys is never *ex opere operato* to merit or strip someone of the
benefits of salvation, but to open or close the gates of both the Christian community and of heaven to anyone, contingent upon his or her faith and repentance
or declination of the same.[29]

Nevertheless, both in Hubmaier's theology and in later Anabaptist practice,
the ban was never exacted as a necessarily permanent condition. Both Hubmaier
and his radical counterparts left open the possibility of restoration into the fellowship. But this was, again, always dependent upon the inner spirit and outer
willingness of the individual. Interestingly, though, the language used by the
Waldshut reformer for church restoration parallels the sacramental language of
spiritual responses necessary before baptism and communion are administered:

> Once the banned person recognizes himself and his misery, 2 Cor.
> 2:1ff., renounces sin in deed, returns, repents, prays God for grace
> and ameliorates his life, immediately the church shall accept him
> again with great joy and with the authority of the keys given to her
> open up again to him the kingdom of Christ, according to the com-
> mand of Christ: 'What you shall loose on earth shall stand loosed
> in heaven as well,' Matt. 18:18. This should happen not just seven
> times but seventy time seven times, Luke 17:4, i.e., four-hundred-
> ninety times, a number which points to the weeks of years of Daniel,
> Dan. 9:24. This is to give us to understand that as often as a sinner
> genuinely finds remorse and sorrow for his sin, it is forgiven him
> through the suffering of Christ. That is proper repentance and re-

---

[27] *Hubmaier*, 421; *Schriften, 375.*

[28] *Hubmaier*, 421; *Schriften, 375.*

[29] Mabry, *Balthasar Hubmaier's Understanding of Faith*, 100.

morse over sin: that one renounces that same sin in deed and henceforth flees, sets aside, and avoids everything whereby he might again
be attracted and drawn again into sin. . . .[30]

Thus, the door inexorably remains open for re-entrance into the community and restoration to its sustaining grace viz. communion. In this way, the church could be the covenantal community, the body of Christ and the nucleus of the king-dom while still understanding itself as a human institution which copes with its foibles and tensions.[31] The harshest of disciplines still does not exclude the pos-sibility of subsequent redemption and inclusion. The key that opens the door in baptism now reopens the door in restoration. In his excellent book, *The Theology of Anabaptism*, Robert Friedmann portrays this potential cycle pictographically

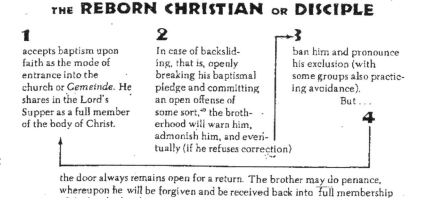

THE **REBORN CHRISTIAN** OR **DISCIPLE**

1

accepts baptism upon
faith as the mode of
entrance into the
church or *Gemeinde*. He
shares in the Lord's
Supper as a full member
of the body of Christ.

2

In case of backslid-
ing, that is, openly
breaking his baptismal
pledge and committing
an open offense of
some sort,[49] the broth-
erhood will warn him,
admonish him, and even-
tually (if he refuses correction)

3

ban him and pronounce
his exclusion (with
some groups also practic-
ing avoidance).
But . . .

4

the door always remains open for a return. The brother may do penance,
whereupon he will be forgiven and be received back into full membership
of the brotherhood.[41]

Hubmaier compared this action of renewal by the church to that of the father to the prodigal son in Jesus' well-known parable. The ban and restoration to good standing then correlate to the sacramental pledges of communion and of baptism, the ban of course relating negatively while Christian restoration associates itself positively. The first key of initiation, between the church's two keys, plays such a vital role in Hubmaier's ecclesiology that its removal or distortion disrupts and destroys the Christian church altogether. Hubmaier wrote:

---

[30] *Hubmaier*, 423-24; *Schriften*, 377.

[31] Robert Friedmann, *The Theology of Anabaptism: An Interpretation* (Scottdale: Herald Press, 1973), 126.

[32] Friedmann, 125. This diagram is used with permission by Wipf and Stock publish-ers.

> Where water baptism in accord with Christ's institution is not reestablished and practiced one does not know who is a brother or sister, there is no church, no brotherly discipline or reproof, no ban, no Supper, nor anything that resembles the Christian stance and nature.[33]

Baptism, as the initiating sacrament, then serves as the keystone for Hubmaier's visible church. The Supper is the sacrament which sustains the baptismal pledge through its reiteration. But the ban merely supports the two sacraments by enforcing the discipline of their associated pledges. Thus, even though it seems to be founded on the same authority, utilizes the same keys and finds its resolution through the same means of penitence, Christian discipline is never labeled by Hubmaier as a "sacrament" and is never accompanied by its own representative sign, as is the case with Eucharist and baptism. One is restored by returning to her baptismal obligations. The re-entrance of the prodigal is celebrated by the community of faith in the same way and through the same theological avenues as Hubmaier's fully developed and demarcated "sacraments". Hubmaier notes that the penitent person "renounces sin in deed, . . . repents, prays God for grace", just as he would do in preparing for baptism or the Supper.[34] The restoration of the wayward Anabaptist through Christian discipline then is not a sacrament in itself but is based upon the sacramental pledge made in baptism and reaffirmed in the Supper.

Preaching

Even though there is little evidence for a concept of preaching as sacrament in Hubmaier's theology, there is nevertheless some association between the act of preaching and the sacraments themselves. Hubmaier spoke and wrote powerfully about the work of preaching:

> [If the] clear and holy Word of God against the images and idols in the Old and New Testaments is earnestly and regularly proclaimed to the people, . . . its strength and power will be put to use and in time will pull down all the images. It is impossible that the Word of God be preached and bring forth no fruit or works in those who hear, for God Himself has sent it forth.[35]

---

[33] *Hubmaier*, 354; *Schriften*, 317.

[34] *Hubmaier*, 423-24; *Schriften*, 377

[35] From Hubmaier's 1522 *Von Klarheit und Gewissheit des Wortes Gottes*, here cited in Armour, *Anabaptist Baptism*, 20.

While the church then carries out its discipleship, God saves, strengthens and reforms through the proclamation of the divine Word. Through this homiletical action, the Spirit of God, who is God's current earthly presence, works within humanity. God's proclamation occurs through both preaching and through the "word symbols" of the ordinances of baptism and communion:

> Accordingly, one should always pay more attention and that more seriously to the things signified by the word symbols than to the symbols themselves. For outside of their signifying, the same mean nothing and are in vain. But the Spirit makes us alive, and the Spirit comes with the Word which then assures the human being of eternal life, as the bread and wine are word symbols of his love.[36]

If the Spirit of God arrives in the hearts of humanity through the Word, and if that Word is both preached and demonstrated symbolically through the ordinances, it is worthy to investigate whether preaching should also be considered on the level of sacrament in Hubmaier's thought.

Following the ascension of Christ, Hubmaier maintained, God assigned to the Spirit the role of life-giving. The Spirit reminds and grants to each believer the promise of God's forgiveness of sins. The Spirit's work is internal, a prerequisite for true sacrament to take place. The preached Word is the Spirit's instrument for repentance, conversion and renewal. Thus, further buttressing his rejection of any *ex opere operato* work in the sacraments, Hubmaier required the inner-workings of the Holy Ghost before any outer ceremony might take place.[37] From this standpoint, Rempel argues that "here the word, without any relationship to the elements, functions sacramentally as the outward sign and means of an inward reality."[38]

At the same time, however, such an understanding once again falls under the rubric of a traditional definition of sacrament as a means or sign of grace and is not wholly consistent with Hubmaier's own significant redefinition. For Hub-

---

[36] *Hubmaier*, 75; *Schriften*, 103. From this point, twentieth century theologian Karl Barth would echo a similar theme early in his *Church Dogmatics*: "Proclamation of the basis of the promise which has been laid once and for all, and therefore proclamation in the form of symbolic action, had to be and to remain essential for [the Reformers]. But this proclamation presupposes that the other, namely, repetition of the biblical promise, is taking place. The former must exist for the sake of the latter, and therefore the sacrament for the sake of preaching, not *vice versa*. Hence not the sacrament alone nor preaching alone, nor yet, to speak meticulously, preaching and the sacrament in double track, but preaching with the sacrament, with the visible act that confirms human speech as God's act, is the constitutive element, the perspicuous centre of the Church's life." See Barth, *Church Dogmatics: The Doctrine of the Word of God*, I.I (Edinburgh: T&T Clark, 1975), 70.

[37] *Hubmaier*, 100-101; *Schriften*, 122.

[38] Rempel, *The Lord's Supper in Anabaptism*, 49.

maier, the sacraments are not the salvific workings of God and signs of his grace directly, though they may remind and assure believers of their forgiveness.[39] Instead, Hubmaier more consistently viewed sacraments as human pledges and responses to that divine intervention that a Christian has received the gospel and will live it out. Sacraments, then, are the fruits of proclamation, the results of the Spirit's workmanship. At the same time, however, proclamation must take place for such sacraments to be valid: "Where there is no proclamation of the word, there is no mass [and no sacraments]".[40] Therefore, Hubmaier required that the Word be proclaimed before both baptism and the Supper are carried out,[41] even as the Word is once again proclaimed through such word symbols.[42] For as Hubmaier patently wrote in the context of his Eucharistic theology: "As often as such commemoration is held, the death of the Lord shall be proclaimed in the tongue of every land. Here all dumb masses fall on one heap."[43]

Faith and the Church

Throughout his Anabaptist life and writings, Hubmaier repeatedly referred to the church as the body of Christ on earth. Modern scholars have made various assertions that the church and its discipleship were central to all of Anabaptist theology.[44] The importance of restoring a community of true believers, then, was extremely important to both Hubmaier and the entire Anabaptist movement of the sixteenth century. Hubmaier, we have seen, understood the church as the possessor of the power of the keys and the administrator of the sacraments. Its community is made up of all who have submitted to the Rule of Christ and its fraternal discipline.

In his *Christian Catechism* Hubmaier wrote:

> The church is sometimes understood to include all the people who

---

[39] See Zwingli, *Huldreich Zwingli's sämtliche Werke* (eds. E. Egli and G. Finster; Leipzig: M. Heinius Nachfolger, 1904), II, 786.

[40] Zwingli, *Huldreich Zwingli's sämtliche Werke* II, 786-787.

[41] *Hubmaier*, 394; *Schriften*, 355-56.

[42] *Hubmaier*, 74; *Schriften*, 102.

[43] *Hubmaier*, 33; *Schriften*, 73.

[44] Franklin H. Littell and Eddie Mabry proposed the former while Harold S. Bender understood the latter. Littell argued that "the dominant theme in the thinking of the mainline Anabaptists was the recovery of the life and virtue of the Early Church." Mabry argued: "The Anabaptist's understanding of the church stood behind all their [sic.] beliefs and practices." See Littell, *The Anabaptist View of the Church: A Study in the Origins of Sectarian Protestantism* (Boston: Starr King Press, 1958), 79; Mabry, *Balthasar Hubmaier's Doctrine of the Church*, 69; and Bender, "The Anabaptist Theology of Discipleship", *MQR* XXIII (1950), 26.

are gathered and united in one God, one Lord, one faith, and one
baptism, and have confessed this faith with their mouths, wherever
they may be on earth. This, then, is the universal Christian corporeal church and fellowship of the saints, assembled only in the Spirit
of God. . . . At other times the church is understood to mean each
separate and outward meeting assembly or parish membership that is
under one shepherd or bishop and assembles bodily for instruction,
for baptism and the Lord's Supper. The church as daughter has the
same power to bind and to loose on earth as the universal church, her
mother, when she uses the keys according to the command of Christ,
her spouse and husband.[45]

In this fascinating passage, Hubmaier revealed his belief that the church is both
local and universal. While the development of much of Hubmaier's ecclesiology transcends the perimeters of this narrow study of his sacraments, it is worth
noting, however, that Hubmaier understood each congregation as holding and
maintaining the right to exercise the divinely-given power of the keys. At the
same time, Hubmaier emphasized an unusual dialectic within Anabaptism with
his comprehension of a visible, yet universal church.[46] One's confession of faith
was not merely relegated to the realm of figure of speech but had to be practiced
within a local community, a microcosm of God's universal fellowship of the
saints. Thus, the importance of faith, discipleship and church were all integral to
the genuine church that Hubmaier's Anabaptism pursued.

Beyond this significant point, Hubmaier often intimated that willing participation through faith in church was the heart of Christian ethics. Conversely, his
writings continued to reflect his medieval training by maintaining the unremit-
ting Catholic argument that outside of the church there was no salvation.[47] Both
the universal and local church maintained the keys which provided necessary
absolution.

What Hubmaier meant by these statements, of course, varied somewhat
from Aquinas, who viewed those outside the church as not having access to the
means of grace through the sacraments.[48] For Hubmaier, the church supplied
both the witnesses for one's initiatory pledge and the necessary covenantal recipients in one's continued pledge of love, the requisite participants in the sac-

---

[45] *Hubmaier*, 351-52; *Schriften*, 315.

[46] In contradistinction to Hubmaier, Estep notes of Anabaptism in general: "The thrust
of Anabaptist ecclesiology was toward the implementation in history of the visible church.
Anabaptism was relatively unconcerned with the idea of the universal, invisible church."
While Estep points out that the concept of a universal church is not completely foreign to
Anabaptism, he argues that "Hubmaier's treatment of the idea is more extensive than that
of most other Anabaptists", *The Anabaptist Story*, 239-40.

[47] *Hubmaier*, 414; *Schriften*, 370.

[48] See Thomas Aquinas, *Catechetical Instructions* (trans. Joseph B. Collins; New
York: Joseph F. Wagner, 1939), art. 10.

raments of baptism and communion respectively. By submitting oneself as faithful to such vows, a Christian conformed to the will of God and the discipline of the fellowship. Thus, while Hubmaier's conception of "sacrament" differed significantly from the Thomistic tradition, the Waldshut reformer's thought resembled Catholic ecclesiology, Erasmus in particular, more than Zwinglian or Lutheran perceptions of the church regarding his continued emphases on the church's saving effects and the power of the keys based on Matthew 16:18-19.

Entering the church through one's baptismal vow, the neophyte is admitted to the "communion of saints" and the "brotherhood of many righteous and believing men, who unanimously confess one Lord, one God, one faith, and one baptism."[49] Additionally, Hubmaier compared this entry to the eight figures aboard Noah's ark, "saved through water" and from the wrath of God's judgment.[50]

Baptism enrolls the believer into the universal church, an action which is salvific:

> Water baptism is given for the forgiveness of sins, Acts 2:38; I Peter 3:21. . . . Therefore, as much as the communion of God the Father, and of the Son, and of the Holy Spirit, yea, also the communion of all the heavenly host and the entire Christian church, and also as much as the forgiveness of sins is important to a person, so much also is water baptism through which he enters and which is embodied in the universal church, *outside of which there is no salvation.*[51]

Significantly, this is no *ex opere operato* divine work but occurs through one's confession of faith: "This outward confession is what makes a church, and not faith alone. . . . And although faith alone makes righteous, it does not alone give salvation".[52] Thus baptism and the Supper require the church's presence and authority, in addition to the profession of one's own faith, in order for salvation to take effect. Consequently, because of its power of the keys, the church of Christ is the only place wherein one may find forgiveness and redemption.[53]

During the incarnation, Jesus maintained the authority to save and condemn. Now in his absence, the church prolongs the life of Christ as his surrogate body who acts in this way in his place. While the Spirit is at work liberating souls to follow, human converts must in turn find entry into Christ's continually incarnate body of the gathered believers. On this point Rempel notes of Hubmaier's church that "because it is composed only of believers, it is literally the embod-

---

[49] *Hubmaier*, 238; *Schriften*, 218.

[50] *Hubmaier*, 117; *Schriften*, 136.

[51] *Hubmaier*, 370-71 [italics mine]; *Schriften*, 335.

[52] *Hubmaier*, 352; *Schriften*, 316.

[53] Armour, *Anabaptist Baptism*, 46.

iment of faith and love. This is the realm of spirit within history. Only spirit can mediate grace. Therefore, ceremonies, which are material but not personal entities, cannot be means of grace."[54] Such strong ecclesio-centrism suggests the possibility of the church, in some sense, as ontologically serving as the essential sacramental reality of the world and the Christian life.[55] While the sacraments utilized the signs of water, bread and wine, the church serves as the *res* to which the signs referred. The covenant community was the ongoing incarnational reality in the world. Christ's radically real absence from this present world allowed for the visible and universal church to take on this meaning. Hubmaier made this point emphatically:

> For he [Christ] is with her [the church] himself by his grace until the end of the world, Matt. 28:20, although bodily he has ascended into heaven where he sits at the right hand of his heavenly Father there in heaven, Mark 16:19; Acts 1:9. Yea, it was in heaven that Stephen saw him; there he sits bodily according to his humanity. He has a particular place 'in heaven, in heaven' and not everywhere, as deity is omnipresent. Yea, neither in the bread nor in the wine nor in other creatures.[56]

Instead, the church serves as Christ's real and incarnate presence on earth. Through its pledges of faith to God and love for one another, the church becomes the medium for sacrament to take place. "Only in a lingering way, which was to be gradually displaced", Rempel observed, "did the Supper [or baptism] continue to be an immediate sign of Christ."[57] The church, in Christ's place, became the spiritual intersection between God and humanity and presented itself as the locality for sacramental covenant to be carried out.

The congregation of believers was the fellowship of the faithful. Hubmaier, like his Anabaptist counterparts, did not divorce faith from ethics. Those who legitimately came to faith in Christ would seek to become a part of his body. One's outward profession of faith in baptism and continued promise to love and live ethically in communion became its touchstones. The sacramental pledges served as the necessary outward confessions of the faithful. Hubmaier wrote in his catechism, then, that the church was built

on the oral confession of faith that Jesus is the Christ, the Son of the

---

[54] Rempel, *The Lord's Supper in Anabaptism*, 83.

[55] Rempel suggests as much for Hubmaier. See Rempel, *The Lord's Supper in Anabaptism*, 85.

[56] *Hubmaier*, 414-15; *Schriften*, 370. Hubmaier parenthetically argued here that "Christ is seated in heaven and not in the fly cupboards", and thus Hubmaier mocked the Catholic use of such profane places to store and protect the supposedly consecrated host.

[57] Rempel, *The Lord's Supper in Anabaptism*, 53.

living God. This outward confession is what makes a church, and not faith alone; for the church that has the power to bind and loose is outward and corporeal, not theoretical, and faith is inward. And although faith alone makes righteous, it does not alone give salvation, for it must be accompanied by public confession.[58]

Faithful participation and confession within the local congregation, with public profession in one's baptism and continued affirmation of faith in communion, are not discretionary activities for Hubmaier's understanding of the genuine believer. These are the hallmarks of Christian obedience and are the church's redemptive necessities.[59] Hubmaier continued to argue that the power of the keys granted the church its salvific authority, and thus the elements themselves carried no sacred ontological effects.[60] One's faith, Hubmaier maintained, would compel the Christian to such action, response and belonging.

Conclusion

The sacramental theology of Balthasar Hubmaier cannot be viewed in a vacuum, isolated from his rest of his thought. While he seemed to place more emphasis on the Supper and baptism in his extant writings, Hubmaier was often writing apologetic works in response to his theological adversaries. The positive outcome of that circumstance is that five centuries later, scholars, clergy and laity may still comb through Hubmaier's prolific works related to these church practices. The unfortunate consequence, though, is that such time of exhaustive defense of the basics of Anabaptism's peculiar church practices may have robbed Anabaptism's greatest theologian of a more systematic presentation of his ecclesiology, Christology and overarching theology.[61] Naturally, to

---

[58] *Hubmaier*, 352; *Schriften*, 315-16.

[59] Pipkin, "The Baptismal Theology of Balthasar Hubmaier", 47.

[60] Armour, *Anabaptist Baptism*, 46.

[61] Robert Macoskey notes "that Hübmaier left no systematic theology behind him is neither proof of his lack of interest in system nor evidence that he lacked ability in this field. Philosophical hairsplitting had been the major interest of his undergraduate experience. He was trained to confound debate opponents with every subtlety of dialectic. He would not have retained the leadership of the debate fraternity at the University of Freiburg if he had been inept at treading his way through elaborate philosophical and theological arguments. Rules learned there could have been applied to this new interest. He might have lived longer and made a greater contribution to the doctrinal literature of the Reformation had he taken this course. Instead, he determined that plain language was needed. When people understood the naked truths of a vital faith, there would be time to put on the clothes of systematic theology". See Macoskey, "The Contemporary Relevance of Balthasar Hubmaier's Concept of the Church", *Foundation* 6 (April 1963), 105.

require of Hubmaier such methodizing would have been anachronistic. Nevertheless, had not this great Anabaptist leader been hunted by politicians and debated by theologians both Catholic and Protestant, his complete thought might have been more thoroughly elaborated and understood.

This chapter has attempted to create cohesion and to assess the trajectory of Hubmaier's theology in many areas conjoined with and related to his sacramental thought. In an attempt to be thorough of this facet of Hubmaier's reflections, this study has, at times, attempted to push Hubmaier to the limit of Anabaptist cogitation by suggesting the potential for other so-called "sacraments" within his ecclesiology. Subsequently, we have seen how penance comes as the prerequisite of one's sacramental pledge, the power of the keys as the necessary authority for the church to evaluate one's faith, the ban as the denial of the backslider from the church's sanctifying work, restoration as acceptance of the repentant similar to the initiation of the neophyte, preaching as the accompaniment and explication of the church's work, faith as the prerequisite and necessity for one's confession to be valid, and the church as the embodiment and witness to the sacramental pledges of each Christian to one another.

All of these aspects of Hubmaier's thought at least border his understanding of "sacrament". Some serve as integral characteristics within his conceptualization of sacramental covenant and even as the building blocks upon which the edifice of his sacraments are built. Yet none of these new suggestions encompasses all the necessary elements of Hubmaier's radical redefinition of "sacrament" to stand as an equal and equivalent partner along side the Lord's Supper and baptism. While Hubmaier mirrored his Protestant contemporaries by maintaining the same two ordinances, as one scholar rightly notes, "Hubmaier's engagement with the Bible moves him farther and farther from traditional sacramental language toward new terms and concepts."[62]

Though very early in his career as a dissident theologian, he defined sacrament as an "outward, visible sign and seal through which we are assured completely of the forgiveness of our sins",[63] Hubmaier later honed and developed his sacramental thought as tied less to the objective promise of God and more directly to the subjective promise of humans. They became for the mature Hubmaier the "commitment by oath and a pledge given by the hand" in response to God's grace.[64] Sacraments then were one's ethical response in Christian obedience to God's saving action. While faith, which is a gift of God, still justifies, the subjective, human response is still requisite for sanctification. Thus the baptismal commitment and the communal pledge of love serve as the true sacraments of the church.[65]

With the possible exception made with the "baptism by blood" in which one

---

[62] Rempel, *The Lord's Supper in Anabaptism*, 63.

[63] Zwingli, *Huldreich Zwingli's sämtliche Werke* II, 786.

[64] *Hubmaier*, 391; *Schriften*, 352.

[65] *Hubmaier*, 391; *Schriften*, 352.

is gruesomely outwardly anointed by one's own internal fluids, (and it is debatable whether this was merely an allusion to or a sacramental replacement for extreme unction and to what degree "baptism by blood" is merely another form of baptismal initiation or segregated as its own sacramental event), no other act other than baptism and the Supper contains all the necessary elements (both responses to faith and corresponding signs) to qualify within Hubmaier's definition of "sacrament". Nevertheless, this is not in any way to diminish these other acts of faith, but only to see them as adjunctive to and supportive of the integral work and worship of the church. Consequently, while the actions and ceremonies outlined in this chapter attend to and buttress one's covenantal pledge of love, they are not self-supportive and sufficient vows in themselves for Hubmaier.

Though radical in his sacramental thought, Hubmaier in no way "spiritualized" the rites of the faith as only internal commitments. Instead, one's "real internal and intensive hunger and thirst" for God must equate to one's outward action, and vice versa.[66] The outward sign must correspond with the inner spirit for a sacrament to be effectual in salvation and witness. As such, Hubmaier's sacramentality encompassed a voluntary response and pledge before God and the community, accompanied by a sign which corresponded to the vow taken. Through such a public means and before the company of the saints in Hubmaier's congregations would Christians find their pledges to be sacramental.

---

[66] *Hubmaier*, 333; *Schriften*, 301.

CHAPTER 5

The Contemporary Relevance and Influence of Hubmaier's Sacramental Thought

One would be hard-pressed not only to answer the question of Hubmaier's modern influence but even his import within the sixteenth century, not to mention among the Anabaptists.[1] Though the Reformed movement might look to Knox and Calvin, Methodists to the Wesleys, and Mennonites to Menno Simons, no one group today points directly to Balthasar Hubmaier as the "father" or founder of its own Christian tradition. Perhaps it is true that Hubmaier had no direct theological descendants.[2] If this is the case, then Robert Macoskey has rightly stated that

---

[1] Menno Simons, the most prolific writer and greatest leader of any subsequent generation of Anabaptists, only makes mention of Hubmaier once in his writings and, in that case, only indirectly by referring to Oecolampadius' correspondence with Balthasar. Nevertheless, the degree of Hubmaier's influence on Menno or any other Anabaptist leader in subsequent years is unclear. See Menno Simons, *The Complete Writings of Menno Simons* (Scottdale: Herald Press, 1956), 695.

[2] A close reading of Anabaptist history indicates Hans (Johannes) Spittelmaier as Hubmaier's successor in Nikolsburg. While Spittelmaier led the Reform Party to maintain its union with the civil authorities and continued the magisterial Anabaptist reformation which Hubmaier initiated, the Party seemed at some juncture to fade from history. Thus, Hubmaier's continuing influence, particularly in terms of his sacramental thought, seems nebulous.

At the same time, however, one cannot discount the scholarship also relating to Hubmaier's influence among the Hutterite fellowship in South Germany, particularly among those disciples of Peter Riedemann. Here, Johann Loserth argues that Riedemann's writings echo all the major themes of Hubmaier, particularly regarding the church and its sacraments. This shall be developed later in this chapter. For the time being, however, we shall observe that Franz Heimann has since argued that Riedemann also portrayed a great deal of independence on these issues, concluding that "though Riedemann seems to be influenced, to a certain extent, by these ideas, there can be no question that the Hutterite brotherhood would not adopt Hubmaier's concept of the church unchanged." See Loserth, "Der Communismus der mährischen Wiedertäufer", in *Archiv für* österr. *Geschichte*, LXXXI (Wien: Adolf Holzhausen, 1894), 226; and Heimann, "The Hutterite Doctrines of Church and Common Life, A Study of Peter Riedemann's Confession of Faith of 1540", *MQR*, XXVI (1952), pt. 1, 32f; pt. 2, 143.

an obscurity compounded by four and a half [now nearly five] centuries of neglect is all that visibly remains of the Hübmaier legacy today. A name which rang loudly in the ears of his contemporaries is now nothing more than a faint echo to be heard by those whose sensitivities are tuned to this Reformation countermelody.[3]

It could be rationalized that Hubmaier had no one to carry on the Hubmaierian torch because his Anabaptist flame, while flickering brightly during its time, was unfortunately also so short-lived. Perhaps had he led a full and productive life, as did his contemporary in Luther or his Anabaptist successor in Menno Simons the following generation, then Hubmaier's view of the church might have established a greater legacy. The fancies of the hypothetical aside, the reality that such a gifted theologian left such a vacuum is particularly striking, even accounting for his and his wife's ghastly executions.

One might wonder, then, why anyone would undertake such an analytical study as this present work beyond its pedantic value. Yet a study not only into the history of the sacramental thought of this figure but also into its abiding historiography within the Christian faith might be both interesting to and revealing of those by whom Hubmaier was revered and of those who might, even unwittingly, recommence Hubmaier's sacramental reasoning, if only typologically.

Mennonites and Other Modern Anabaptists[4]

Mennonites, Amish, and Hutterites are traditionally seen as among the most direct inheritors of Anabaptism.[5] Menno Simons, after whom the Mennonites are named, served as Dutch Anabaptism's early organizer, laying the groundwork for the continuing Anabaptist community in Holland and north Germany.

---

[3] Macoskey, "Contemporary Relevance of Balthasar Hubmaier's Concept of the Church", *Foundations* 6 (April 1963), 102.

[4] Much of the substance of this section is taken from the forthcoming book chapter by Brian C. Brewer, "Anabaptist Sacramentalism and Its Contemporary Appropriation", in *Marginal or Mainstream?: Anabaptists, Mennonites and Modernity in European Society* (eds. Mark Jantzen and Mary Sprunger; Cornelius H. Wedel Historical Series; North Newton: Bethel College, 2011).

[5] Donald B. Kraybill, *Who are the Anabaptists?: Amish, Brethren, Hutterites, and Mennonites* (Scottdale: Herald Press, 2003), 7. Kraybill lists the Brethren (originally known as German Baptist Brethren) in addition to these other three groups, but he notes: "Strictly speaking, the Brethren are not an organic offshoot of sixteenth-century Anabaptism", 11. For further study of modern Anabaptists in connection with their sixteenth century roots, see Donald B. Kraybill and Carl Desportes Bowman, *On the Backroad to Heaven: Old Order Hutterites, Mennonites, Amish, and Brethren* (Baltimore: Johns Hopkins University Press, 2001), 1-19.

From this sect came offshoots in the Waterlanders in 1557 and the Amish in 1693. Mennonites have spread their influence well beyond a corner in mainland Europe now throughout the continent, to North America, and beyond.

Interestingly, during a dialogue and exchange of papers between Mennonites and representatives of the Reformed tradition, Marlin E. Miller explained the modern Mennonite and Anabaptist traditions' abandonment of the term "sacrament":

> Although the various Mennonite traditions have frequently differed on the theological categories which they have used to speak about baptism, they have shared a common rejection of traditional sacramental understandings and practice. During the last three centuries this common stance has usually included a strong preference for an alternative theological vocabulary as well. Terms such as 'ordinance,' 'sign,' and 'symbol' have become commonplace and have almost entirely replaced the concept of sacrament.[6]

At the same time, Marlin acknowledged that the overall rejection of such terminology was not always the case within the Anabaptist tradition and that "early reinterpretation of sacrament is instructive for understanding the core convictions regarding baptism in the Mennonite traditions and for evaluating the theological validity of their formulations."[7] Through such an admission, Miller turned to the writings of Pilgram Marpeck and Balthasar Hubmaier. Both Marpeck and Hubmaier allowed for the term "sacrament" to abide in their theologies as each became Anabaptist, yet they reinterpreted its meaning by utilizing classical philology in seeking the etymology of the word from the Latin as a "covenant" or "solemn pledge". Thus, baptism (and inherently the Lord's Supper) became means for public commitment of faith and discipleship.

Like Hubmaier, Marpeck then argued for something more substantial than a purely sacramentarian or Zwinglian view of the ordinances. In his writing entitled, "What the Word Sacrament Really Means and is", Marpeck explained:

> Sacrament is a Latin word derived from *sacer, sacra, sacrum,* and it means holy . . . . Sacrament refers to anything done in connection with an oath or a similar obligation, and refers to an event that is special and holy or a work that has that kind of connotation; similarly, the knight commits himself to serve his lord by the raising of a finger in battle where, on his honor and with his oath, he commits himself not to yield in combat. *Now, the raising of his finger is not the battle, nor a fight, nor endurance, nor is it victory; the action is a covenant, made in the firm hope that, according to the command*

---

[6] Marlin E. Miller, "Baptism in the Mennonite Tradition", *MQR* 64 (July 1990), 240.
[7] Miller, 240.

> *and the desire of his Lord, he will diligently attack the enemy of his*
> *Lord, even risking his life until death.*[8]

Likewise, Marpeck likened the sacraments to the probable response of a person upon receiving a gift. The recipient would likely return thanks to the giver through some meaningful, demonstrable action. For Marpeck, then, the "sacrament is not to be understood as a single essential thing, but only as the act that is carried out. If the act is carried out with an oath or a similar commitment, then it can be called a sacrament."[9]

What is important about Marpeck's comments is that they demonstrate a continuation of sacramental thought first formulated by Hubmaier for Anabaptism, a sacramentalism which perceives the ordinances as more than rites which simply follow divine commands or carry out symbolic actions. As Timothy Reardon notes of Marpeck's theology: "Sacrament is instead an incarnational act where the church lives as Christ on earth: first, in the action of baptism, and subsequently, in the life of baptism. Sacrament itself is a meeting of the divine and creation, the pinnacle of which is accomplished in the incarnation of Christ."[10] The sacraments act as witnesses to what God has already accomplished in the heart of the new Christian and in her congregation. Marpeck's use of the word "witness" then is not as a passive event but as a kinetic occurrence which necessitates the participation of the Christian and his church. These actions become the incarnational reality when believers consciously and wholeheartedly partake in them. This new, Anabaptist approach would, controversially but understandably, preclude young children from sacramental participation because they were incapable of manifesting and articulating their beliefs in God and acquiescing to the church's discipline.[11]

Marpeck refers to this sacramentalism as "embodied action", understanding baptism as a Christian's pledge to follow Christ and to join in Christ's suffering and the Supper as the corporate recommitment to the baptismal promise. Christians spiritually encounter the Holy Spirit in the sacraments through the co-witnessing signs of the inner reality. However, such action does not happen mechanically. The elements must be received in faith, as the Spirit works within each person, for the ordinance to be a genuine "sacrament" as a co-witness to the Spirit's work. Marpeck then concluded,

> Thus you can see how both baptism and the Lord's Supper are
> called sacraments, namely, because both of them take place with a

---

[8] Pilgram Marpeck, *The Writings of Pilgram Marpeck* (Transl. and eds, William Klassen and Walter Klaassen; Scottdale: Herald Press, 1978), 169 [editor's italics].

[9] Marpeck, 170.

[10] Timothy W. Reardon, "Pilgram Marpeck's Sacramental Theology: Based on His Confession of 1532", *MQR* 83 (April 2009), 294-95.

[11] Readon, 311-13.

commitment and sanctification, which is actually what a sacrament is. For merely to plunge somebody into water or to baptize them is no sacrament. You must baptize in such a manner that the one who is baptized dies to his sins in a sincere way and in the power of a living faith in Christ. From henceforth, he commits himself to a new life, and only then is baptism a true sacrament, that is, when the content and action of baptism happens with the commitment to a holy covenant. It is the same way with the Lord's Supper.[12]

Marpeck, along with Hubmaier, provides the believers' church with another appropriation of Anabaptist sacramentalism in the Swiss and South German Anabaptist context. Rejecting the Catholic notion of the sacraments as effecting salvation in and of themselves *ex opere operato*, the Anabaptist sacramentalism that developed after Hubmaier also rejected both the popular Spiritualism that diminished the importance of outward ceremonies and even the Zwinglian idea of the bread, wine and water as merely symbols. The elements were not effective without the reception of faith. For Marpeck, the Anabaptist congregation was obligated to practice the ordinances in order to experience their co-witnessing power through the Holy Spirit.

Moreover, what is surprising to many contemporary Anabaptist historians is that this new understanding of sixteenth century Anabaptist sacramentalism was not limited to Hubmaier amd Marpeck, or even Swiss and South German Anabaptism. In the decade following Hubmaier's death a similar sacramental theology was mirrored by many Dutch Anabaptists, most particularly their greatest early theologians Dirk Philips (1504-1568) and Menno Simons (1496-1561). Though the Dutch Anabaptists are often regarded as sacramentarian (i.e., they regarded the ordinances as symbolic only), a closer investigation into Philips' and Simons' early thought reveals a more moderating and theologically nuanced sacramentalism.

Anabaptism in Holland may well have drifted towards extremism without firm leadership. However, Obbe and Dirk Philips joined Menno Simons to influence the Dutch towards a moderate Anabaptism in order to sustain the movement and avert its trajectory toward becoming theologically peripheral. Complementing his brother's gifts for organization, Dirk Philips provided significant theological guidance for the movement.[13] Interestingly, Dirk differentiated somewhat between the terms "ordinance" and "sacrament."[14] Along with

---

[12] Marpeck, 171-72.

[13] Cornelius J. Dyck, *An Introduction to Mennonite History*, 3rd ed. (Scottdale: Herald Press, 1993), 101.

[14] For a fuller explanation of this differentiation between "ordinance" and "sacrament" in Dirk Philips' and Menno Simons' writings, see William Echard Keeney, *The Development of Dutch Anabaptist Thought and Practice from 1539-1564* (Nieuwkoop: B. de Graaf, 1968), 74.

the two sacraments of baptism and the Supper, Dirk listed general "ordinances" by which a believer can know Christ: ordination, footwashing, church discipline, brotherly love (the new law), and the mandate to keep the commandments of Christ. Moreover, regarding church ceremonies, Dirk demarcated baptism and the Lord's Supper as "sacramental signs" which direct the believer to "the true and only [real] sign of grace" in Christ Jesus. Dirk further explained:

> Thus Christ fulfills in us what the sacraments signify. Therefore, whenever we utilize or receive the external signs of baptism and the Lord's Supper, we look not primarily upon the external sign but upon Jesus Christ himself, 'from whose fullness we have all received grace upon grace.'[15]

In other words, Dirk established that the sacraments represented externally what God granted internally.[16] While the other four "ordinances" represent the horizontal relationship between believers in fellowship, that Dirk utilized the term "sacrament" for the other two ordinances seems to underscore their special status in the vertical, divine-human encounter. Although Dirk referred to them as sacramental signs, these signs were nevertheless still tethered to the work of the Spirit. As William Keeney wrote of both Dirk Philips and Menno Simon's sacramentalism:

> though they treated the sacraments as signs or symbols, it is incorrect to say that to them they were "only" or "merely" signs and symbols. The sacraments were closely correlated with the spiritual reality or true being which must support or sustain the outward or external expression. Menno and Dirk's tendency to look upon the commands of Christ as positive law and their reaction against any form of sacramentarianism may obscure the fact that their view was dynamic and not static or formal. Nevertheless, their view of the sacraments had a certain mystical quality. . . .[17]

Just as Simon's contributions to Anabaptist sacramentalism mirrored the thoughts of his friend and colleague, Dirk Philips, Menno's notion of sacrament was also congruent with Hubmaier's and Marpeck's understanding. Menno often defined the sacraments as human responses to God's grace and, like the Swiss and South German Anabaptists previously outlined, saw baptism and the Supper as pledges to God and the fellow congregants that believers would follow Christ according to their church's discipline. For example, in articulating

---

[15] Dirk Philips, *The Writings of Dirk Philips, 1504-1568* (Trans. and eds., Cornelius J. Dyck, William E. Keeney, and Alvin J. Beachy; Scottdale: Herald Press, 1992), 40.

[16] Philips, 116.

[17] Keeney, *The Development of Dutch Anabaptist Thought and Practice*, 76.

the requirement for each candidate to experience a new life in Christ as prerequisite for the outward ceremony of baptism to be administered, Menno explained that "in the spiritual strength which we have received, we henceforth bind ourselves by the outward sign of the covenant in water which is enjoined on all believers in Christ."[18] Sacraments then served as covenantal commitments made by believers to God and to one another. But Hans Jürgen-Goertz observes that this pledge, for Menno,

> not only affirmed the salvific action of God in man, but also occupied a special place within it. Only through confession, that is to say water-baptism, did God's action become redemptive reality, as if God felt himself bound by man's acceptance of his gift of grace. In this sense, Menno regarded baptism as more than a mere symbol of obedience, occasionally speaking of its effects and of the 'forgiveness of our sins in baptism.' By this he meant that, through the act of confession, what man confessed was actually effected.[19]

Resembling Marpeck's comprehension of the rites, Menno furthered explained that "the believing receive remission of sins not through baptism, but in baptism",[20] as the Holy Spirit works within the newly baptized through his or her faith in Christ. The water itself, then, does not ontologically change the baptizand, but God, who uses the element of water, and one can extrapolate the same for the bread and wine in Communion, will transform the willing believer through such rites nevertheless.

Many sixteenth century Anabaptists then took a nuanced, middle position regarding the sacraments in contradistinction both with the Catholic notion of the sacraments as *ex opere operato* transmitting grace on the one hand and the Zwinglian concept of them as symbolic ceremonies devoid of God's active working on the other. This middle position, however, becomes harder to trace among Anabaptists in the decades to follow. Given that its reception has receded in modern Anabaptism, it would likely be hypothesized that this view faded as the Radical Reformation matured in its subsequent decades. Regardless, while it is difficult to determine whether such thought continued uninterruptedly in the following centuries among Mennonites and other Anabaptists, upon closer investigation one may readily see that significant descendants of the wider Anabaptist movement replicating a variation of this sacramentalism in our modern period.

Although most Mennonites have abandoned the terminology of "sacrament",

---

[18] Menno Simons, *The Complete Writings of Menno Simons* (ed. J.C. Wenger; Scottdale: Herald Press, 1956), 125.

[19] Hans Jürgen-Goertz, *The Anabaptists* (London: Routledge, 1996), 84.

[20] See John Horsch, *Menno Simons: His Life, Labors, and Teachings* (Scottdale: Mennonite Publishing House, 1916), 261.

undoubtedly out of fear of misinterpretation, Hubmaier's insistence upon water baptism as a sign of a Christian's commitment still lingers. Miller then concludes,

> Because divine grace is primarily a power which restores fallen human nature and enables the response of obedient faith, the sacramental significance of baptism focuses upon the believer's confession of faith and pledge. Any understanding of baptism which can be enacted not only independently of the believing response of faith and commitment, but even without emphasizing that the believing response and commitment is an essential part of the divinely initiated covenantal transaction of which baptism is the sign, represents a different understanding of both divine grace and sacramental reality.[21]

Said more succinctly, while the Mennonites do not claim Hubmaier as their founder, his sacramental thought, though perhaps more indirectly that directly, may still affect modern Mennonite theology and church practice.[22] Hubmaier's enormous literary output was useful to subsequent Anabaptists and their leaders. Modern scholars have observed this most empirically from the Hutterian Brethren who were to follow. Upon Hubmaier's death, the Hutterite *Chronicle* records:

> Two hymns are still in our brotherhood which this Balthasar

---

[21] Miller, 243.

[22] Interestingly, though perhaps incidental to the center of this present study, twentieth century Mennonite theologian John Howard Yoder has called for a new or renewed understanding of sacramentalism within the church. Here, Yoder argues the need to resurrect a "sacramental realism" in which baptism and the Lord's Supper represent the egalitarian family of God. For Yoder, this intones both spiritual and economic commonality: "When the family head feeds you at his or her table, the bread for which he or she has given thanks, you are part of the family. . . . To be immersed and to rise from the waters of the *mikvah* may be said to symbolize death and resurrection, but really it makes you a member of the historical community of the new age." For Yoder, the *meaning* of the sacraments are not nearly as important as their ontological nature: that one is part of the new people. When Christ says, for instance, "whenever you do this, do it in my memory", Jesus is not discussing Eucharistic theory but the ordinary partaking of food for the body. The communal meal is emblematic of material and economic solidarity. Thus, the sacraments are not nearly as powerful in symbol as they are in reality. As such, Yoder argues this as the basis for disavowing all non-voluntary practice of the rites. While one might see some parallel with Hubmaier's continued sacramentality, Yoder's implications tend more towards communal value especially in baptism, while Hubmaier's sacraments inexorably pointed towards their covenantal qualities. See Yoder, "Sacrament as Social Process: Christ the Transformer of Culture", in *The Royal Priesthood: Essays Ecclesiological and Ecumenical* (Grand Rapids: Eerdmans, 1994), 364-67.

> Hubmaier composed. There are also other writings by him from which one learns how he had so forcefully argued the right baptism, and how infant baptism is altogether wrong, all this proved from the Holy Scriptures. Likewise, he brought to light the truth of the Lord's Supper, and refuted the idolatrous sacrament and the great error and seduction by it.[23]

Clearly, then, Hubmaier's influence regarding the sacraments retained some life beyond his own. Perhaps no one person accommodated the Waldshut reformer's corpus more than Peter Riedemann. In his study of Reidemann's use and appropriation of Hubmaier's works within his own confession for the Hutterite community, Franz Heimann particularly observes the exact parallels in their *ordo salutis* and the sacraments. Here, Heimann writes of Riedemann that:

> The teaching concerning the right sequence of preaching the Word, hearing, change of life, and baptism, seems to be derived from Hubmaier. In addition, Riedemann seems to have borrowed from him almost in its entirety the polemic against infant baptism with all its numerous arguments and reasons, in which polemic Hubmaier nearly exhausted his theological capacity. There is also a fairly complete agreement of the *Rechenschaft* with Hubmaier's teaching concerning the 'Fellowship of the Lord's Table,' whose inner communion must already be present prior to the breaking of bread. Likewise we find already in Hubmaier the teaching of the Christian brotherhood or church (*Gemineschaft*), which exercises inner discipline by brotherly punishment and the ban.[24]

Thus, the very doctrines on which this study focused most particularly and the actual facets of theology on which Hubmaier could be accused of being at least intimating or adjoining the sacramental are those which were passed down to the Hutterite community through Peter Riedemann. Michael Sattler, in turn, is noted in his liberal use of Riedemann in his formulation of the *Schleitheim Articles* in 1527.[25]

Regardless, Riedemann even sustained the sacramental language employed by Hubmaier regarding the rite of baptism as effecting regeneration.[26] To be clear, Hubmaier never associated baptismal regeneration with the water itself during his Anabaptist days. Instead, Hubmaier saw baptism as one's induction into the community of salvation in the church. On these points, at least,

---

[23] See A.J.F. Zieglschmid (ed.), *Die älteste Chronik der Hutterischen Brüder: Ein Sprachdenkmal aus frühneuhochdeutscher Zeit* (Ithica: Cayuga Press, 1943), 52.

[24] Heimann, 144.

[25] Heimann, 142-44.

[26] Heimann, 143.

Riedemann seemed to trudge along in Hubmaier's footprints, elongating the marks of his predecessor's theological sojourn.[27]

The Baptists[28]

At the same time, interestingly, the group that has most overtly clamored to Hubmaier's principles and explored potential relationships with his Anabaptist thought has been the Baptists.[29] Baptists still argue today, though not as rau-

---

[27] Though it may be stretching Hubmaier beyond the boundaries of his own Anabaptist sacramentalism, some thought which parallels his own has infiltrated into at least one non-Anabaptist, magisterial and Reformed confession of faith. The Heidelberg Catechism, which is typically attributed to Melanchthon, has more recently come under dispute regarding its authorship, whether Melancthonian, Calvinistic or Zwinglian in origin. Yet one passage in particular sounds somewhat vaguely familiar to students of Hubmaier: "Sacraments", it says, "are ceremonies, instituted by God and added to the promise of grace, so that by them he might represent the grace promised in the gospel, that is, the communication of Christ and all his benefits; and so that, *as if by visible pledges and public testimonies*, he might give assurance that this promise most certainly belongs to and will be eternally valid for all those who use these ceremonies in true faith, and so that those who use them might, on their part, bind themselves to persevere in true faith and piety toward God", here cited in Lyle D. Bierma, "The Doctrine of the Sacraments in the Heidelberg Catechism: Melancthonian, Calvinist, or Zwinglian?" *Studies in Reformed Theology and History*, no. 4 (Princeton: Princeton Theological Seminary, 1999), 9 [italics mine]. While portraying a more objective working of God than Hubmaier would have, the catechism's sacramentalism still demonstrated subjective qualities, particularly of pledge and testimony which might intimate not only Zwinglian but also Hubmaierian influence.

[28] Much of the content of the following section is taken from Brian C. Brewer, "Signs of the Covenant: The Development of Sacramental Thought in Baptist Circles", *Perspectives in Religious Studies* 36, no. 5 (Winter 2010), 407-20, particularly from the section "The Historic Rise of Baptist Sacramentalism", 412-16. It is reused here with permission.

[29] Werner O. Packull has suggested that the reason for the Baptist dominance in Hubmaierian scholarship may be as much because Mennonites had at one point all but abandoned the figure as because Baptists were attracted to him. Writing on the subject of Mennonite historiography, Packull argued: "What did not serve apologetic ends was pushed to the periphery as aberration, half-Anabaptist (*Halbtäufer*), or peripheral figures (*Randfiguren*). Such selectivity", Packull continued, "truncated and fragmented the Anabaptist movement, leaving scholars with too many anomalies. Balthasar Hubmaier, a key Anabaptist theologian who did not fit the sectarian, pacifist Bender model, had to be abandoned to Baptist scholars." See Packull, *Hutterite Beginnings: Communitarian Experiments during the Reformation* (Baltimore: The Johns Hopkins University Press, 1995), 4.

cously as in decades past, over the historical link between Anabaptism on mainland Europe and its own Baptist origins among English Separatists. Such scholarship has most particularly focused on the early Baptist John Smyth and his interaction with a group of Collegiant Mennonites, called Waterlanders, in Holland.[30] Regardless of this particular debate, however, any direct connection between the Baptist tradition and Balthasar Hubmaier is much more difficult to establish. Nevertheless, many Baptist historians see in Hubmaier at least a prototype of the Baptist cause. Writing for an American Baptist journal, Robert Macoskey opined that Hubmaier was "a spiritual ancestor of modern American Baptists if ever there was one."[31]

Even though some Baptists in Europe have utilized the term "sacrament" in reference to the ordinances of baptism and communion, most sacramental Baptists do not associate their theology with Hubmiaer's radical new definition as pledge or promise but instead hold on to a traditional view that the material elements become vehicles of grace. In his *History of the English Baptists*, A.C. Underwood records what he perceived as a change in understanding of the sacraments among such Baptists. While he herein discusses baptism, the spirit of the text also relates to the sacramental understanding of communion as well:

> The older Baptists were, in the main, contented to set forth a symbolic view of baptism which reduced it to a mere sign. For them, it symbolized the inward experience of conversion, and the experience of dying to the old sinful life and rising again to newness of life in Christ. It was also an act of obedience to a command of Christ, and the symbolic utterance of the candidate's purpose to live for Him and join His people. Largely under the influence of the writings of Dr. H. Wheeler Robinson, many English Baptists have abandoned this view in favor of a sacramental interpretation of believers' baptism. They reject as superstitious the *ex opere operato* doctrine of the sacraments; and resolutely refuse the make baptism necessary for salvation. Personal response to the grace of God in Christ is the only thing that can, in their view, make a man a Christian. Baptism without conversion is, therefore, nothing and no baptism. They point out, however, that in the New Testament the gift of the Spirit is associated with the baptism of believers, and that as a matter of fact the actual experience of those baptized believers carries them beyond mere symbolism. Their baptism is an unforgettable religious experience of the first rank, in which God does something for them in response to their repentance and faith. They receive from Him a further endowment of the Spirit and further power to walk in new-

---

[30] H. Leon McBeth, *The Baptist Heritage: Four Centuries of Baptist Witness* (Nashville: Broadman Press, 1987), 44.

[31] Macoskey, 99.

> ness of life. . . . Clearly, then, their baptism is something more than
> a declaratory act on their part; it is a genuine sacrament: a means of
> grace in which God, in response to their faith, uses material media as
> the vehicle of His grace.[32]

In his excellent historical study of Baptist sacramentalism, Stanley K. Fowler observed a strong presence of sacramental theology both in the early Baptist confessions and among notable seventeenth and eighteenth century Baptist figures.[33] Thus, in contradistinction to Underwood, Fowler has demonstrated that the early British Baptists appropriated a free church sacramentalism, which we argue is similar to that espoused by Hubmaier a century prior.

However, even before the Baptists founded their churches in Britain, a brand of sacramentalism manifested in its founding congregation in Holland under the leadership of John Smyth. In his *Short Confession of Faith in XX Articles*, written in Holland in 1609, Smyth noted that one of the principal duties of the church was "administering the sacraments" of baptism and the Supper. Baptism was articulated as an "external sign" of a spiritual reality. However, as Fowler carefully observed, Smyth did not explain his view of the timing of this reality in association with the sign. Thus, whether the external sign enacted the internal reality or whether is simply followed it was left unclear in this document.

Nevertheless, following Smyth's application to join the Waterlander Mennonite Church in Holland, the latter group required Smyth and his congregation to sign *A Short Confession* of thirty-eight articles to determine the English Separatist group's affinity to their own beliefs. Within the statement, which Smyth and his church readily signed,[34] was a description of "the two sacraments appointed by Christ" in which baptism and the Lord's Supper were called "outward visible handlings and tokens" which portrayed both God's work and the Christian's or congregation's response. Regarding the former sacrament, the confession further explained: "Therefore, the baptism of water leadeth us to Christ, to his holy office in glory and majesty; and admonisheth us not to hang only upon the outward, but with holy prayer to mount upward, and to beg of Christ the good thing signified."[35] Thus while Smyth's own statement on the sacraments was nebulous regarding their effectiveness, the Waterlander confession, which the majority of the heretofore first Baptist congregation signed, articulated a sense of God's mysterious action in the outward rite itself.

---

[32] A.C. Underwood, *A History of the English Baptists* (London: The Kingsgate Press, 1947), 268-69.

[33] See Stanley K. Fowler, *More Than a Symbol: The British Baptist Recovery of Baptismal Sacramentalism* (Carlisle: Paternoster, 2002), 10-57.

[34] Jason K. Lee, *The Theology of John Smyth: Puritan, Separatist, Baptist, Mennonite* (Macon: Mercer Press, 2003), 87.

[35] Here cited in William L. Lumpkin, *Baptist Confessions of Faith* (Philadelphia: Judson Press, 1959), 98.

However, sacramentalism did not cease among Baptists when Smyth and most of his English Separatist congregation pledged their commonality with the Dutch Mennonites. Instead, a line of sacramental continuity germinated, though with marked variation, among numerous Baptist witnesses through the next two centuries. Several seventeenth century denominational documents appear to be instructive to this end.

The Particular Baptist *Second London Confession* (1677) noted that the sacraments of baptism and the Lord's Supper were bonds and pledges of the participants with God. Its terminology and definitions of the sacraments were uncannily similar to Hubmaier's. Regarding the Supper, for instance, the confession further explained that "worthy receivers, outwardly partaking of the visible Elements in this Ordinance, do then also inwardly by faith, really and indeed, yet not carnally, and corporally, but spiritually receive, and feed upon Christ crucified & all the benefits of his death."[36] The body of Christ was therefore not present physically but made spiritually available through the faith of the gathered community of believers, just as present, the confession related, "as the Elements themselves are to their outward senses".[37]

While some scholars might attribute this sacramental quality within the Particular Baptist tradition to its Reformed origins, what is fascinating is the presence of sacramentalism among the early General Baptists, too. For instance, the General Baptists' *Orthodox Creed* (1678) noted: "Those two sacraments [baptism and the Lord's Supper] are ordinances of positive, sovereign, and Holy institution, appointed by the Lord Jesus Christ, the only Lawgiver."[38] To be clear, the mere presence of the word "sacraments" in an historic document does not necessitate sacramentality. Instead, many seventeenth century Baptists appeared to use the words "sacrament" and "ordinance" interchangeably with great variation from other Baptists or even without much reflection on the meaning of such terminology. However, the *Orthodox Creed* demonstrated further sacramental development for its representative churches. Regarding the Lord's Supper, for instance, the creed noted:

> The supper of the Lord Jesus was instituted by Him . . . for the confirmation of the faithful believers in all the benefits of His death and resurrection and spiritual nourishment and growth in Him; sealing unto them their continuance in the covenant of grace and to be a band and pledge of communion with Him, and an obligation of obedience of Christ, both passively and actively, as also of our communion and union each with others, in the participation of this Holy

---

[36] *Second London Confession*, here cited in Lumpkin, 291.

[37] *Second London Confession*, here cited in Lumpkin, 291.

[38] *The Orthodox Creed*, here cited in *Baptist Confessions, Covenants, and* Catechisms (eds. Timothy and Denise George; Nashville: Broadman and Holman Publishers, 1996), 112.

sacrament.[39]

That the Supper is a "band and pledge" which spiritually seals and nourishes the believers in Christ denotes the same kind of sacramentalism which Hubmaier had previously defined for the free church tradition. It highlights the active work of both God and the confessing congregant in a covenantal renewal through the bread and cup.

These confessional examples do not appear to be aberrant comments made unreflectively but, instead, seem to correspond to the thought of some of the leading Baptist authorities of the early Baptists. One of the earliest Baptist leaders to espouse a Baptist sacramentalism was the Particular Baptist pastor Robert Garner (d. 1649). Garner's short book, *A Treatise of Baptisme,* published in 1645, served as an apologetic work against pedobaptism. Yet, in arguing against the practice of infant baptism, Garner underscored the power of calling the Triune God upon the baptizands:

> Believers (in submitting to this Ordinance) have the name of the Father and of the Sonne, and of the holy Spirit called upon them therein. . . . [F]or these words, Baptizing them in the Name of the Father, and of the Sonne, and of the Holy Spirit, carry the force of a promise in them: for in that the Lord hath commanded his servants to baptize believers in his Name, to Put or Call his Name upon them in baptisme he saith Amen to it, he confirmeth the word of his servants, he performeth what he promiseth to them.[40]

According to Garner, in order for baptizands to have the name of God placed upon them as a sign of their acquiescence to be God's children and as members of God's people, candidates must be mature enough to understand and consciously submit to the same. Only then does the rite serve as a demarcation of God's promise to save and provide for the new believers. Consequently, sacramentalism is not rejected in Garner's apologetic against infant baptism. Paradoxically, infant baptism is rejected because of the nature of Garner's sacramental thought. Thus, baptism serves as a covenantal sign which combines both a human and a divine promise, like that outlined in Hubmaier's sacramental thought. This covenantal work by both God and the believers incorporates the latter into the church, granting them spiritual communion with other Christians, uniting new believers in the death and resurrection of Christ Jesus to the effect that "the strength of the body of sinne is more subdued, and they are more enabled to walk in newnesse of life",[41] and conveying God's divine assurance of

---

[39] *The Orthodox Creed,* here cited in George (eds), *Baptist Confessions, Covenants, and Catechisms,* 116.

[40] Robert Garner, *A Treatise of Baptisme* (London: n.p., 1645), 10-11.

[41] Garner, *A Treatise of Baptisme,* 17.

forgiveness upon them. The enactment of the divine-human covenant demonstrates a sacramentality in which God actually acts upon that which God had promised. The baptismal waters serve as a sign, confirmation, and seal whereby Christians are actively but mysteriously united with Christ and his church.

This notion of a believer's mystical union through the waters of baptism was repeated in the writing of Particular Baptist Henry Lawrence a decade later. In his systematic work titled, *Of Baptism*, first published in 1659, he notes that through the sacrament of baptism, Christ becomes the "middle person, the bond" between God and the baptizand.[42] Baptism serves to assure and seal the Christian in this covenantal relationship. This "sealing" is not to be interpreted as figurative language in Lawrence's work. What apparently is described in baptism applies also to the Supper:

> This is that which is the effect of Baptisme, and which Baptisme seals up to you; for what Baptisme findes it seals, although it doeth also exhibit more of the same kind; Baptisme and so all the ordinances of Christ, those we call Sacraments, seale up what is already, else how could it be a seale, but doth also conveigh more of the same.[43]

Therefore, Lawrence, like Garner, granted that in baptism (as well as in the Supper for Lawrence) God places in the sacrament what God established in faith, strengthening and securing believers through the rite. Provided the believers consciously respond to God, the Spirit provides them the security and confidence of their salvation through the elements of baptism and the Supper.[44] This understanding may well go beyond Hubmaier's own definition. For Hubmaier, the sign merely represented what the promise entailed spiritually. For these Baptists, the signs themselves apparently were seen to be used by God. Regardless, the notion of both divine and human participation in covenant with one another through the rite remains intact.

But this notion of Baptist sacramentalism was not reserved for Particular Baptists only, as previously demonstrated through the General Baptists' *Orthodox Creed* (1678). One of the most notable leaders of the General Baptists in their first century of existence was Thomas Grantham (1634-1692). Grantham described baptism as the "ordinary way of God's communicating the grace of the Gospel . . . as a means where in not only the Remission of our sins shall be granted us, but as a condition whereupon we shall receive the gift of the Holy Ghost." For Grantham, baptism "was fore-ordained to signfie and sacramentally to confer the grace of the pardon of sin, and the inward washing of the Con-

---

[42] Henry Lawrence, *Of Baptism* (Amsterdam?, n.p., 1646), 2.
[43] Lawrence, *Of Baptism*, 22-23.
[44] Lawrence, *Of Baptism*, 109-11.

science by Faith in the Bloud of Jesus Christ."[45] Thus, while the faith of the
believer was contingent upon receiving this divine promise, God nevertheless
communicates divine grace through the Holy Spirit in the waters of baptism.

Likewise, Grantham used sacramental language for Communion:

> Can anything be more effectually spoken to unite the members
> of Christ or will any man say these things are not spoken of this
> ordinance? . . . Yea here Christ gathers his people together at his own
> Table as one family. And it is that Table to which all saints are to
> approach with such preparation as may render them fit for communion
> in that mystical body, the Church, which is also called Christ because
> of that unity they have in him and one another in him.[46]

Grantham, then, equated one's union with Christ with one's union with
Christ's church, a concept shared by the Anabaptists in general and Hubmaier
in particular a century and a half before Grantham's writings. Additionally, the
Lord's Supper served for Grantham as the binding sacrament in which a believer
joined both Christ and Christ's corporate Body. He concluded by noting that the
purpose of the sacrament of communion was "to assure the saints as by a pledge
or token that the new testament is ratified and confirmed by the death of the
testator, so that whether we regard the certainty of sufficiency of the gospel, both
declared in this ordinance as much as any other."[47] This sign becomes effective
when appropriated experientially, a concept parallel to Hubmaier's sacramental
thought. Thus, like Hubmaier and other Anabaptist and Baptist sacramentalists,
Grantham rejected the Catholic *ex opere operato*, mechanical notion of the
sacraments' effects while emphasizing their actualization when appropriated
experientially by faith and personal commitment.

William Mitchill (1662-1705) serves as a final Baptist individual to exemplify
early Baptist sacramentalism for this chapter. In his work, *Jachim and Boaz*,
published posthumously in 1707, Mitchill wrote:

> Sacraments are holy Signs of the Covenant of Grace immediately
> instituted by Christ, to represent him and his Benefits, and to confirm
> our Interest in him, and solemnly to engage us to the Service of
> God in Christ, according to his Word: There is in every Sacrament a
> spiritual Relation, or a Sacramental Union between the Sign, and the
> thing signified: Whence it comes to pass that the Names and Effects

---

[45] Thomas Grantham, *A Sigh for Peace: or The Cause of Division Discovered* (London: n.p., 1671), 87-88; here cited in Fowler, *More than a Symbol*, 28.

[46] Grantham, *Christianismus Primitivus: or The Ancient Christian Religion*, II/II/6 (London: Francis Smith, 1678); here cited as "The Primitive Christian Religion", in Freeman et al. (eds), *Baptist Roots*, 95.

[47] Grantham, *Christianismus Primitivus*, 95.

of the one is ascribed to the other: The Grace which is exhibited in or by the Sacraments rightly used, is not conferred by any power in them, neither doth the Efficacy of a Sacrament depend upon the Piety of Intention of him that doth administer it, but upon the Work of the Spirit, and the Word of Institution, which contains, together with a Precept authorizing the use thereof, a Promise of benefit to the worthy Receivers. There be only two Sacraments ordained by Christ our Lord in the Gospel, that is to say, Baptism and the Lord's Supper, neither of which ought to be administered but by a Minister of the Word lawfully called.[48]

Utilizing much of the language of the *Westminster Confession*, Mitchill appropriated a magisterial Protestant sacramentalism through a Baptist soteriology. Thus, like his Baptist predecessors previously cited, the sign of the covenant is made effective both by the Holy Spirit and by genuine confession of faith of the human participant. Without the latter, the Spirit does not move and the rite is impotent. But with the faith in the promise by the believer, the sign of the covenant in both baptism and communion becomes an effective sign.

From these Baptist leaders, one might conclude as Philip Thompson did regarding the writings of Thomas Grantham: "A non- or anti-sacramental label attaches to this view only with great difficulty."[49] Furthermore, one may readily see a strong similarity between the early sacramental Baptist understanding of the rites and Hubmaier's Anabaptist thought a century prior. Stanley Fowler cites similar expressions of Baptist sacramentalism in the works of Benjamin Keach (1640-1704), John Gill (1697-1771), Abraham Booth (1734-1806), Anne Dutton (1692-1765), Andrew Fuller (1754-1815), John Ryland, Jr. (1753-1825), and numerous others through the eighteenth and even nineteenth centuries.[50] Therefore, many Baptists continued the vocabulary and theology of Protestant sacramentalism while appropriating the meaning of the rites within their free church ecclesiologies. Balthasar Hubmaier may well have laid the foundation for subsequent Anabaptists and Baptists alike in their understanding of a free church sacramentalism.

Thus, while many English Baptists have now reclaimed the sacraments as such, and while they have also rejected a transubstantiative quality to them, they also seem to have added to what would be Hubmaier's understanding of

---

[48] Originally cited in "William Mitchill's Jachin and Boaz", *Transactions of the Baptist Historical Society* 3 (1912-1913), 160; here cited in Fowler, *More Than a* Symbol, 31. Original copies of Mitchill's *Jachin and Boaz* are extremely rare. However, portions of this book are cited also in Abel Jones Parry, *History of the Cloughfold Baptist Church, from 1675-1875* (Manchester: John Heywood, 1876), 62-82.

[49] Philip E. Thompson, "A New Question in Baptist History: Seeking a Catholic Spirit Among Early Baptists", *Pro Ecclesia* 8, no. 1 (Winter 1999), 67.

[50] See Fowler, *More Than a* Symbol, 29-85.

the *ordo salutis.* Now in the British Baptist understanding, baptism and communion are not only human responses to God's initiating grace, they are also means by which God provides a further manifestation of God's gift.[51] Thus, one cannot safely attribute to Hubmaier such influence in their sacramental shift. The Baptist sacramental understanding is similar to Hubmaier's, but in many cases it has variations foreign to the Waldshut reformer.

Baptists in America, particularly in the South, are much more reluctant to use the term altogether and tend to rebuff, perhaps more emotionally than theologically, any hint of "sacramentality".[52] For instance, in a sermon titled "Baptist Sacramentalism", Southern Baptist historian Robert A. Baker wrote that sacramentalism

> represents a radical revision of fundamental beliefs, not an inciden
> tal idea on the margin of Baptist convictions. American Baptists be
> lieve what they do about the ordinances because of what they believe
> about the lordship of Jesus Christ, the work of the Holy Spirit, the
> priesthood of believers, the function of ministry, and other central
> doctrines. This innovation puts all of these fundamental doctrines out
> of focus. Even the English use of the word 'sacrament' has unsavory
> connotations. It sounds strange on Baptist lips. It is the historic word
> of the Roman Catholic Church by which they teach boldly that the
> materials of the sacraments work of themselves

. . . .[53]

Baker then pled for Baptists in America to instead "magnify the work of Christ in their hearts", devoting themselves to Scripture instead of attempting to make baptism and the Lord's Supper "more meaningful by such false interpreta-

---

[51] In 1983, Michael J. Walker, an English Baptist, wrote about the need to retrieve "the sacrament of baptism out of the Zwinglian shadows" and described baptism as "a place of rendezvous between God and man, an integral part of that process of conversion". See Walker, "Baptist Worship in the Twentieth Century", in *Baptists in the Twentieth Century* (ed. K.W. Clements; London: Baptist Historical Society, 1983), 25. Additionally, Baptist New Testament scholar George Beasley-Murray writes: "The idea that baptism is a purely symbolic rite must be pronounced not alone unsatisfactory, but out of harmony with the New Testament itself. . . . The Apostolic writers make free use of symbolism of the baptismal action; but they go further and view the act as a symbol with power, that is, a sacrament." Beasley-Murray then explains: "In baptism the Gospel proclamation and the hearing of faith become united in one indissoluble act, at one and the same time an act of grace and faith, and act of God and man." See George Beasley-Murray, *Baptism in the New Testament* (New York: Macmillan, 1962), 263, 272.

[52] As such, John Howard Yoder referred to Baptists as "radicalized Zwinglians". See Yoder, "Sacrament as Social Process: Christ the Transformer of Culture", in *The Royal Priesthood: Essays Ecclesiological and Ecumenical* (Grand Rapids: Eerdmans, 1994), 367.

[53] Robert A. Baker, "Baptist Sacramentalism", in *Chapel Messages* (Grand Rapids: Baker Book House, 1966), 24.

tion".[54]

Clearly, if Baker's comments are in any way representative of most Southern Baptist sentiments regarding "sacramentalism", then little consideration of or relation to Hubmaier's radical redefinition has been established among them. Thus, save for Hubmaier's views on war and sectarianism, Baptists would find few distinct parallels with Hubmaier's thought over against that of several other of Hubmaier's Anabaptist contemporaries. It seems curious, then, why a number of Baptist historians, whether British or American, continue to long for such connection if Hubmaier's sacramentalism is incongruent with Baptist views.[55]

However, in their *Baptist Manual of Polity and Practice*, Norman Maring and Winthrop Hudson make some basic observations regarding Baptist perspectives and misunderstandings of "sacrament" which seem pertinent to this theme:

> For centuries a sacrament has been commonly defined as 'an outward and visible sign of an inward and spiritual grace.' In such a definition there is nothing inherently offensive to Baptist doctrine. Usage of the term, however, conveys to some an impression that goes beyond this definition. It suggests that a sacrament is the means by which some change is brought about in an almost mechanical way. This understanding, though not necessarily confirmed by official theologies, seems to minimize the need for faith on the part of a recipient. Thus actual practice has often magnified the degree of institutional control over God's grace and minimized human response.[56]

If Maring and Hudson portray the Baptist theological landscape accurately, then, as with Hubmaier's theology, the term "sacrament" need not be dismissed on the grounds of emotionalism and misunderstanding. Instead, a greater emphasis upon human response could be placed by radically redefining "sacrament" among Baptists for our time. In so doing, Baptists could continue to emphasize personal experience and confession of faith while binding such confessions more strongly with their corresponding symbols through a sacramental vocabulary. Balthasar Hubmaier's sacramental thought might become a fitting

---

[54] Baker, 28.

[55] See, for instance, Henry C. Vedder, *A Short History of the Baptists* (Valley Forge: Judson Press, 1907), 145-66 and Freeman, McClendon, and da Silva (eds), *Baptist Roots*, 32-40, for two examples of Baptist historians who include Hubmaier as a contributor to Baptist history.

[56] Norman H. Maring and Winthrop S. Hudson, *A Baptist Manual of Polity and Practice* (Valley Forge: Judson Press, rev. ed., 1991), 145-46.

and readily accessible model for Baptist liturgical renewal.[57] Jonathan Rainbow observed:

> For Zwingli, baptism was a *mere sign*. For Hubmaier, it was *more than a sign*. Baptists historically belong in the high baptismal tradition which sees baptism as the expression and embodiment of the saving work of God, the *sacramentum fidei*, not just an act of obedience tacked on. Baptists historically have known how to embrace Peter's declaration, 'Baptism now saves you' (I Pet 3:20), not because they ascribe a crude, magical saving power to the rite as such, but because they consider, on the basis of an open and personal confession, that the person coming to the water believes in Jesus Christ, and that there is an inner reality to which the baptism corresponds. Baptism is not magic, but it is more than a sign. That is the heart of what the Reformation Anabaptists were saying.[58]

If Baptists are then going to claim Hubmaier, for which there is at least some argument typologically (and probably not directly albeit this is what the old Landmarkist movement[59] may well have done), then they need to decide whether the term "sacrament" is useful. Is their disdain for it, especially prevalent among Southern Baptists, out of anti-Catholic anxieties, from the influence of the Stone-Campbell tradition in America, or from a more well-reasoned sacramentarianism? If not the latter, then perhaps Hubmaier's suggestion of transposing sacrament from the rite itself to the human's pledge of love, a public confession of inward grace, might be helpful in furthering the development of Baptist and free church doctrine. Consequently, Hubmaier's sacramental thought might continue to live and breathe in a world which now might more greatly appreciate his synthetic appropriation of traditions and Scripture.

---

[57] Andrew Fuller, an early Southern Baptist theologian, also wrote coterminously to Hubmaier on at least the subject of baptism. Fuller described the rite as "an act by which we declare before God, Angels, and men, that we yield ourselves to be the Lord's; that we are dead to the world . . . and risen again to 'newness of life'". Fuller, like Hubmaier and especially Pilgrim Marpeck, likened the sacrament to a soldier's oath of allegiance and to a military uniform. We make our pledge to God, like a military oath, but it is publicly stated before witnesses, like a uniform identifying to others of one's commitment to special service. Fuller is here cited in Maring and Hudson, 152-53.

[58] Jonathan H. Rainbow, "'Confessor Baptism': The Baptismal Doctrine of the Early Anabaptists", in *Believer's Baptism: Sign of the New Covenant in Christ* (eds. Thomas R. Schreiner and Shawn D. Wright; Nashville: Broadman and Holman, 2006), 206.

[59] For a thorough evaluation of the Baptist Landmarkist or Successionist theory, see W. Morgan Patterson, *Baptist Successionism: A Critical View* (Valley Forge: Judson Press, 1969), esp. 13-29.

Karl Barth

It seems wholly implausible to suggest a connection between a twentieth century reformed theologian with a sixteenth century Anabaptist. Nevertheless, a typology between Karl Barth, a Reformed Swiss village pastor-made-professor and leader of Neo-Orthodox theology, and Balthasar Hubmaier should not be hastily dismissed. In a fascinating study, John Howard Yoder argued that Barth's trajectory of thought was that of a free churchman. Here he cited parallels between Karl Barth and Anabaptism on such topics as simple Bible reading and hermeneutics; socialistic commitments; ecclesiology; Barth's openness to dialogue late in life with Zinzendorf, Moravians and Mennonites; pacifism; and perhaps most prominently, on baptism.[60] An extension of Yoder's thought would be to suggest that Karl Barth moved, at least typologically, in parallel theological fashion with Hubmaier, especially regarding baptism.

Additionally, Karl Barth may have even shared a similar passion regarding the power of proclamation with Hubmaier. Both theologians saw a need to tie or associate the sacramental events of baptism and the Supper with preaching of the Word. On this subject, for instance, Hubmaier stated that "he who does not proclaim the Word of God is not celebrating mass".[61] Barth would seem to agree, arguing:

> there is preaching in the full sense only where it is accompanied and explained by the sacraments. . . . Because both the sacraments and preaching can take place meaningfully only in the church, it is true of both that they are legitimate only in their relation to one another. Preaching . . . is legitimate, then, only when it does not seek to be anything other than a commentary, an interpretation of the sacraments, a reference to the same thing, but now in words.[62]

---

[60] John H. Yoder, "Karl Barth: How His Mind Kept Changing", in *How Karl Barth Changed My Mind* (ed. Donald K. McKim; Eugene, OR: Wipf & Stock Publishers, 1998), 166-71.

[61] *Hubmaier*, 28; *Schriften*, 787.

[62] Karl Barth, *Homiletics* (Louisville: Westminster/John Knox Press, 1991), 58. At the same time, Hubmaier's notion of preaching serving the sacraments is not novel in its general argument. Even Augustine referred to preaching as an "audible sacrament", and orthodox theologian John Breck indicates that the divine word, like sacramental grace, depends upon the cooperation between God's initiative and human receptivity. See John Breck, *The Power of the Word in the Worshipping Church* (Crestwood, N.Y.: St. Vladimir's Seminary Press, 1986), 9. Additionally, one might easily observe other contemporary theologians who share such a high view of preaching. Geoffrey Wainwright resounds both Hubmaier's and Barth's themes while even tightening the preaching task to sacramental worship by utilizing Eucharistic language for the homiletic act. Wainwright would argue that preaching is not simply located in the context of sacramental worship; it is, itself, a liturgical act. See both Wainwright's *Doxology: The Praise of God in Worship, Doctrine and Life. A Systematic Theology* (New York: Oxford University Press, 1980), esp. 177-180 and 328-9, and his articles "Preaching as Worship" and "The Sermon and the Liturgy" both in *Greek Orthodox Review* 28 (Winter 1983), 325-336 and 337-349, re-

However, the subject of baptism may provide the most fodder for portraying the Hubmarian and Barthian kinship. Karl Barth shocked the theological world in 1943 with his landmark lectures on baptism.[63] Although he came from the Reformed tradition in which infant baptism was commonplace and accepted practice, Barth did not defend this view. Instead he argued:

> Baptism without the willingness and readiness of the baptised is true, effectual and effective baptism; but it is not correct; it is not done in obedience, it is not administered according to proper order, and therefore it is necessarily clouded baptism. It must and ought not to be repeated. It is, however, a wound in the body of the Church and a weakness for the baptised, which can certainly be cured but which are so dangerous that another question presents itself to the Church: how long is she prepared to be guilty of the occasioning of this wounding and weakening through a baptismal practice which is, from this standpoint, arbitrary and despotic?[64]

Such a citation portrays both differences and similarities with Hubmaier. While Hubmaier would demand for baptism to be repeated, Barth would not, only complaining of its distorted practice. Nevertheless, both men saw baptism as a primary issue in order to usher in needful church reform. In his lecture, Barth also sounded a theme which comes eerily close to Hubmaier's covenantal understanding of the sacrament:

> Christian baptism is in essence the representation (*Abbild*) of a man's renewal through his participation by means of the power of the Holy Spirit in the death and resurrection of Jesus Christ, and therewith the representation of man's association with Christ, with the covenant of grace which is concluded and realized in Him, and

---

spectively. Lastly, for further research on this sacramental association with proclamation, see Carol M. Noren's discussion of theological views through the history of the relationship between the homily, liturgy and the sacraments in her article, "The Word of God in Worship: Preaching in Relation to Liturgy", in *The Study of Liturgy* (New York: Oxford University Press, 1992), 33-51.

[63] Robert Short, among others, called Barth's *Die kirchliche Lehre von der Taufe* "a bombshell on the playground of the theologians". See Robert L. Short, "Karl Barth's Final Plea", *Religion in Life* 40, no. 4 (Winter 1971), 479.

[64] Karl Barth, *The Teaching of the Church Regarding Baptism* (London: SCM Press, 1967), 40-41.

with the fellowship of His Church.[65]

Here one may easily observe both Barth's covenantal language for baptism and its association both with one's relationship to Christ and to the church. Additionally, the act of baptism represents the spiritual response having already taken place. For Barth, just as with Hubmaier, baptism did not bring about the salvation of humans (*causative*), but attested to their salvation by the symbolic representation of their renewal in Christ (*cognitive*). It is here that both theologians also depart from their Reformed counterparts. In holding that cognizance is the work and word of Christ as a divine gift of salvation, they both concluded that it must follow that the baptized have a capacity to understand the truth of such a gift and be ready and willing to submit themselves to God's directives. Thus, only adults who were willing to respond to God's offer of grace were adequate recipients and participants in water baptism. Here Barth again seems to echo Hubmaier:

> Neither by exegesis nor from the nature of the case can it be established that the baptized person can be a merely passive instrument (*Behandleter*). Rather it may be shown, by exegesis and from the nature of the case, that in this action the baptized is an active partner (*Handlender*) and that at whatever stage of life he may be, plainly no *infans* can be such a person.[66]

So important was this issue in Barth's thought that Barth worked to complete the "fragment" volume of his twelve volume magnum opus *Church Dogmatics* to answer this sacramental issue systematically. The Swiss theologian had already developed a pattern of ending volumes with a section or tome on relevant ethics. Having completed three sections of his fourth volume, *The Doctrine of Reconciliation*, at age eighty, Barth found himself in poor health and with deteriorating vigor.[67] But after a respite of renewed strength, he felt compelled to write one section on the ethics of reconciliation: his "fragment" on baptism (IV. 4). Essentially, Barth, similar to Hubmaier, broke the sacrament of baptism down into two parts: baptism with the Holy Spirit, which is God's objective and salvific working in humanity, and baptism with water, which is humanity's subjective response in faith. They are, dialectically, separate yet connected:

> The two elements in the foundation of the Christian life, the objective and the subjective, are to be correlated as well as distinguished. Only as (I) the divine change makes possible and demands human

---

[65] Barth, *The Teaching of the Church Regarding Baptism*, 9.

[66] Barth, *The Teaching of the Church Regarding Baptism*, 41.

[67] Geoffrey W. Bromiley, *An Introduction to the Theology of Karl Barth* (Grand Rapids: Eerdmans, 1979), 239.

decision as conversion from unfaithfulness to faithfulness to God, and only as (2) this human decision has its origin wholly and utterly in the divine change, does there come about the foundation of the Christian life and the existence of a man who is faithful to God. Only as the two are seen together in differentiated unity can one understand them. The act of God in this event is thus to be construed strictly as such, and the act of man in the same event is also to be construed strictly as such. Each of the elements both individually and also in correlation, and therefore the totality of the event, will be misunderstood if it is either separated from or, instead of being distinguished, mixed together or confused with the other. Baptism with the Holy Spirit does not exclude baptism with water. It does not render it superfluous. Indeed, it makes it possible and demands it. Again, baptism with water is what it is only in relation to baptism with the Holy Spirit. . . . To say this is to say that in the one event of the foundation of the Christian life we have the wholly different action to two inalienably distinct subjects. On the one side is the action of God in His address to man, and on the other, made possible and demanded thereby, the action of man in his turning towards God. On the one side is the Word and command of God expressed in His gift, on the other man's obedience of faith required of him and to be rendered by him as a recipient of the divine gift. Without this unity of the two in their distinction there could be no Christian ethics. To see their distinction in unity is especially important at this point where we are concerned with the beginning of the relation between God who commands in His grace and the responsible action of the man who is grateful to this God.[68]

Following a close reading of both Hubmaier and Barth one might readily deduce certain parallels in one another's theology in at least this aspect of their sacramental thought. Both theologians tended to separate, yet keep in close proximity, the objective saving work of God through the gift of grace and the subjective yet significant response of humanity to the gift through baptism. Both refer to the former as "baptism with the Spirit" and the latter as "baptism with water" and both would argue for the appropriateness of the response to come only after a person recognized and might confess God's previously received gift. While Hubmaier may have placed more importance on the liturgical pledge previous to the rite, and while Barth may have been more open to recognizing the legitimacy, though distortion, of infant baptism, these two thinkers, separated by four centuries, manifest surprising parallels in the development of their thinking.

---

[68] Karl Barth, *Church Dogmatics: The Doctrine of Reconciliation*, IV.4 (fragment) (Edinburgh: T&T Clark, 1969), 41.

Additionally, both Hubmaier and Barth saw the correction of infant baptism with confessional baptism as integral in reforming and restoring the church to a greater purity. The call for ethics, humanity's proper response to God's grace, was the means for such church renewal. Thus, while he may never have reflected on the radical insights of his theology as characteristically Anabaptist in trajectory, Karl Barth manifested in his mature thought an example of Hubmaierian principles being appropriated typologically in modern theology.

Naturally, such a parallel between thinkers separated by four centuries might be overstated. Hubmaier generally retained his sacramental language through his mature Anabaptist thought while redirecting it to a Christian's response in covenant to God. Barth, on the other hand, tended to reject such sacramental vocabulary save for his analysis of the Second Person of the Trinity. Barth considered Jesus Christ in the Incarnation, the true breaking-in of divine into humanity, as the greatest representation of sacrament. Such Christocentrism, which led him to supralapsarianism, ultimately transformed Barth's final position on baptism. While in his earlier volumes (CD I.1-2), Barth had argued that both baptism and the Supper were sacramental, now they served as human acts in response to God. Barth believed that the current use of such vocabulary as "sacrament" inferred an erroneous notion that associated divine energies mediated through human actions, implying that God could be coerced by humans to serve humanity's needs. Consequently, the idea of baptism and the Lord's Supper as sacraments required a "cautious and respectful demythologizing" that is expedient and practical.[69] Thus, Barth categorized baptism and the Lord's Supper not only as church ordinances but also as Christian ethics.

For Barth, because Jesus Christ in the incarnation is the only sacrament, baptism and the Lord's Supper do not repeat the incarnation but only bear witness to it. They in themselves cannot infuse grace into believers.[70] Regardless of Barth's reluctance to utilizing the terminology, the purpose and definition of baptism and the Supper and his insistence upon understanding the rites' cognitive role over against any causative capacity are uncannily similar characteristics to Hubmaier's Anabaptist themes. Consequently, that one touted by many as the greatest theologian of the twentieth century,[71] particularly in light of the recent resurgence of interest in Barth, might echo free church themes articulated by Hubmaier, especially regarding the sacraments, is worthy of noting.

---

[69] Karl Barth, *Church Dogmatics* IV.4 (fragment), 13-14.

[70] Short, 482.

[71] For instance, John Cobb writes: "It would be hard to doubt that Barth is the greatest theologian of our century." See John B. Cobb, Jr., "Barth and the Barthians: A Critical Appraisal", in *How Karl Barth Changed My Mind*, 172.

Free Church and Ecumenical Dialogue

Beyond such parallels and typologies, Balthasar Hubmaier may provide help to free church traditions in their continuous dialogue with various other Christian traditions. Hubmaier's attention to the power of the keys might well inform Mennonites in their understanding of their rites and need for church discipline as well as underscore their divergence in interpreting Christ's remarks to Peter from that of the Roman Catholic Church. Carl Leth has noted that "surprisingly, Hubmaier stands much closer to the Catholic tradition than to Luther or Zwingli in his understanding of the keys granting effective power associated with the remission of sins. In fact, he shares with Thomas Aquinas the belief that the power of the keys may be effectively exercised through human initiative."[72] If the free church, particularly the Mennonite tradition, then wished to deepen its historical understanding of its practices through Hubmaier's influence, Hubmaier's writings, in turn, would aid modern Anabaptism in any ecumenical discussions with Catholicism. Consequently, both traditions may see value in their shared understanding of the keys' importance and find a bridge between their otherwise rather discrepant theologies.

With the exception of various "high church" pockets within the Baptists and Disciples of Christ, the believers' church has generally rejected the term "sacrament". Yet, like Barth, it might find in Hubmaier a more appropriate understanding of the term to be appropriated within its own distinct theology so that sacramentality might be revived without the assumptions of any causative action. This understanding centers on the cognitive role of the human for the purpose of reminding him of Christ's work on his behalf and presenting him with the mechanism to respond in faith through his pledge to God. The importance Hubmaier placed on the cognitive role in his sacramental theology might bring might bring greater understanding between the free church and its Christian counterparts today.

Lastly, Balthasar Hubmaier's emphasis on tangible responses to God's grace via the sacraments provides a solution to a gamut of theological traditions' ethical decay. Hubmaier's liturgies of the Supper and baptism portray the need to incorporate prayer, confession, and heartfelt response to God encompassed by a strong sense of divine covenant within the worship of God itself. Hubmaier's understanding of the sacraments keep the sovereignty of God and the importance of Christian piety within a healthy tension. His eclectic theological synthesis represents one of the greatest assortments of theological variety assimilated into cohesive Christian thought. From this vantage point, Arnold Snyder observed that "Hubmaier stands not only at the beginning of the Mennonite denominational tradition, he is speaking out of a common Christian understanding that reaches back through medieval Christianity to a common biblical and apostolic understanding of what it means to be a faithful follower

---

[72] Leth, 115.

of Christ."[73] Thus, Hubmaier may well have been an unwitting ecumenist before his own time. Regardless, Balthasar Hubmaier's sacramental theology might not only have presented solutions for church reform within his own day but also suggests possibilities for renewal within our own time.

---

[73] Arnold Snyder, "Modern Mennonite Reality and Anabaptist Spirituality: Balthasar Hubmaier's Catechism of 1526", *The Conrad Grebel Review* 9 (Winter 1991), 48-49.

Conclusion

Recent scholarship has typically viewed the study of Anabaptism through ecclesiological, soteriological or ethical lenses. Such approaches, while generally accurate, nevertheless tend to diminish Anabaptism's diversity in origins, emphases, traditions and theology. Though one may readily observe how such theological issues as the nature of the church, salvation and Christian disciple are important to Balthasar Hubmaier, early Anabaptism's greatest theologian, one cannot simultaneously conclude that Hubmaier was therefore typical among the movement's first leaders.

Thankfully, various scholars have undertaken studies into Hubmaier's doctrines of baptism and the Lord's Supper, particularly over the twentieth and early twenty-first centuries. Yet, until recently, no one study had outlined Hubmaier's sacramental theology comprehensively.[1] One must consider this to be a glaring oversight, since Hubmaier's understanding of the church practices of baptism, communion and the ban are inextricably related to one another as well as to his Anabaptist theology as a whole.

Several students of Hubmaier have correctly portrayed him as the most conservative among early Anabaptists, as the former priest retained much of his medieval Catholic training. This present study has substantiated this claim and taken the logical step of analyzing Hubmaier from this conventional standpoint. Furthermore, this work has demonstrated how Hubmaier's medieval influences and training provided the theological rudiment for much of his mature Anabaptist sacramentality and his consistent emphasis on the church as the source of one's faith, sustenance and salvation.

This is not to exaggerate the claim of Hubmaier's unicity. Most of the doctrinal matters which concerned Hubmaier concerned other Anabaptists and vice versa, particularly their mutually strong interest in reforming, or even restoring, the church to what might be viewed as its New Testament practices. Nevertheless, Balthasar Hubmaier may well have developed the argument for instituting adult baptism (and thus most often employing a "rebaptism" of Christians) and an understanding of the Supper (as memorial to Christ and unifying to the church, Christ's present earthly Body) by a significantly disparate approach from other, lesser trained Anabaptists because of his interminably lingering Catholicity.

---

[1] Kirk R. MacGregor's *A Central European Synthesis* and this present book remain the only two works which have attempted a comprehensive sacramental theology of Hubmaier.

A number of subsequent Anabaptists, such as Pilgram Marpeck, Dirk Philips, and Menno Simons, understood the ordinances as "sacraments". Yet Hubmaier may well have developed Anabaptist sacramentalism for the first generation of Anabaptism.

Hubmaier lived and wrote during an age in which Catholic sacramentalism dominated. While the church had already begun to diversify in its practice and understanding of the rites locally,[2] the seven sacraments of the medieval church were nevertheless customarily viewed as appropriating the objective workings of God *ex opere operato*. The priest, acting on behalf of God and God's representative church, bestowed upon the parishioner the experience of salvation, forgiveness and restoration to a good standing with God through the elements within the Latin rites. The elements themselves carried such power as God's designated gifts to the church. Thus the church became the means by which the Christian found and maintained salvation.

Only a handful of years before Hubmaier began writing his extant works, Luther had begun to question both the number of sacraments in the church and the Catholic notion of transubstantiation in the Eucharist. Significantly, Luther brought to bear the importance of human reception and comprehension before and during the church's rites. Luther, Zwingli, and other new reformers would argue that faith must precede the signs for the sacraments to be in any way effective. Hubmaier resonated with this thinking, yet he applied this notion much more radically to his reformation designs than did any of his magisterial reformed counterparts.

We have seen how dramatically Hubmaier changed the center and meaning of the sacraments from objective acts in the rites of water, wine and bread, to subjective and anthropologic responses through a Christian's pledge to love God and the community in both baptism and the Lord's Supper. For Hubmaier, then, that which is "sacramental" is not dispersed in those symbolic acts. Instead, the symbolic acts of pouring, eating, and drinking symbolically reenact the previous covenantal acts of pledging oneself through confession of faith to God and through mutual submission to and love for the congregation.

Throughout Hubmaier's argument, the church plays the central role in administering the sacraments. Here again, Hubmaier did not completely divorce himself from his Catholic training. Instead, the church still retained salvific authority through the power of the keys. While he may have mitigated the authority of the clergy, Hubmaier in no way diminished the important role of the church. Instead, the congregation as a community retained this authority of binding and loosing. Consequently, the congregation itself remained the context within which one was baptized, received and shared communion, and from which the apostate was banned. All of these rites carried eternal ramifications

---

[2] See Old, 4-6.

with them. Hubmaier even required believer's baptism as an authentication of one's Christianity. In a dialogue treatise in which he recorded his debate with Oecolampadius in August of 1525 on the topic of infant baptism, Hubmaier maintained this point: "I confess we do not consider believers as Christians, so long as they do not accept the Christian symbols, no matter how holy they are otherwise. For this way Christ wanted to gather a people to himself by the sacramental symbols."[3]

Thus, Hubmaier's sacramental emphasis is part and parcel of his strategy for revitalizing the church. One's heartfelt baptism through confession of sins and faith in God becomes the gateway into a new, believers' church. The pledge of one's genuine expression of love and mutuality for other Christians becomes the reminder for each Christian to be responsible in her Christian ethics throughout her life. Conversely, the threat of the ban grants the church its necessary tool for accountability. In all of these things, the church becomes the stage and setting for one's genuine response in Christian faith and life. Thus, in this sense, Balthasar Hubmaier maintained much of his Roman Catholic sacramentality.

Hubmaier resounded these themes repetitively because he saw a proper sacramental understanding and practice in the church as the *sine qua non* for restoring its spiritual vitality.[4] Yet, most of his contemporaries rejected Hubmaier's apparent sacramental accentuation. In response, Hubmaier contended even against strong criticism:

> So all of those who cry: 'Well, what about water baptism? Why, all the fuss about the Lord's Supper? They are after all just outward signs! They're nothing but water, bread and wine! Why fight about that?' They have not in their whole life learned enough why the signs were instituted by Christ, what they seek to achieve or toward what they should finally be directed, namely to gather a church, to commit oneself publicly to live according to the Word of Christ in faith and brotherly love, and because of sin to subject oneself to fraternal admonition and the Christian ban, and to do all of this with a *sacramental* oath before the Christian church and all her members, assembled partly in body and completely in spirit, testifying publicly, in the power of God.[5]

Again, Hubmaier located the power of the sacraments within the church, as these oaths were the subjective adhesive commitments mirroring the objective binding of the Spirit of God. The elements themselves no longer conveyed grace but the act of pledging oneself God and to the others in love, devotion

---

[3] Hubmaier, "On Infant Baptism Against Oecolampad", *Hubmaier*, 292; *Schriften*, 268.

[4] e.g., Hubmaier's well-known phrase: "Where there is no water baptism, there is no church", etc. *Hubmaier*, 127; *Schriften*, 145.

[5] *Hubmaier*, 384 [italics mine]; *Schriften*, 346.

and service sustained its sacramental meaning. While the priest was still charged with presiding over such rites, the sacraments were now performed in correspondence with and by the authority of the entire congregation as a whole.

This comprehension certainly portrayed the anthropological trends of his age. Nevertheless, the sacraments were, for Hubmaier, far more than individual fruits of one's faith. The sacraments, though now assigned to the realm of subjective retroaction instead of objective and divine gifts, were nonetheless still centered in and administered by the church. The church would be renewed along Hubmaierian lines by becoming the locality in which the Christian responded to the divine rather than simply passively receiving God's blessings.

Consequently, Balthasar Hubmaier may well provide today's free church tradition a vocabulary that has heretofore been rejected by them because of a wide-sweeping relinquishment of sacramental terminology to "mainline" Christianity. By redefining "sacrament" altogether, Hubmaier provided a means by which free church congregations may articulate and even strengthen their own beliefs of genuine faith, while at the same time express their theology to an oft still misunderstanding public both from within and without their congregations.

For Hubmaier, these thoughts were more than concepts relegated to the pages of formal theological writings, though the Waldshut reformer certainly made a lasting contribution in this realm. Beyond this legacy in writing, Hubmaier's understanding of these sacramental practices was a call to arms to reform the church into a genuine community of faith and Christian discipline. The sacraments were always both one's oath to love God and community through faith and a believer's response to God's grace. Grace is not conferred through the elements themselves. Instead, the elements point beyond themselves, symbolizing the faith already appropriated in the hearts of responsive Christians.

Hubmaier would not concede this new understanding even in the days before his execution. Thus, while Hubmaier's life was cut short, his work remains, awaiting a greater appreciation and employment by the descendants of Anabaptism and by the church universal. For Hubmaier the sacramental promises of Christians in response to their gracious God embodied the immortal verities of faith and love. These covenantal pledges in baptism and the Lord's Supper were at least part of the immortal truth in which Balthasar Hubmaier deeply believed, and for which he lived and ultimately died.

Bibliography

Primary Sources

Aquinas, T., *Catechetical Instructions* (trans. Joseph B. Collins; New York: Joseph F. Wagner, Inc., 1939).

Bernard of Clairvaux, "On the Second Baptism", in *Sermons for the Seasons and Principal Festivals of the Year* (trans. a priest of Mount Mellary; Westminster, MD: Carroll Press, 1950).

Biel, G., *Epitome et collectorius ex Occamo circa quatuar Sententiarum libros* II. (Tübingen, n.p., 1501/Frankfurt: Minerva, 1965).

Cyprian, "Epistola ad Fortunatum de exhortaione martyrii", *Patrologiae Cursus Completus: Series Latina* IV, col. 654 (ed. J.P. Migne; Paris: Garnier Frères,1844).

__, *Epistle LXXXII.* from *The Ante-Nicene Fathers*, vol. 5 (eds. Alexander Roberts & James Donaldson; Peabody: Hendrickson Publishers, 1995).

Erasmus, D., "De Libero Arbitrio Diatribe", in *Quellen zur Geshictge des Protestantimus,* VIII (Leipzig: A Deischert'sche, 1910).

__, *The Education of a Christian Prince* (ed. Lester K. Born; New York: Norton, 1968).

Garner, R., *A Treatise of Baptisme* (London: n.p., 1645).

George, T. and D. (eds), *Baptist Confessions, Covenants, and Catechisms* (Nashville: Broadman and Holman Publishers, 1996).

Grantham, T., *A Sigh for Peace: or The Cause of Division Discovered* (London: n.p., 1671).

Hubmaier, B., *Balthasar Hubmaier: Theologian of Anabaptism* (eds. H. Wayne Pipkin and John H. Yoder; Scottdale, PA: Herald Press, 1989).

__, *Balthasar Hubmaier Schriften* (eds. Gunnar Westin and Torsten Bergsten; ütersloh: Verlagshaus Gerd Mohn, 1962).

Karlstadt, A., *Karlstadts Schriften aus den Jahren 1523-1525* (Halle: Max Niemeyer, 1957).

Kessler, J., *Johannes Kesslers Sabbata mit kleineren Schriften und Briefe* (ed. Emil Egli and Rudolph Schoch; St. Gallen: Fehrsche Buchhandlung, 1902).

Lawrence, H., *Of Baptism* (Amsterdam?, n.p., 1646).

Lumpkin, W.L. (ed.), *Baptist Confessions of Faith* (Philadelphia: Judson Press, 1959).

Luther, M., *D. Martin Luthers Werke* I & IV (Weimar: Böhlau, 1883).

__, "The Pagan Servitude of the Church", in *Martin Luther: Selections from his Writings* (ed. John Dillenberger; New York: Anchor Books/Doubleday, 1962).

__, "The Babylonian Captivity of the Church", *LW* 36. Word and Sacrament, I (ed. Abdel Ross Wentz; Philadelphia: Muhlenberg Press, 1959).

Marpeck, P., *The Writings of Pilgram Marpeck* (trans. and eds., William Klassen and Walter Klaassen; Scottdale: Herald Press, 1978).

Oecolampadius, J., *Briefe und Akten zum Leben Oekolampads: Zum 400jährigen Jublilaeum der Basler Reformation* I (ed. Ernst Staehelin; Leipzig: M. Heinsius Nachfolger, 1927; New York, 1971).

Philips, D., *The Writings of Dirk Philips, 1504-1568* (trans. and eds., Cornelius J. Dyck, William E. Keeney, and Alvin J. Beachy; Scottdale: Herald Press, 1992).

Simons, M., *The Complete Writings of Menno Simons* (ed. J.C. Wenger; Scottdale: Herald Press, 1956).

Tertullian, *On Baptism*, in *Ante-Nicene Fathers*, vol. III (eds. Alexander Roberts and James Donaldson; Peabody: Hendrickson Publishers, 1995).

Zwingli, U. *Early Writings* (ed. Samuel Macauley Jackson; New York: G.P. Putman's Sons, 1912; repr. Durham, NC: The Labyrinth Press, 1987).

__, *Huldreich Zwinglis sämtliche Werke* I & II (eds., Emil Egli and G. Finsler; Leipzig: M. Heinius Nachfolger, 1904/1908).

__, *Huldreich Zwingli: The Reformer of German Switzerland, 1484-1531* (trans. Samuel Macauley Jackson; New York: G.P. Putman's Sons, 1901).

__, *Huldruch Zwingli Writings* I & II (trans. E.J. Furcha, ed. H. Wayne Pipkin; Allison Park, PA: Pickwick Publications, 1984).

__, *Huldrych Zwingli* (ed. G.R. Potter; New York: St. Martin's Press, 1977).

__, *Selected Works of Huldreich Zwingli* (ed. Samuel Macauley Jackson; Philadelphia: University of Pennsylvania, 1901).

__, *Zwingli and Bullinger* (ed. G.W. Bromiley; The Library of Christian Classics XXIV. Philadelphia: Westminster Press, 1963).

__, *Zwingli: Commentary on True and False Religion* (eds. S.M. Jackson and C.N. Heller Durham, NC: Labyrinth Press, 1981).

Secondary Sources

Armour, R.S., *Anabaptist Baptism: A Representative Study* (Scottdale, PA: Herald Press, 1966).

__, "The Theology and Institution of Baptism in Sixteenth-Century Anabaptism", *Mennonite Quarterly Review* 38 (July 1964), 305.

Bainton, R.H., "The Left Wing of the Reformation", *Journal of Religion* 21 (1941), 124-34.

Baker, R.A., "Baptist Sacramentalism", in *Chapel Messages* (eds. H.C. Brown, Jr. and Charles P. Johnson; Grand Rapids: Baker Book House, 1966), 23-28.

Barth, K., *Church Dogmatics* 1.1: *The Doctrine of the Word of God* (eds.

G.W. Bromiley and T.F. Torrance; Edinburgh: T&T Clark, 1975).

__, *Church Dogmatics* IV.4: *The Doctrine of Reconciliation* (fragment) (eds. G.W. Bromiley and T.F. Torrance; Edinburgh: T&T Clark, 1996).

__, *Homiletics* (Louisville: Westminster/John Knox Press, 1991).

__, *The Teaching of the Church Regarding Baptism* (London: SCM Press, 1967).

Beachy, A.J., *The Concept of Grace in the Radical Reformation* (Nieuwkoop: B.D. Graaf, 1977).

Beasley-Murray, G., *Baptism in the New Testament* (New York: Macmillan, 1962).

Bergsten, T., *Balthasar Hubmaier: Anabaptist Theologian and Martyr* (ed. W.R. Estep, Jr.; Valley Forge, PA: Judson Press, 1978).

__, *Balthasar Hubmaier: Seine Stellung zu Reformation und Täufertum, 1521-1528* (Kassel: J.G. Oncken, 1961).

Bierma, L.D., "The Doctrine of the Sacraments in the Heidelberg Catechism: Melanchtonian, Calvinist, or Zwinglian?", *Studies in Reformed Theology and History*, no. 4 (Princeton: Princeton Theological Seminary, 1999).

Breck, J., *The Power of the Word in the Worshipping Church* (Crestwood, NY: St. Vladimir's Seminary Press, 1986).

Brewer, B.C., "Anabaptist Sacramentalism and Its Contemporary Appropriation", in *Marginal or Mainstream?: Anabaptists, Mennonites and Modernity in European Society*, Cornelius H. Wedel Historical Series (eds. Mark Jantzen and Mary Sprunger; North Newton: Bethel College, 2011).

__, "Radicalizing Luther: How Balthasar Hubmaier (Mis)Read the 'Father of the Reformation'", *Mennonite Quarterly Review* 84, no. 1 (January 2010), 95-115.

__, "Signs of the Covenant: The Development of Sacramental Thought in Baptist Circles", *Perspectives in Religious Studies* 36, no. 5 (Winter 2010), 407-420.

Bromiley, G.W., *An Introduction to the Theology of Karl Barth* (Grand Rapids: Eerdmans, 1979).

Clasen, C-P., *Anabaptism: A Social History, 1525-1618* (Ithica, NY: Cornell University Press, 1972).

Cobb, J.B., Jr., "Barth and the Barthians: A Critical Appraisal", in *How Karl Barth Changed My Mind* (Eugene, OR: Wipf and Stock Publishers, 1998), 172-177.

Cummins, D.D., *A Handbook for Today's Disciples in the Christian Church (Disciples of Christ)* (St. Louis: Chalice Press, 1991).

Driedger, M., "The Intensification of Religious Commitment: Jews, Anabaptists, Radical Reform, and Confessionalization", in *Jews, Judaism, and the Reformation in Sixteenth-century Germany* (eds. Dean P. Bell and Stephen G. Burnett; Boston: Brill, 2006), 269-99.

Durnbaugh, D.F., *The Believers' Church: The History and Character of Radical Protestantism* (Scottdale, PA: Herald Press, 1968).

Dyck, C.J., *An Introduction to Mennonite History*, 3rd ed (Scottdale, PA: Herald Press, 1993).

Estep, W.R., *The Anabaptist Story: An Introduction to Sixteenth-Century Anabaptism* (Grand Rapids: Eerdmans, 1996).

__, "The Anabaptist View of Salvation", *Southwestern Journal of Theology* 20, no. 2 (Spring 1978), 32-49.

__, "Balthasar Hubmaier: Martyr without Honor", *Baptist History and Heritage* 13 (Apr. 1978), 5-10.

Everts, W.W., Jr., "Balathazar Hubmeyer", *Baptist Review,* no. 10 (1881), 201-222.

Fast, H., *Quellen zur Geschicte der Taufer in der Schweiz, Zweiter Band, Ostschweiz* (Zurich: Theologischer Verlag, 1957).

Finger, T. "Sacramentality for the Catholic-Mennonite Theological Colloquium (April 2005).

Fowler, S.K., *More Than a Symbol: The British Baptist Recovery of Baptismal Sacramentalism* (Carlisle: Paternoster, 2002).

Freeman, C.W., James Wm. McClendon, Jr., and C. Rosale Velloso da Silva (eds), *Baptist Roots: A Reader in the Theology of a Christian People* (Valley Forge, PA: Judson Press, 1999).

Friedmann, R., *The Theology of Anabaptism* (Scottdale, PA: Herald Press, 1973).

Friesen, A., *Erasmus, the Anabaptists, and the Great Commission* (Grand Rapids: Wm. B. Eerdmans, 1998).

Hall, T., "Possibilities of Erasmian Influence on Denck and Hubmaier in their Views on the Freedom of the Will", *The Mennonite Quarterly Review* 35 (April 1961), 149-70.

Heimann, F., "The Hutterite Doctrines of Church and Common Life, A Study of Peter Riedemann's Confession of Faith of 1540", *The Mennonite Quarterly Review* 26 (Jan. – Apr. 1952), pt. 1: 22-47.

Horsch, J., *Menno Simons: His Life, Labors, and Teachings* (Scottdale, PA: Mennonite Publishing House, 1916).

Iserloh, E., "Die Eucharistie in der Darstellung des Johannes Eck", in *Reformationsgeschichtliche Studien und Texte* 73/74 (Münster: Westfalen, 1950).

Janz, D.R., "Late Medieval Theology", in *The Cambridge Companion to Reformation Theology* (David Bagchi and David C. Steinmetz; Cambridge: Cambridge University Press, 2004).

Johnson, T.E., "Initiation or Ordination? Balthasar Hubmaier's Rite of Baptism", *Studia Liturgica* 25 (1995), 68-85.

Jürgen-Goertz, H., *The Anabaptists* (London: Routledge, 1996).

Keeney, W.E., *The Development of Dutch Anabaptist Thought and Practice from 1539-1564* (Nieuwkoop: B. de Graaf, 1968).

Klaassen, W., *Anabaptism: Neither Catholic nor Protestant* (Waterloo, ON: Conrad Press, 1973).

__, "The Rise of the Baptism of Adult Believers in Swiss Anabaptism", in *Anabaptism Revisited* (Scottdale: Herald Press, 1992).

__, "Speaking in Simplicity: Balthasar Hubmaier", *Mennonite Quarterly Review* 40 (Apr. 1966), 139-47.

Klager, A.P., "Balthasar Hubmaier's Use of the Church Fathers: Availability, Access and Interaction", *Mennonite Quarterly Review* 84, no. 1 (January 2010), 5-65.

Kraybill, D.B. and Carl Desportes Bowman, *On the Backroad to Heaven: Old Order Hutterites, Mennonites, Amish, and Brethren* (Baltimore: Johns Hopkins University Press, 2001).

Kraybill, D.B., *Who are the Anabaptists?: Amish, Brethren, Hutterites and Mennonites* (Scottdale, PA: Herald Press, 2003).

Lee, J.K., *The Theology of John Smyth: Puritan, Separatist, Baptist, Mennonite* (Macon: Mercer Press, 2003).

Leth, C.M., "Balthasar Hubmaier's 'Catholic' Exegesis: Matthew 16:18-19 and the Power of the Keys", in *Biblical Interpretation in the Era of the Reformation* (eds. Richard A. Muller and John L. Thompson; Grand Rapids: Wm. B. Eerdmans, 1996).

Littell, F.H., *The Anabaptist View of the Church* (Boston: Starr King Press, 1958).

Loserth, J., "Balthasar Hubmaier", *Mennonite Encyclopedia* 2 (1956), 826-834.

__, "Der Communismus der mährischen Wiedertäufer", in *Archiv für* österr. *Geschicte*, LXXXI (Wein: Adolf Holzhausen, 1894).

__, *Doktor Balthasar Hubmaier und die Anfänge der Widerfäufer in Mähren* (Brünn: R.M. Rohrer, 1893).

Mabry, E.L., *Balthasar Hubmaier's Doctrine of the Church* (Lanham: University Press of America, 1994).

__, *Balthasar Hubmaier's Understanding of Faith* (Lanham: University Press of America, 1998).

__, "The Baptismal Theology of Balthasar Hubmaier" (Ph.D. diss., Princeton Theological Seminary, 1982).

McBeth, H.L., *The Baptist Heritage: Four Centuries of Baptist Witness* (Nashville: Broadman Press, 1987).

McClendon, J.W., Jr., "Balthasar Hubmaier, Catholic Anabaptist", in *Essays in Anabaptist Theology* (Elkhart, IN: Institute of Mennonite Studies, 1994), 71-85.

McGlothlin, W.J., "An Anabaptist Liturgy of the Lord's Supper", *Baptist Review and Expositor* 3 (1906), 82-83.

MacGregor, K.R., *A Central European Synthesis of Radical and Magisterial Reform: The Sacramental Theology of Balthasar Hubmaier* (Lanham: University Press of America, 2006).

__, "Hubmaier's Concord of Predestination with Free Will", *Direction* 35, no. 2 (Fall 2006), 279-99.

Macoskey, R.A., "Contemporary Relevance of Balthasar Hubmaier's Concept of the Church", *Foundations* 6 (April 1963), 99-122.

Maring, N.H. and Winthrop S. Hudson (eds), *A Baptist Manual of Polity and Practice* (Valley Forge: Judson Press, rev. ed. 1991).

Mau, W., *Balthasar Hubmaier*, in *Abhandlungen zur mittleren und neueren Geschicte*, XL (eds. Georg von Below et al.; Berlin & Leipzig: Walter Rothschild, 1912).

Miller, M.E., "Baptism in the Mennonite Tradition", *Mennonite Quarterly Review* 64 (July 1990), 230-58.

Moore, W., "Catholic Teacher and Anabaptist Pupil: The Relationship Between John Eck and Balthasar Hubmaier", in *Archiv für Reformationsgeschicte* 72 (1981), 79-93.

Neumann, G.J., "The Anabaptist Position on Baptism and the Lord's Supper", *Mennonite Quarterly Review* 35 (Apr. 1961), 140-48.

Noren, C.M., "The Word of God in Worship: Preaching in Relation to Liturgy", in *The Study of Liturgy* (New York: Oxford University Press, 1992), 33-51.

Old, H.O., *The Shaping of the Reformed Baptismal Rite in the Sixteenth Century* (Grand Rapids: William B. Eerdmans, 1992).

Packull, W.O., "Balthasar Hubmaier's Gift to John Eck, July 18, 1516", *The Mennonite Quarterly Review* 63 (Oct. 1989), 428-32.

__, "Denck's Alleged Baptism by Hubmaier: Its Significance for the Origin of South German-Austrian Anabaptism", *Mennonite Quarterly Review* 47 (Oct. 1973), 327-38.

__, *Hutterite Beginnings: Communitarian Experiments during the Reformation* (Baltimore: The Johns Hopkins University Press, 1995).

Parry, A.J., *History of the Cloughfold Baptist Church, from 1675-1875* (Manchester: John Heywood, 1876).

Patterson, W.M., *Baptist Successionism: A Critical View* (Valley Forge: Judson Press, 1969).

Pipkin, H.W., "The Baptismal Theology of Balthasar Hubmaier", *Mennonite Quarterly Review* 65 (Jan. 1991), 34-53; and in *Essays in Anabaptist Theology* (Elkhart, IN: Institute of Mennonite Studies, 1994), 87-103.

__, *Scholar, Pastor, Martyr: The Life and Ministry of Balthasar Hubmaier (ca. 1480-1528)* (Prague: International Baptist Theological Seminary of the European Baptist Federation, 2008).

Rainbow, J.H., "'Confessor Baptism': The Baptismal Doctrine of the Early Anabaptists", in *Believer's Baptism: Sign of the New Covenant in Christ* (eds. Thomas R. Schreiner and Shawn D. Wright; Nashville: Broadman and Holman, 2006).

Reardon, T.W., "Pilgram Marpeck's Sacramental Theology: Based on His Confession of 1532", *Mennonite Quarterly Review* 83 (April 2009), 293-317.

Rempel, J.D., *The Lord's Supper in Anabaptism: A Study in the Christology of Balthasar Hubmaier, Pilgrim Marpeck, and Dirk Philips* (Scottdale, PA: Herald Press, 1993).

___, "Mennonite Worship: A Multitude of Practices Looking for a Theology", *Mennonite Life*, vol. 55, no. 3 (September 2000).

Sachsse, C., *D. Balthasar Hubmaier als Theologe* (Berlin: Trowitzsch & Sohn, 1914).

Scott, T., "Reformation and Peasants' War in Waldshut and Environs: A Structural Analysis", in *Archiv für Reformationsgeschicte* 69 (1979), 82-102; 70 (1979), 140-69.

Short, R.L., "Karl Barth's Final Plea", *Religion in Life* 40, no. 4 (Winter 1971), 479-88.

Sider, R.J., *Andreas Bodenstein von Karlstadt: The Development of His Thought, 1517-1525* (Leiden: E.J. Brill, 1974).

Snyder, A., "Modern Mennonite Reality and Anabaptist Spirituality: Balthasar Hubmier's Catechism of 1526", *The Conrad Grebel Review* 9 (Winter 1991), 37-51.

Stacy, R.W., "Baptism", in *A Baptist's Theology* (ed. R. Wayne Stacy; Macon, GA: Smyth & Helwys, 1999), 153-74.

Stayer, J.M., "Anabaptists and future Anabaptists in the Peasants' War", *Mennonite Quarterly Review* 62 (Apr. 1988), 99-139.

___, *The German Peasants' War and the Anabaptist Community of Goods* (Montreal: McGill-Queen's University Press, 1991).

Stealey, S.L., "Balthasar Hubmaier and Some Perennial Religious Problems", *The Review and Expositor* XL, no. 4 (Oct. 1943), 403-22.

Steinmetz, D.C., "The Baptism of John and the Baptism of Jesus in Huldrych Zwingli, Balthasar Hubmaier and Late Medieval Theology", in *Continuity and Discontinuity in Church History* (eds. F. Forrester Church and Timothy George; Leiden: E.J. Brill, 1979), 169-81.

___, *Luther in Context* (Grand Rapids: Baker Academic, 2002).

___, *Reformers in the Wings* (Oxford: Oxford University Press, 2001).

___, "Scholasticism and Radical Reform: Nominalist Motifs in the Theology of Balthasar Hubmaier", *Mennonite Quarterly Review* 45 (Apr. 1971), 123-44.

Thompson, P.E., "A New Question in Baptist History: Seeking a Catholic Spirit Among Early Baptists", *Pro Ecclesia* 8, no. 1 (Winter 1999), 51-72.

___, *Reformers in the Wings* (Philadelphia: Fortress Press, 1971).

Toulouse, M.G., *Joined in Discipleship: The Shaping of Contemporary Disciples Identity* (St Louis: Chalice Press, 1997).

Underwood, A.C., *A History of the English Baptists* (London: The Kingsgate Press, 1947).

Vedder, H.C., *A Short History of the Baptists* (Valley Forge: Judson Press, 1907).

___, *Balthasar Hübmaier: The Leader of the Anabaptists* (New York: G.P. Putnam's Sons, 1905).

Wainwright, G., *Doxology: The Praise of God in Worship, Doctrine, and Life* (New York: Oxford, 1980).

__, "Preaching as Worship", *Greek Orthodox Review* 28 (Winter 1983), 325-36.

__, "The Sermon and the Liturgy", *Greek Orthodox Review* 28 (Winter 1983), 337-49.

Walker, M.J., "Baptist Worship in the Twentieth Century", in *Baptists in the Twentieth Century* (ed. K.W. Clements; London: Baptist Historical Society, 1983).

White, J.F., *The Sacraments in Protestant Practice and Faith* (Nashville: Abingdon Press, 1999).

Williams, G.H., *The Radical Reformation* (Philadelphia: Westminster Press, 1962).

Williamson, D.T., "The 'Doctor of Anabaptism' and the Prince of Humanists: Balthasar Hubmaier's Contact with Erasmus", *Erasmus of Rotterdam Society Yearbook Twenty- Seven* (2007), 37-58.

Windhorst, C., "Balthasar Hubmaier: Professor, Preacher, Politician", in *Profiles of Radical Reformers* (ed. Hans-Jürgen Goertz; Scottdale, PA: Herald Press, 1982), 144-57.

__, "Das Gedächtnis des Leidens Christi und Pflichzeichen brüderlicher Liebe: zum Verständnis des Abendmahls bei Balthasar Hubmaier", in *Umstrittenes Täufertum, 1525-1975* (ed. Hans-Jürgen Goertz; Göttingen: Vandenhoeck & Ruprecht, 1977),111-37.

__, *Täuferisches Taufverständnis: Balthasar Hubmaiers Lehre Zwischen Traditioneller und Reformatorischer Theologie* (Leiden: E.J. Brill, 1976).

Yoder, J.H., "Balthasar Hubmaier and the Beginnings of Swiss Anabaptism", *Mennonite Quarterly Review* 33 (Jan. 1959), 5-17.

__, "The Believers' Church Conferences in Historical Perspective", *Mennonite Quarterly Review* 65 (Jan. 1991), 5-19.

__, "Karl Barth: How His Mind Kept Changing", in *How Karl Barth Changed My Mind* (ed. Donald K. McKim; Eugene, OR: Wipf and Stock Publishers, 1998), 166-71.

__, "Sacrament as Social Process: Christ the Transformer of Culture", in *The Royal Priesthood: Essays Ecclesiological and Ecumenical* (Grand Rapids: Wm. B. Eerdmans, 1994), 359-73.

__, *Täufertum und Reformation in der Schweiz*, pt. 1, *Die Gespräche zwischen Täufern und Reformatoren, 1523-1538* (Karlsruhe: H. Schneider, 1962).

Zeman, J.K., *The Anabaptists and the Czech Brethren in Moravia 1526-1628: A Study of Origins and Contacts* (Paris/The Hague: Mouton, 1969).

Zieglschmid, A.J.F. (ed.), *Die* älteste *Chronik der Hutterischen Brüder: Ein Sprachdenkmal aus frühneuhochdeutscher Zeit* (Ithica: Cayuga Press, 1943).

General Index

PATERNOSTER

STUDIES IN CHRISTIAN HISTORY AND THOUGHT

New titles in the series, 2012

Michael Brealey, *Bedford's Victorian Pilgrim. William Hale White in Context* – 9781842277850 - £24.99

Raymond Brown, *Spirituality in Adversity. English Nonconformity in a period of Repression 1660-1689* – 9781842277850 - £34.99

Larry Siekawitch *Balancing Head and Heart in Seventeenth Century Puritanism. Stephen Charnock's Doctrine of the Knowledge of God* – 9781842276709 - £24.99

Michael Parsons (ed.), *Since we are Justified by Faith. Justification in the Theologies of the Protestant Reformation* – 9781842277775 - £24.99

Adam Hood (ed.), *John Oman: New Perspectives* – 9781842277317 - £24.99

Some future titles in the series

Van Vliet, *Marrow of the Theology and Piety of the Reformed Traditions* - 9781842273944

Clifford B. Boone, *Puritan Evangelism: Preaching for conversion in late-seventeenth century English Puritanism as seen in the works of John Flavel* - 9781842277843

Aaron T. O'Kelley, *Did the Reformers Misread Paul? A Historical-Theological Critique of the New Perspective* - 9781842277942

Brian Talbot, *In the Shadow of Geneva* - 9781842277959

Michael Pasquarello, *Hugh Latimer* - 9781842277973

Martin Wellings (ed.), *Protestant Nonconformity and Christian Missions* - 9781842277980

Edwin E. M. Tay, *The Priesthood of Christ in the Atonement Theology of John Owen (1616-1683)* - 9781842277997

Roger Standing, *The Forward Movement: evangelical pioneers of 'Social Christianity'* –9781842278031

Michael Parsons (ed.), *Aspects of Reformation. Reforming Theology and Practice* - 9781842278061

Other available titles

[volumes published *before* 2008 are half price while stocks last: contact paternoster@authenticmedia.co.uk]

David Thompson, *Baptism, Church and Society in Britain. From the Evangelical Revival to* Baptism, Eucharist and Ministry – 9781842273937 (2009) - £19.99

Tom Aitken, *Blood and Fire, Tsar and Commissar. The Salvation Army in Russia (1907-1923)* – 9781842275115 (2007) - £24.99 £12.50

Byung-Ho Moon, *Christ the Mediator of the Law. Calvin's Christological Understanding of the Law as the Rule of Living and Life-giving* – 9781842273180 (2006) - £29.99 £15.00

Andrew Partington, Church and State. *The Contribution of the Church of England Bishops to the House of Lords during the Thatcher Years* – 9781842273340 (2006) - £29.99 £15.00

Linda Wilson, *Constrained by Zeal. Female Spirituality amongst Nonconformists, 1865-1875* – 9780853649724 (2006) - £24.99 £12.50

Anthony Rich, *'Discernment' in the Desert Fathers* – 9781842274316 (2007) - £29.99 £15.00

Anna Robbins, *Ecumenical and Eclectic. The Unity of the Church in the Contemporary World* – 9781842274323 (2007) - £24.99 £12.50

Anthony Cross, *Ecumenism and History* – 9781842271353 (2005) - £29.99 £15.00

Jack Whytock, *An Educated Clergy. Scottish Theological Education and Training in Kirk and Session, 1560-1850* – 9781842275122 (2007) - £24.99 £12.50

Alan Sell, Enlightenment, Ecumenism, Evangel. Theological Themes and Thinkers, 1550-2000 – 9781842273302 (2005) - £29.99 £15.00

Kevin Hester, *Eschatology and pain in St Gregory the Great* – 9781842274378 (2007) - £19.99 £10.00

Michael Thomas, *The Extent of the Atonement. A Dilemma for Reformed Theology from Calvin to the Consensus* – 9780853648284 (1997) - £24.99 £12.50

Ruth Gouldbourne, *Flesh and the Feminine. Gender and Theology in the Writings of Casper Schwenckfeld* – 9781842270486 (2004) - £24.99 £12.50

Tim Larsen, *Friends of Religious Equality. Nonconformist Politics in Mid-Victorian England* – 9781842274026 (2007) - £24.99 £12.50

Stuart Clarke, *The Ground of Election. Jacob Arminius' Doctrine of the Work and Person of Christ* – 9781842273982 (2006) - £19.99 £10.00

Andrew Daunton-Fear, *Healing in the Early Church. The Church's Ministry of Healing and Exorcism from the First to the Fifth Century* – 9781842276235

(2009) - £19.99

Alan Sell, *Hinterland Theology. A Stimulus to Theological Construction* – 9781842273319 (2008) - £39.99

Carole Spencer, *Holiness – the Soul of Quakerism* – 9781842274392 (2008) - £29.99

M. Knell, *The Immanent Person of the Holy Spirit from Anselm to Lombard: Divine Communion of the Spirit* – 9781842275610 (2009) - £24.99

William Evans, *Imputation and Impartation. Union with Christ in American Reformed Theology* – 9781842274361 (2008) - £24.99

Harold Hill, *Leadership in the Salvation Army. A Case-Study in Clericalism* – 97812842274293 (2006) - ~~£29.99~~ £15.00

Mark Garcia, *Life in Christ. Union with Christ and the Twofold Grace in Calvin's Theology* – 9781842275726 (2009) - £29.99

Tim Grass, *The Lord's Watchman. Edward Irving* – 9781842274262 (2011)- £24.99

Dennis Ngien, *Luther as a Spiritual Advisor* – 9781842274613 (2007) - ~~£19.99~~ £10.00

Brian Shelton, *Martyrdom from Exegesis to Hippolytus. The Early Church's Presbyter's Commentary on Daniel* – 9781842275689 (2008) - £24.99

John Darch, *Missionary Imperialists? Missionaries, Government and the Growth of the British Empire in the Tropics, 1860-1885* – 9781842275603 (2009) - £24.99

Stephen Orchard, *Nonconformity in Derbyshire. A Study in Dissent, 1600-1800* – 9781842276204 (2009) - £19.99

Shawn Wright, *Our Sovereign Refuge. The Pastoral Theology of Theodore Beza* – 9781842272527 (2004) - ~~£24.99~~ £12.50

Martin Sutherland, *Peace, Toleration and Decay. The Ecclesiology of Later Stuart Dissent* – 9781842271520 (2003) - ~~£24.99~~ £12.50

Donald Fortson, *Presbyterian Creed. A Confessional Tradition in America, 1729-1870* – 9781842274248 (2009) - £24.99

Colin Bulley, *The Priesthood of Some Believers. Developments from the General to the Special Priesthood in the Christian Literature of the First Three Centuries* – 9781842270349 (2000) - ~~£29.99~~ £15.00

Galen Johnson, *Prisoner of Conscience. John Bunyan on Self, Community and the Christian Faith* – 9781842272237 (2003) - ~~£24.99~~ £12.50

James Bruce, *Prophecy, Miracles, Angels and Heavenly Light. The*

Eschatology, Pneumatology and Missiology of Adomnan's Life of Columba – 9781842272275 (2004) - ~~£24.99~~ £12.50

Alan Sell & Anthony Cross, *Protestant Nonconformity in the Twentieth Century* – 9781842272213 (2005) - ~~£29.99~~ £15.00

Clark and Trueman, *Protestant Scholasticism. Essays in Reassessment* – 9780853648536 (1998) - ~~£29.99~~ £15.00

Crawford Gribben, *Puritan Millennium. Literature and Theology, 1550-1682* – 9781842273722 (2008) - £24.99

J.S. Yuille, *Puritan Spirituality. The Fear of God in the Affective Theology of George Swinnock* – 9781842275627 (2008) - £24.99

William Black, *Reformation Pastors. Richard Baxter and the Ideal of the Reformed Pastor* – 9781842271902 (2004) - ~~£29.99~~ £15.00

C. Clement, *Religious Radicalism in England, 1535-1565* – 9781842278449 (1997) - ~~£29.99~~ £15.00

Jeff McInnis, *Shadows and Chivalry. C.S. Lewis and George MacDonald on Suffering, Evil and Goodness* – 9781842274309 (2007) - ~~£19.99~~ £10.00

Susan Tara Brown, *Singing and the Imagination of Devotion. Vocal Aesthetics in Early English protestant Culture* – 9781842274071 (2008) - £19.99

Orchard & Briggs, *The Sunday School Movement. Studies in the Growth and Decline of the Sunday School* – 9781842273630 (2007) - ~~£19.99~~ £10.00

Mark Thompson, *A Sure Ground on Which to Stand. The Relation of Authority and Interpretive Method in Luther's Approach to Scripture* – 9781842271452 (2004) - ~~£29.99~~ £15.00

Guy Richard, *The Supremacy of God in the Theology of Samuel Rutherford* – 9781842275740 (2008) - £24.99

Roy Kearsley, *Tertullian's Theology of Divine Power* – 9780946068616 (1998) - ~~£19.99~~ £10.00

Brian Kay, *Trinitarian Spirituality. John Owen and the Doctrine of God in Western Devotion* – 9781842274088 (2008) - £19.99

Garnet Milne, *The Westminster Confession of Faith. The Majority Puritan Viewpoint on Whether Extra Biblical Prophecy is Still Possible* – 9781842275214 (2007) - ~~£24.99~~ £12.50